MANAGING

An Introduction to its Political Economy and
Public Policy

Edited by

Richard Maidment and
Grahame Thompson

Foreword by Gillian Peele

SAGE Publications

London • Newbury Park • New Delhi

PUBLISHED IN ASSOCIATION WITH

The Open
University

First published 1993
©The Open University 1993

SAGE Publications Ltd
6 Bonhill Street
London EC2A 4PU

SAGE Publications Inc
2455 Teller Road
Newbury Park, California 91320

SAGE Publications India Pvt Ltd
32, M-Block Market
Greater Kailash–1
New Delhi 110 048

British Library Cataloguing in Publication Data

Managing the UK
  I. Maidment, Richard
  II. Thompson, Grahame

ISBN 0–8039–8850–8
ISBN 0–8039–8851-6 pbk

Library of Congress catalog card number 93–085427

Edited, Designed and Typeset by the Open University.
Printed in the United Kingdom by
Cromwell Press, Broughton Gifford,
Melksham, Wiltshire

CONTENTS

ACKNOWLEDGEMENTS

This book arises from the Open University Course D212 'Running the Country' which presents a wide-ranging introduction to the political economy of the UK. It is an accompanying volume to *Markets, Hierarchies and Networks: The Coordination of Social Life* (eds. Thompson, G., Frances, J., Levačić, R., and Mitchell, J.; Sage, London, 1991). We would like to record our thanks to all the members of the original D212 'Running the Country' course team for the collective contribution they made to earlier versions of the chapters included here. In addition we would like to extend our thanks to David Wilson of the Open University Publishing Division for so ably arranging the book's external publication and to Anne Hunt and Tom Hunter for secretarial and editing services respectively.

Grateful acknowledgement is made to the following sources for permission to reproduce material in this book:

Chapter 1: Figure 1.4: Parker, H.M.D. (1957), *Manpower*, reproduced with the permission of the Controller of Her Majesty's Stationery Office; Figure 1.6: Hennessy, P. (1989), *Whitehall*, George Weidenfeld and Nicolson Ltd. Table 1.1: Hennessy, P. (1989), *Whitehall*, George Wedenfeld and Nicolson Ltd. *Chapter 2:* Table 2: adapted from Williamson, O.E. (1985), *The Economic Institutions of Capitalism*, The Free Press, New York. *Chapter 3:* Figure 1 and Table 1: Scott, J. and Griff, C. (1984), *Directors of Industry, the British Corporate Network, 1904-76*, Basil Blackwell Ltd. *Chapter 5*: Figure 1: Williams, K., Williams, J. and Haslam, C. (1987), *Economy and Society*, Vol 16, No 3, Routledge; Table 1: adapted from Rhys, G. (1988), 'Economics of the motor industry', *Economics*, Winter 1988. *Chapter 6*: Table 1: Arnold, E. (1983), *Competition and Technological Change In The Television Industry*, D.Phil Thesis, University of Sussex. *Chapter 8*: Figures 1 and 2: Levačić, R. (1993), 'Local management of schools as an organization form: theory and application', *Journal of Education Policy*, Taylor and Francis Ltd. *Chapter 9*: Figure 1: Harrison, S., Hunter, D.J. and Pollitt, C. (1990), *The Dynamics of British Health Policy*, Unwin Hyman, © Harrison, S., Hunter, D.J. and Pollitt, C., 1990. *Chapter 10*: Table 1: CIPFA (1989), *Local Government Trends*, Chartered Institute of Public Finance and Accountancy. *Chapter 11*: Figure 1: adapted from Dunleavy, P. (1991), *Democracy, Bureaucracy and Public Choice*, Harvester Wheatsheaf; Figure 2: adapted from Dunleavy, P. (1985), 'Bureaucrats, budgets and the growth of the state', *British Journal of Political Science*, Cambridge University Press; Tables 1 and 2: adapted from Drewry, G. and Butcher, T. (1991), *The Civil Service To-day*, Basil Blackwell Ltd. *Chapter 12*: Jackson, P.M. (1992), 'Economic policy', in Marsh, D. and Rhodes, R.A.W. (eds.), *Implementing Thatcherite Policies: Audit Of An Era*, Open University Press.

FOREWORD

It is a great pleasure to be able to write an introduction to *Managing the UK*. This book develops a new approach to the problems of coordinating British society and sheds new light on the interaction of some of the fundamental processes of governing an advanced industrial society in the late twentieth century. The chapters cover many of the traditional topics which one might expect to find on a British government course such as the civil service and local government. However, it also reflects the shifting boundaries of the public sector and the development of new approaches to public management in the key areas of education and the health service. In addition the book includes a consideration of policy areas which present novel problems for the economy and society — for example the management of hi–tech industries such as television — as well as sectors of industry (such as car manufacturing) where there has been extensive exposure to international influences. It fully recognizes the impact of British membership of the European Community. The book thus captures, to a much greater extent than many traditional texts, the interaction of public and private decision making and the reality of the contemporary world where very little of significance can be seen purely in terms of the nation–state.

Moreover, unlike many rather static approaches to the study of British government and politics, *Managing the UK* makes the process of decision making central to all its discussions and focuses on the dynamic aspects of coordination. One of the most significant features of the policy process is that it involves individuals and groups reacting to a series of problems which may be presented simultaneously rather than singly. The environment of the policy maker — whether in the public or the private sector is complex and multi-faceted; and the decision-making process is accordingly much less tidy than many portrayals of government would suggest.

Although the authors of this book are very much aware of the empirical detail of their subject matter, they have been anxious to inform their discussion of the issues surrounding the coordination of British society with a challenging theoretical component. The use of three explanatory models — hierarchy, markets and networks is extremely stimulating and allows the reader to develop their own insights and analytical powers about the most appropriate methods of coordination for particular policy areas. The models are not of course entirely value free. The concepts of hierarchy, of the market and of networks have each generated a literature of their own and have their own disciplinary and ideological associations. As the readers become familiar with the models and use them to illuminate the empirical material, they will find themselves introduced to a range of inter-disciplinary analyses. Indeed one of the particularly impressive features of the text is the way it facilitates independent thought and highlights the different perspectives which may be taken on familiar themes and problems. The use of different levels of analysis and the advantages of a cross–disciplinary approach to issues are indeed inherent to the whole design of the book.

It should be noted that the use of the three basic models of hierarchy, markets and networks is a particularly pertinent approach to the study of decision making at the present time. The period since the 1970s has seen renewed intellectual interest in the role of markets and, of course, there have been in Britain a number of efforts to introduce markets into sectors hitherto dominated by hierarchical styles of decision making. It is to be hoped that *Managing the UK* will prompt extensive and dispassionate reflection on both the advantages and the limits of the market as a method of coordination as well as on the merits and demerits of other modes of coordination.

Finally, although enough historical detail has been included to enable the reader to appreciate how social and political institutions have evolved in the United Kingdom, the focus is very much on contemporary issues. The opportunity has also been taken to raise important yet contentious issues — for example about the bias of elites in hierarchical decision-making systems and networks.

In summary this text offers its readers an unusual opportunity to enhance their critical understanding of the forces shaping the country and is a very welcome addition to the literature on British Government.

Gillian Peele

Lady Margaret Hall,
Oxford.
May 1993

INTRODUCTION

Richard Maidment and Grahame Thompson

Managing the United Kingdom has become an increasingly difficult and controversial process. The increased difficulties arise because the UK has become a more complex society with a seeming loss of homogeneity and common purpose. In addition it has become more internationally interdependent, which has made it difficult for both public and private agents to manage their own domestic affairs without paying attention to the growing international constraints, and indeed opportunities, on their activities. The process of social management has become more controversial as a result of the emergence of new ideologically based political forces which have made a claim on expertise in organizing social, political and economic life. These have challenged much of the conventional wisdom on these matters. In its turn, this has given rise to the development of new combinations of mechanisms that speak to the task of modernizing and restructuring large parts of British public and private life, and the institutions that have traditionally been responsible for running these. The main purpose of this book is to explore the nature of this new situation in a systematic way; to both provide a framework in which the novel features of managing the UK can be understood and to analyse the important arenas of UK social, political and economic life where these novel features have had their most significant impact.

To do this, the book concentrates upon two main tasks. The first is provided by the opening three substantive chapters which provide the intellectual framework for the book. In these chapters the idea of three different 'models of coordination' are elaborated; hierarchy, markets and networks. These three chapters act as the analytical spine for the eight chapters that follow. The models of coordination represent an abstract 'ideal type' for each of the coordination mechanisms they focus upon. The objective is both to describe the way the different models give an intellectual purchase on the analysis of social existence as at the same time they seek to differentiate themselves from one another. However, each of these models is not meant to represent the complexity of social existence in its entirety or in isolation. As the later chapters show, that existence always involves the deployment of a combination of the models to make any adequate sense. The subsequent analyses demonstrate that the complexity of social relations is such that any single model of coordination is unable to successfully untangle that complexity and describe the totality of the social process.

The eight chapters that follow these first three are aimed at the second task. They provide a series of case studies of important parts of the privately and publicly organized UK social fabric. Each of these

1

chapters utilizes the three models to highlight the changing way the institutional and relational aspects of that part of the UK focused upon is managed. They take a central area of UK economic, social or political life and subject it to an analysis in the context of the three models to see first how the historical emphasis has changed in the manner of their coordination, and secondly, how that coordination is contemporarily being recast in the light of the growing complexity and controversial nature of the programmes of performance assessment as mentioned above.

Managing the UK clearly implies a programme of overt attempts to coordinate and control. It raises the notion of policy, whether that be the policy adopted by a privately owned firm or of a publicly operated institution like a school. Thus we interpret policy widely in this book; to mean any conscious attempt to mobilize resources and personnel to achieve an objective. All social agents thus have policies and programmes, and it is towards the nature of these that the eight case study chapters are directed. They deal with a range of institutions, industries, areas and levels of coordination and their operation. Some concentrate upon a single institutional manifestation like the school system or hospitals. Others look towards a discrete area of activity like television, the motor industry, the hi-tech consumer electronics industry or housing. Others look towards a distinct level or institution of government, such as the local authorities and their relationship to central government or the operation of the Civil Service. These case studies are designed to illustrate the range of activity at present under transformation in terms of their coordinative structures. They are not fully comprehensive in coverage but represent discrete arenas of activity. The features and processes highlighted in each are, however, indicative of general trends throughout the UK. Together they give a very clear picture of the nature of the contemporary political economy of the UK overall, concentrating on the processes involving, and problems confronting, those attempting to manage it in its various guises.

The final chapter offers a wide ranging overview of the present configuration of the UK as a whole, linking the case studies with the models and situating these within the context of the UK's deeper and more structural governing mechanisms. This chapter raises issue about the general nature of the UK state, its economy and society, considered in the light of the case studies and models of coordination. It also asks whether we can say something of a macro nature about the condition and trajectory of the UK's overall political economy.

As suggested above, each of the case studies tackles its concerns in the light of all three of the models discussed in the first three chapters. But there is also some division of labour between them in terms of the emphasis they give to one or other, or to a combination, of the models. Broadly speaking Chapter 4 on television considers the way hierarchy might progressively be giving way to the market as the dominant mode of organizing domestic television broadcasting as the industry rapidly globalizes in scope. Chapter 5, on the automobile industry, considers the way a privately organized sector, traditionally subject to market processes (though with a good deal of historical public sector involvement), is being reshaped on an international scale by the operation of newly invigorated competitive forces. This chapter implicates the two main ways the market mechanism is considered in Chapter 2; as a static equilibrium producing system on the one hand or as a dynamic disequilibrium producing one on the other. The following chapter on the consumer electronics industry (Chapter 6), whilst inevitably dealing with the market as a coordinating mechanism is also particularly concerned with the network model. It considers the way indigenous firms can organize to form a defensive network type lobbying body in the face of an external threat from foreign suppliers. In Chapter 7, on the provision and organization of housing, the emphasis returns to the relationship between hierarchy and market, but this time set within the context of a set of overt (and changing) government policy initiatives. This remains a theme in the following two chapters, where schools and hospitals are considered (Chapters 8 and 9). Here it is the way the internal reorganization of these two traditionally publicly provided services is increasingly involving the substitution of a hierarchical mode of organization by forms of quasi- or internal-markets. However, both of these also involve strong elements of networking. And it is with the case of local government in Chapter 10 that we encounter the network model more centrally. But here again hierarchy and the market are strongly implicated, particularly as local government services are increasingly being subjected to the dictates of central government, and in this process local government itself is being exhorted to become more sensitive to market-based pressures. Finally, in Chapter 11, it is the quintessential hierarchical organization of the Civil Service that is the subject of market base performance and efficiency pressures that forms the focus for the analysis.

The innovative nature of this book is the way the case studies just outlined are systematically related to the notions of hierarchy, markets and networks as developed in Chapters 1, 2 and 3. The main intellectual work involves the linking of these two elements in the book, something the authors of the chapters have been at pains to do with some care. But this also remains an intellectual task for the reader as well. Not everything can be explained with the aid of our models of coordination; they are not totally exhaustive as explanatory categories. We have chosen to concentrate upon them as a kind of intermediate theoretical exercise. From the point of view of this book they represent neither simple descriptive devices nor mega-theoretical systemic perspectives. The models are practically orientated and deliberately limited in extent; analytical devices that suit a modest, but we would argue robust, intellectual objective — to provide a concrete understanding of the current restructuring and transformation in the social organization of a country like the UK. Of the three models, hierarchy and the market are probably the best known, most widely analysed and elaborated. Networks are relatively underdeveloped in these terms. Chapters 1, 2 and 3 bring all three into a common framework, however; they explain the distinctive features of each, analyse their strengths and weaknesses, and compare and contrast them. Whilst it is perhaps tempting to see the current era as one in which it is the market mechanism that is progressively and whole-heartedly displacing the hierarchical mode as the dominant model of social coordination, the analyses of this book will provide an antidote to this common (miss)conception by indicating the complexity of the relationships between all three modes both historically and in the contemporary period.

CHAPTER 1:
COORDINATION BY HIERARCHY

Jeremy Mitchell

1   Introduction

There are essentially three broad ways in which actions or policy are managed and coordinated in Britain today, namely: by hierarchy, by market and by networks In this chapter we are concerned with the first of these, *hierarchy*, and the role of bureaucracy in British government. However, hierarchy is a complex idea so in this chapter I want to try to answer such questions as 'What is meant by hierarchy?', 'What are the constituent elements of a hierarchy?', 'How do these elements relate to each other?', and, more importantly, 'How do they act together?', or even more generally, 'What processes or activity make up hierarchical coordination?' After we have looked at the nature and structure of hierarchy we can then go on to ask what hierarchies actually do.

But of course the focus of this chapter is not solely theoretical. This chapter is concerned with looking at how things happen in Britain today and after outlining the basic nature of hierarchy it will look at the existence of hierarchies as a mode of coordination in Britain, and how they function in practice.

However this is only one part of the story. Hierarchies are not just a mechanism for coordinating processes and activities. They also have a life of their own, their own internal dynamics. Hierarchies are staffed by people and we need to look at the divergence between the ideas of hierarchies as coordination mechanisms and the way that hierarchies actually function since the way that they function may influence how they coordinate. So we must discuss some of the problems of hierarchies, the gap between the intention and the reality. But note too that not everything is 'run' through hierarchical coordination, it cannot explain everything. Although hierarchy is particularly associated with the role of government there has recently been a change of emphasis in such coordination. Within the past ten years government has changed the pattern of some of its activities. Industries such as gas and the telephone system, which were previously state monopolies, have been privatized and their ownership transferred from the public to the private sector. But much of the overall structure of these industries, how they are run, has remained the same, their internal organization has remained hierarchical. So this is a change from public hierarchy to private hierarchy. But how are these private sector hierarchies coordinated? When they were still in the public sector we would have said that they were 'run' by ministers and civil servants and by the networks within and between ministries. Now such enterprises are regulated and constrained more by competition with alternative sources of energy or other telephone services, that is by the market, although it is of a regulated kind. So the story of government management over the last decade is a complex one. The change suggests that some aspects of hierarchical coordination remain constant, whether the organization is private or public, and that the processes of coordination within hierarchies in both sectors can be seen as relatively comparable. However, the nature of coordination between hierarchies may also have changed significantly. Finally, there may have been changes in the structure and operation of the hierarchy itself: the numbers of levels may have decreased or the relationship between individuals within a hierarchical organization may have changed. Structures may have become 'flatter' or 'looser' — changes which could affect both activity within hierarchies and their effectiveness as agencies of coordination and management.

A hierarchy is a mechanism for getting things done and as such it is used both by government and non-governmental organizations. A hierarchy can be discerned within the public sector or private sector firms such as ICI, or indeed within some voluntary sector organizations such as Oxfam. They all have certain common structural features and a common organizational logic. So much of the discussion of hierarchical organization, both positively and negatively, applies directly to the public sector and to more market led organizations. However, between the two areas of activity the overall purpose of hierarchical coordination may not be so clear.

Within the private sector firms exist to manufacture goods or offer services, to make a profit and thus to continue to exist and/or show a return on capital for their shareholders. But why is there hierarchical coordination by government? What is government trying to do? In general, it is trying to manage the state and perform those functions that citizens expect of government. However, such a general answer covers a very wide variation in government action.

Consider two very distinct sets of activity, leisure pursuits and the prison service. On one hand, government makes no direct claims upon how people spend their leisure time. It is up to individuals to decide what to do and how to do it, how to allocate time, effort and other resources. On the other hand, government does have a fairly direct say in the running of the prison service and the life of those who are serving prison sentences. It indirectly influences where they go, what they do and so on and this will continue to be the case even if the running of prisons is transferred to a private contractor. But most government activity falls somewhere between these two extremes. Governments may not order matters extensively or in detail, but they often lay down broad rules or limits within which much activity takes place. To go back to the leisure example, the government may not say how leisure time is spent but it will have an indirect influence on what is done through laws relating to cinema safety, the opening hours of public houses, the use of cars or the transfer of money abroad, as well as regulating hours of work or the length of the working life. In such areas of activity the state lays down a framework within which behaviour can take place, the state provides a regulatory framework for much activity within society.

This difference in the nature of public and private hierarchies also suggests differences in the coordination between them. Private sector organizations sell goods and services within a competitive market place. Failure to do so effects their ability to continue. Public sector hierarchies are not so constrained. Their coordination is by political action or through existing structures or individuals. They are relatively autonomous in an economic sense. So there is a major difference between public and private hierarchies. But what is meant by a hierarchy?

2 What is hierarchy?

The idea of hierarchy and hierarchical coordination is both simple and complex. The idea of an organizational structure, of different levels of activity of the division of a task into sub-tasks and their allocation to different individuals, is straightforward but this simple idea is separate from understanding how hierarchy works. Is hierarchical coordination effective because of the relationships between the individuals within organizations and if so what are the relationships involved?

The activities of government we are mostly concerned with are hierarchies associated with large-scale organizations and in particular those that are part of the administrative structure of the civil service. The picture many people have of such large organizations is that drawn from television programmes like the classic BBC comedy series *Yes Minister*, a world which is very much concerned with its own internal problems rather than its supposed external purposes. This structure and its operation seems to bear little relationship to the jobs for which such organizations are supposed to exist. Indeed they seem characterized by their own peculiar logic, a structure of internal rules and rewards, a culture which bears little relationship to the 'real' world. Those who work within them seem to spend more time realizing personal organizational goals than they do serving the overt purposes of the hierarchical organization itself. It is these aspects of hierarchies and bureaucracies that have passed into popular consciousness either as a source of comedy as in *Yes Minister*, or in a more oppressive way through novels by Kafka or George Orwell.

It is important here to distinguish between hierarchy as an abstract idea and hierarchy in practice. Some understanding can be gained both of the idea and the practice by examining the functions of a school.

For most people formal education begins at the age of five and ends at the age of sixteen or in some cases eighteen. The child enters the school, is placed within a larger group of children of roughly the same age and is taught by a number of teachers. Over time the pupil progresses through the school and receives instruction in a number of different areas, those of the core curriculum and other subjects. But what has all this got to do with hierarchy? Well, in the later stages of their school career pupils are often taught particular subjects by particular individual teachers, history by a history teacher, mathematics by a mathematics teacher, business studies by a business studies teacher and so on. At the start of their school career the pupil may well have been taught by one or a few teachers who cover the whole range of subjects, but beyond a certain age there is a degree of subject specialization amongst teachers.

In the family there is a two level hierarchical relationship between parents and children and to some extent this carries over to the relationship between teachers and their pupils. Here too there is an element of authority in this relationship although there may be a higher degree of consent to that authority as well. However, within a large school the organization of teachers may also be hierarchical; typically there will be several teachers for each subject. Normally one person would be the head of department or the head of that area of specialization. As such they will be responsible for coordinating all the teaching and the teachers within this area assigning them to particular classes or to teach particular parts of their subject — say GCSE history. These heads of department will be responsible to the head teacher, who will be responsible to the school governors. This overall structure of school organization can be represented as in Figure 1.1.

Much of the internal activity of teaching is coordinated by the head teacher and senior teachers: for example in the construction of the timetable which lays out the basic framework that governs the allocation of pupil to teacher. But many of the decisions that are implemented by hierarchies are taken outside the structure which does the implemen-

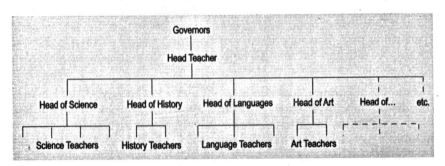

Figure 1.1   A school hierarchy

tation. In terms of the school this will be decisions taken by the board of governors or by the relevant Education Department or by external authorities such as examination boards. It is important to remember that the hierarchical structure of Figure 1.1 is there to coordinate the processes within the school in response to the decisions taken elsewhere, and to produce particular results in the light of those decisions.

Within some schools there is a parallel pupil hierarchy that is separate from that of the teaching staff, although the two may well be linked to effect the internal coordination of school activity outside of classroom instruction. Some of the government of a school may well be carried on through a pupil hierarchy of prefects and form monitors which is analogous to the hierarchy of teachers. However the important point to note is that within a school the teaching hierarchy is characterized by task specialization. Some teachers have specific areas of knowledge and expertise. It may be possible for a language teacher to teach both French and German but it is very unlikely that they could teach mathematics or physics. Their capabilities are only transferable to a very limited degree. So it is with hierarchies in general: not only are they characterized by differences in power and authority between the different levels of the hierarchy but they also typically have a differentiation of areas of competence and specialization between individuals within the same level.

The school structure exists to implement decisions that are often taken elsewhere; they transmit policy 'downwards'. The overall task is sub-divided into sub-tasks performed lower down the structure. With such a structure there may not be much capacity for the transmission of information in the reverse direction upwards from 'bottom' to 'top'. But not all hierarchies are of this simple form, and we need to look at more complex structures to explore the nature of hierarchy and hierarchical coordination in more detail.

3 Bureaucracy and organizations

Simple hierarchies have relatively few levels of authority, but they do have two important features which are common to all hierarchies. First, there is a stratification of power between the levels in such structures. Those at the 'top' have power, those at the 'bottom' are in a subordinate position and normally follow directives from those at the top of the hierarchy. In the case of the chain of command within the army, those at the 'bottom' are there to carry out orders from above which are transmitted to them through the various intermediate levels of the army command structure. Second, there may be a degree of task specialization amongst those who are at equivalent positions within a hierarchy, in the case of the school the history teacher could not teach mathematics, and vice versa.

Both of these are general characteristics which we find in larger, complex, multilevel hierarchies. We usually refer to such organizations as bureaucracies and they share some of the characteristics identified in the earlier cases. Within larger bureaucracies processes are also broken up into subprocesses with one or more elements of the overall process supervised by one or more individuals. Each individual will be supervised by a superior to whom he or she is accountable and so on. This relationship of superior to subordinates means that such complex hierarchies are typically pyramidal in structure with each individual at a given level having one superior but a number of subordinates. One result is to concentrate direction and control so large organizations can be run and coordinated by a relatively small number of coordinators (managers, leaders, etc.). This is true of the government sector too.

The expansion of state activity in Britain since 1945 has brought with it a need for greater organizational supervision or control. In Britain, as in other countries, increased state activity has resulted in bureaucratic expansion too; the growth of government has brought with it an increase in the size and functions of the civil service. The bureaucracy is in theory the neutral arm of a democratically accountable state subject to political control, the servant and not the master of government. How can we analyse and understand the complex hierarchy of contemporary government bureaucratic administration, the way that government coordination runs state activity?

One way to understand the characteristics of hierarchies is to look at how an individual works within such a hierarchical organization, that is at the nature of the bureaucrat's career. Previously we examined hierarchy in terms of the family and the school. For most individuals the other common experience is that of work. Here the variation in individual experience may be much greater than either in family life or in education and so it is less easy to discuss in general terms. But let us suppose that after leaving school the individual joins a large firm such as BP, British Telecom or ICI. (Note that we are here discussing this in terms of the private sector organizations but the individual could just as easily join some public sector organization. Although the jobs may differ the work situation may well be comparable.) The individual could be recruited to do a specific task — something to do with oil production for BP or a telephone engineer for British Telecom, or a process manager for ICI. Once they have joined a large organization many individuals will follow a career within that particular company. Such a career often involves job development and promotion. Within their career the activities and responsibilities of the individual changes over time. Most large-scale firms have a structure which can be characterized as an extensive hierarchical organization, see Figure 1.2.

A career within a company may well involve a change in location within the organizational structure of the company over time. What can this career tell us about the nature of hierarchy in general? The in

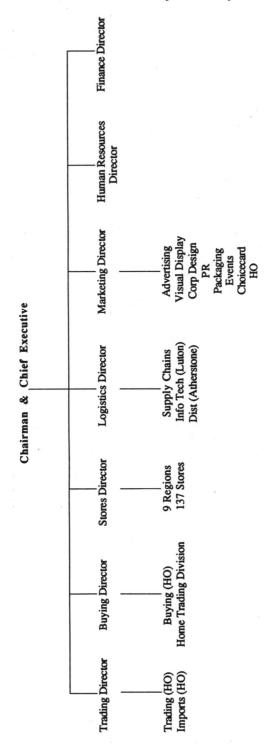

Figure 1.2 Organizational chart for a large company

dividual may start off by performing a particular task: they may have
been recruited for that specific purpose and given training to help them
discharge one particular job: they will be located within one specific
level of the company's organization. There will be a matching of the
specialization of the task to the training and skills of the individual.
The amount of autonomy or discretion within the job will probably be
limited, he or she may not be called upon to exercise their own judgement but will be following a particular set of rules or carrying out a particular set of tasks. However, as the individual is promoted within the
organization, as they move up from level to level and come to occupy
more authoritative positions within the hierarchy, this will change.
The range of tasks for which they are responsible increases and becomes
more general, and at the same time they may well gain greater autonomy for the carrying out of such tasks. As they are promoted they become less dependent upon orders from above and are able to make more
independent decisions. At the same time as they move up and are given
more authority they will have a greater number of direct and indirect
subordinates, the number increasing as they rise higher within the
firm or organization. Note that we have now moved from a discussion
of the nature of hierarchy to an implicit analysis of the way that hierarchies operate. Some consequences of this change depend upon our
assumptions of what are the general characteristics of hierarchies
themselves. We have assumed that hierarchies have a pyramidal
structure.

Hierarchy is a structural mechanism for bringing about coordination,
of running a large and complex organization, of making a large number
of individuals act together for a collective purpose, of producing desired end results, in short it is a way of 'getting things done'. The
pyramidal structure reinforces the earlier suggestion as to how this
coordination is effected, how hierarchical coordination works. A task,
or policy, or project, is progressively broken down into discrete elements
which are entrusted to individuals to carry out or supervise. The
overall process is factored into a number of subprocesses which
collectively make up the original objective. For government this type
of activity can be seen at its most direct and straightforward in
emergency situations when it is thought necessary to control all aspects
of the allocation of a desired good or service. In the Second World War,
for example, it was necessary to supervise the supply of labour. The
normal peacetime workings of the labour market were not thought able
to match labour inputs to the tasks that were essential for the fighting
and winning of the war. So the supervision and control of the labour
market was handed over to a hierarchical organization, it became part
of the Ministry of Labour.

As the official historian of the period comments:

> ...by the summer of 1943 a vast organization had evolved,
> stretching from the War Cabinet into intermediate levels to

the local offices of the Ministry of Labour ... when the Minister of Labour had taken decisions on major questions of manpower policy, it became the responsibility of the Ministry of Labour to carry them into effect. This involved the construction of schemes together with the machinery for putting them into effect...

(Parker, 1957, pp. 212 and 214)

The actual administrative machinery is shown in Figure 1.4 — note the hierarchical form of the organization, the sub-division of the overall tasks of the ministry and so on, and indeed the overall bureaucratic structure.

But Parker notes that the recruitment and mobilization of labour 'could not be considered in isolation but had to be closely integrated into the activities of other ministries ... all this involved frequent and prolonged discussions with other departments, and sometimes with employers and trade unions ...' (Parker, 1957, pp. 217–18) In other words, the coordination of the labour market was carried out by activities within departments and involved coordination between other departments and organizations as well. Such inter-organizational coordination could itself be hierarchical — carried out in accordance with directives from the War Cabinet — or it might be done in other ways. This also suggests the importance of the wider context of government activity. Separate departments need to work together and such overall coordination may be both hierarchical — linked to the overall structure of government — and take place through non-hierarchical channels.

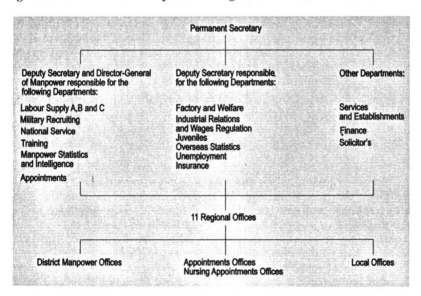

Figure 1.3   *Organization of the Ministry of Labour*
Source: Parker, H. , 1957

However even in these circumstances, with extensive direction from the top, the process of administration and control involved more than just a flow of directions 'downwards' through the established hierarchical structure. This is an important modification of the argument so far. The discussion of war-time organization of labour hastended to imply that it was merely the putting into effect of orders that were taken elsewhere. However many hierarchical structures respond tochanges in their external environment. Coordination in a changing environment is a much more dynamic process than that implied by the simple ideas of a command structure with which we have so far been concerned. Again an analogy with an everyday activity can tell us something about the processes involved, driving a car gives some idea of the complexity of coordination within a changing environment.

The actual process of driving requires the use of several different limbs to effect particular subprocesses of the overall activity: using the clutch, the gears, the steering, the brakes and so on. The overall driving of the car is controlled by the coordination of these separate activities via the central nervous system. As you drive you respond to changes in the external environment, the traffic, the changing topography of the road, the lighting conditions and so on. These impinge upon you via various sensory organs and responses to them are coordinated by the brain. However, unlike direction from the top, where the task was subdivided and delegated to other agencies lower down in the hierarchical organization, the actual environment itself within which coordination takes place is changing. So in a parallel manner coordination within any hierarchy may not be just a matter of administration or regulation. As the external environment changes it can become necessary to redefine hierarchical activity in response to such changes. While there is a flow of 'commands' from top to bottom within a hierarchy, there is at the same time another flow of information which reflects these changes. This flow may well be in the 'reverse' direction, 'up' the hierarchy. For example, a salesperson may be responsible for selling his or her company's products and in selling them they may well notice which products sell more than others and to whom they sell. Such information, passed back up the hierarchy to those in charge of marketing, could effect not only the range of products manufactured but also the way in which they are sold, and so on. This suggests that the nature of the individual task at specific levels in a hierarchy will itself be constantly redefined, and that all actors in the organization may have some degree of autonomy.

So the original simple idea of hierarchy as an implementing structure provides only a partial understanding of the actual nature of modern bureaucracy particularly within such large-scale organizations as firms or government agencies. It is the combination of the basic structural aspect of hierarchies together with the process of the institution at work, its dynamic element, which gives rise to the particular problems of hierarchy as a model of coordination. It is the structure, *and* the processes that arise within the structure, that produce particular patterns of activity and behaviour which we will analyse later. Hierarchies exist independently of those who work in them but at the same time they are composed of these individuals. Although you may work for a particular company, and may leave to work elsewhere, that company carries on existing *after* you have left its employment; the structure, and the structural continuity of hierarchy is important.

4 The civil service in Britain

What we have established so far is that hierarchy is an effective mode of coordination within large-scale organizations. Such organizations are frequently bureaucratic in the senses defined by Weber who stressed the rule based nature of behaviour in bureaucracies and the relationship between this and rational administration. He saw extensive activity by a democratic state as only possible through bureaucracy. He also stressed the distinctive nature of the bureaucratic career with the absence of a link between performance and reward, promotion on merit and recruitment based on universalistic criteria. Weber saw work in a bureaucracy as different from other types of employment — and as explaining some of the processes through which hierarchies function.

While other commentators would agree with some elements of Weber's analysis they also point to a distinction between public and private hierarchies: those who work in a public hierarchy do not themselves own the resources of the bureaucracy. This is not necessarily the case in a private hierarchy and may influence both the behaviour of individuals and the processes within such organizations. This difference has also been linked to the perceived inefficiency of bureaucracies (see for example, Beetham, 1991) although the hierarchical structure does imply that there are common processes in both public and private bureaucracies. But if hierarchy is an effective way of organizing or coordinating large-scale structures and processes, whether public or private, are there particular problems with hierarchical management for state organizations? The period after 1945 saw a growth of state activity. For a variety of reasons Government assumed greater responsibility for many areas of social and economic life. More than this Government itself became one key agent of coordination within British society. State activities derive from a desire either to plan or to control important sectors of the economy — in the control of the labour supply in wartime for example — or merely a wish to influence or regulate discrete and important areas such as broadcasting One consequence of this growth in government has been a growth in the size and number of agencies designed to implement and coordinate government policy. In particular a growth in the size and complexity of the civil service itself.

And by its very nature the civil service is hierarchical. It is a bureaucracy in the sense defined by Weber with all the benefits that he outlined, and with some of the consequences that Beetham (1991) suggests for public sector organizations too. Indeed there is a tendency to conflate hierarchical/bureaucratic coordination with civil service/governmental action. This is only partially justifiable. Hierarchical coordination is certainly one element of how the government runs the country, but hierarchical coordination is also found within the organizational structures of large-scale private sector firms. After the expansion of wartime planning and control between 1939–1945, the same pattern of administration was applied to many areas during the war — food, fuel and so on. At the end of the war, the apparatus was partially dismantled although some of the rationing mechanisms remained until the 1950s. It provided a model for subsequent comprehensive planning initiatives. But the change of government after 1945 brought with it a changing definition of the role and range of governmental activity. Under the Labour government between 1945 and 1951 the extension of the range of governmental responsibilities led to a redrawing of the boundaries between the state and society after 1945. The extension of government agencies which were designed to oversee and coordinate areas of social and economic life created other problems. An increase in the number of agencies brought difficulties of inter-agency coordination and a need for more extensive networks within the community of civil servants and politicians.

For much of this post-war period, successive governments of both parties accepted this enlarged responsibility for economic management and for the wider provision of other social services. One can summarize this complex process by suggesting that the post-war period saw the growth both of the welfare state and an extension of government regulation in other areas of social life. This is not a process which was either uncontested or confined to the United Kingdom only. There were equivalent developments in many other European democracies during this period. However, the change of government in 1979 brought a change of emphasis both in defining the range of governmental responsibilities and the mechanisms through which these responsibilities were discharged. In addition, a further level of such coordination was added through Britain's membership of the European Economic Community after 1973. This supra-national level of regulation forms the background to the government coordination which is carried out by bureaucratic or hierarchic organizations in the UK. But before discussing how they 'work' we need a brief overview of the structure of British government as a whole and the role of hierarchical coordination within it.

5 Central government

Central government in Britain is conventionally thought of in terms of the Whitehall departments — Defence, Health, Education and so on — as well as their outstations. These are staffed by civil servants with a top level of political control. To these we can add local government which in many of its activities acts as an agency of central government.

The internal workings of departments follow the bureaucratic workings that have been discussed so far, and indeed the same type of analysis applies to the working of local government too; there is a general pattern of bureaucratic administration. In addition, the relationship between the two levels of government is itself hierarchical with many of the actions of local government dependent upon central government policy making.

There are a number of qualifications that can be added. Such a description may apply to the administration of policy but takes little account of current changes in the structure of the civil service, and says nothing about the overall coordination of government in Britain.

Recent initiatives, such as *The Next Steps* programme, may alter the existing structure of government. A change to executive agency status would alter the formerly hierarchical relationship between an agency and the parent department but would not affect the hierarchical relationships and processes within the agency itself (see Chapter 11).

Overall coordination of government policy takes place within the 'core executive', the complex set of institutions and actors that forms the topmost layer of British government. It includes 'the Prime Minister, the Cabinet, Cabinet Committees, the coordinating departments (number 10 Downing Street, the Treasury, Cabinet Office, the law officers, and the intelligence services), and an extensive network of interdepartmental committees' (Dunleavy, 1990, pp. 101–2) So policy coordination in central government is effected both through hierarchy and other non-hierarchical mechanisms.

The actual internal workings of a department are discussed later but since 1945 there has been a great expansion of the overall scope of government and big government brought big administrative problems. The growth of government activity led to a growth of the public sector. (The term the 'public sector' can refer to both people employed in state owned industries and people employed in the civil service.) Figure 1.4 shows the growth of civil service employment in Britain over the period 1938 to 1986.

The graph in Figure 1.4 clearly shows the growth in the number of people involved in public sector management but what it does not show is how these personnel are distributed between departments of government, between the sexes or between the regions of the United Kingdom, or indeed between lower and higher administrative grades. Nor does it distinguish between industrial civil servants and administrators.

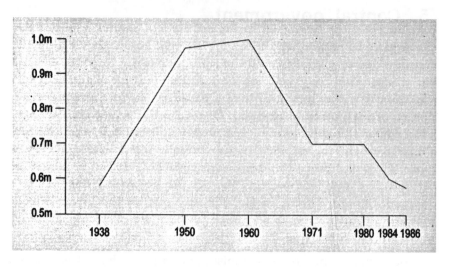

Figure 1.4   *Civil service employment: 1938–1986*

A recent study has described the condition of the civil service as follows:

> ...the civil service in its crudest division can be separated into two main categories; 500,419 non industrial officials, and 105,593 industrials (of whom nearly 30,000 were craftsmen of various kinds). The non industrials divided almost evenly between men and women, though the bulk of the women work in the lower two grades of the administrative hierarchy.
>
> *(Hennessy, 1989, pp. 529–30).*

Two points can be made which bring out important cultural aspects of the civil service. The first is that it is indeed a hierarchy — there is a strict structure of merit and/or responsibility and authority. The senior management and policy-making part of the civil service has seven categories with fewer in each category or grade as one goes up the hierarchy (see Table 1.1).

Table 1.1 shows that there were 12,000 individuals at the lowest grade of the hierarchy — Principal — in 1987, and that this grade was larger in size than the sum of all the higher senior grades. The same is almost strictly true for all the grades. This is merely what we expect in a hierarchical administrative structure with an individual at each level having a large number of subordinates.

The second characteristic of the civil service is shown by the gender division revealed in Table 1.1, the overall ratio of male to female within the higher civil service is roughly 12 : 1 for the senior grades as a whole, with the ratio increasing to about 40 : 1 for the top two grades. This suggests that the informal culture of the civil service is overwhelmingly a male one and this in turn may have consequences for the way that coordination is carried out. Of course the senior civil service

Table 1.1 Civil service unified grades (1987)

Grade	Men	Women	Total
1 (Permanent Secretary)	38	1	39
2 (Deputy Secretary)	133	3	136
3 (Under Secretary)	467	22	489
4 (Supervising grade)	163	7	170
5 (Assistant Secretary)	1,955	153	2,108
6 (Senior Principal)	3,483	251	3,734
7 (Principal)	10,909	983	11,892

Source: HM Treasury (reproduced from Hennessy, 1989)

service is not alone in having this problem — the world of ministers and the world of senior management in industry in the private sector show a very similar imbalance. However, since the non-industrial civil service is almost equally divided between men and women there must be some categories in which women predominate. In the lower ranks of the administration group, such as administrative officer or administrative assistant, women outnumber men by roughly three to one, as they also do in the local officer second grade of the social security category. This reflects the historic cultural position of women both in such organizations and in society generally. However this analysis of personnel and personnel growth is only one way of looking at the civil service since 1945. Another way would be to look at life within a department — to describe the civil service within a particular ministry.

The Department of the Environment was created in 1971 by the merger of the Ministry of Housing and Local Government with the Ministry of Public Buildings and Works. It is an important department headed by a Minister who now sits in the Cabinet. The department can be thought of as typical being involved in a variety of regulatory and administrative activity, that is, it is an organizational structure which is intended to fulfil some overall coordination function. Some idea of the scope of the department is shown by an outline of its organizational structure (Fig. 1.5).

The structural outline of the department is typically pyramidal with a few individuals supervising the activity of many. However, the organizational outline, which indicates the overall range of department activities too, gives no indication of the actual dynamics involved in

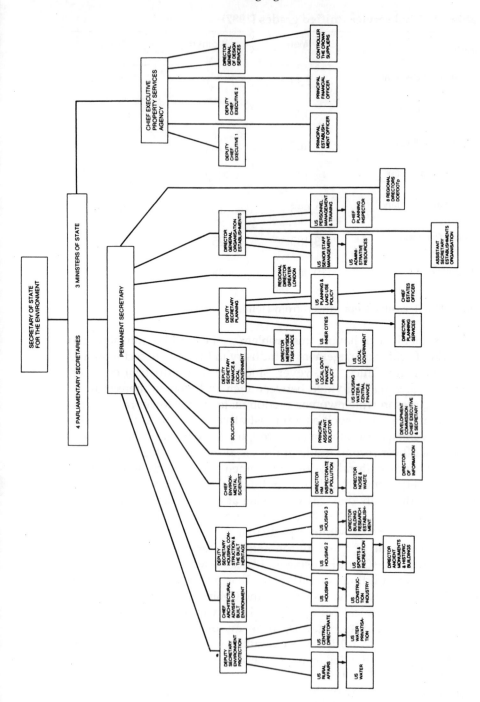

Figure 1.5   *Department of the Environment*
Source: Hennesey, 1989

administration. It is similar to the general behaviour of bureaucracies but the relationship between Minister and Permanent Secretary is also important. The Permanent Secretary links political decisions to administrative process and, as the senior civil servant in a department, can have a crucial influence on departmental policy. The role of a Permanent Secretary may be close to that of a senior manager in the private sector. A recent study of the Department of the Environment took this parallel further.

> The DOE, in addition to its core functions of local government and housing, is a bit like a Whitehall holding company in the range of activities it supervises to a greater or lesser extent at arm's length. It is the classic quangoid department operating through a network of statutory bodies, some of which are big spenders and employers...
>
> Taken together with its traditional functions, its quangoid empire makes the DOE one of the hardest departments to run, particularly when the huge management problem of the Property Services Agency (the old Ministry of Works) is added. Yet the DOE was in the van of the movement for managerial improvement after 1979.
>
> *(Hennessy, 1989, pp. 440–1.*

This managerial improvement was initially centred in such areas as monitoring financial information but it has since spread to take in more fundamental alternatives to hierarchical coordination within British government.

The Department of the Environment is just one of forty or so ministries in British government. These have resulted from the growth and extension in government activity which can be traced in part to the changing responsibility of government after 1945. However it is one thing to outline a structure of these organizations, to say in theory how this hierarchical coordination is effected, how government aims, policies or objectives are linked to the environment in which they work. But it is quite another to see how these organizations actually work in practice. One consequence of suggesting that there is a hierarchical mode of coordination, and that such coordination is carried out by bureaucratic organizations, is to suggest that there is a general way in which all departments work in British government today. It is to the general workings of hierarchies and bureaucracies that we now turn.

6 Working in a hierarchy

We can extract some defining characteristics of a bureaucracy from the previous discussion, and from this see how bureaucracies work, how they carry out hierarchical coordination. Two of the more important characteristics were discussed in the first two sections: the stratified and hierarchical nature of bureaucracy on the one hand and task specialization on the other. The world of the bureaucrat is formed by rules which define and determine their sphere of competence. The nature of the work in many government departments is impersonal; cases or activities are processed according to specific rules and precedents. The bureaucrat is appointed on merit, often through an open competitive examination, and promoted on the same basis. Work as a civil servant or bureaucrat is considered to be a full time career with little or no interchange within employment in the private sector. What makes it distinct from other types of employment in similar large organizations is that the bureaucrat is protected from the public and has a guaranteed independence *vis-à-vis* both superiors and subordinates; their salary is to a large extent independent of the quality of their performance, and derives from their position within the organizational hierarchy.

There is a great variety in the type of work carried out within the civil service as part of the overall hierarchical coordinating activity of government. Most civil servants carry out routine tasks, with little discretion or use of initiative. Such tasks are defined from above in the manner suggested earlier, and they are in turn related to the overall organization of the department. This is not in itself surprising since most government activity is concerned with implementing existing policies rather than initiating new ones. So most activity of the majority of civil servants will be concerned with 'running the machine', that is with the on-going coordination of government activities. However, as critics have pointed out, this kind of routine hierarchical coordination does have a number of problems. But what is it actually like to be a 'hierarchical coordinator'? What is it like to work within a bureaucracy?

Most bureaucracies are a stable environment in which individual bureaucrats follow well-established sets of rules and most analyses of bureaucracy start with these generalized characteristics of the organizational context to draw a rather unflattering picture of bureaucratic hierarchy. For example, they may suggest that there is little in the way of incentives for individuals within such organizations as rewards are not directly derived from an individual's performance. So such structures may be inefficient in some sense. Secondly, other authors stress the routine nature of the work within bureaucracy. Much activity is concerned with following rules. This, and the logic of bureaucratic coordination, contribute to the fragmentation of policy making. Thirdly, the insulation of individuals within large-scale structures can lead to goal displacement in which individuals become more concerned with organizational life itself rather than with the intended functions of such organizations. Not all of these are problems in all bureaucracies. But many commentators suggest that private sector hierarchies have problems which are parallel to those in the public sector hierarchies. However, as governments have grown the problems of public sector bureaucracies have grown too and it may be that bureaucrats have their own reasons for running departments and organizations, their own goals and objectives and these can be different from their 'real' purposes.

7 Alternatives to hierarchy

Are there any alternatives to the managing/coordinating role of government bureaucracy? One approach to the problem of hierarchical coordination is to ask two basic although slightly different questions: Why do hierarchies exist? and, in particular, Why do government bureaucratic hierarchies exist? In part the answer to these questions is an outline of how and why governments 'do' things, and one answer for British government in the 1990s is that the extent of government activity today is the result of the growth in the period after 1945 when there was an increase both in regulation and direct state activity. The Labour government of the period between 1945 and 1950, took control of some industries which had previously been within the private sector and also considered that some aspects of social life should be subject to greater governmental oversight. The mechanism for coordinating activity in both cases was through bureaucratic hierarchy and partly as a result, the size of the civil service hierarchy grew throughout this period. However, if hierarchy is a general way of coordinating complex activities then some of the same processes will be at work in the private sector and account for the hierarchical growth of large firms. As firms grow so the organizational structures of such firms may grow too. This growth may be further increased by processes of merger and internationalization.

If we inquire further into the 'why' of government action we might find that in some cases there was an economic rationale for this action. Some industries were felt to be natural monopolies which should be regulated by government in the public interest rather than left to operate for their own self-interest within the wider economy. In other cases there were public goods involved and it was argued that these could only be provided by state action. Since such goods, of which defence is one example, were felt to be necessary or desirable this implied that the government itself should be involved in their production. In still other cases the actions of some economic agents produced spillover effects such as pollution which could only be controlled through government activity, they were not eliminated by the actions of the market. All of these can be related to general economic ideas of market failure.

However, underlying these actions there was also a response to the perceived defects of the market as revealed by the economic problems of the 1930s. One response to the depression of the inter-war years was that the government itself should assume overall responsibility for regulating economic activity, and the social consequences of that activ-

ity. After 1945 politicians felt that government should take a much
more active role within the management of the economy and that, more
importantly, it was possible to design better outcomes for the overall
economic process than could be produced by unregulated market forces on
their own. This type of hierarchical coordination is known as planning.
One example of state planning in post-war Britain is discussed in Chapter 9. The Conservative government of the day wished to improve the
provision of health care and to do this they produced a national plan
which related anticipated national needs to specific actions such as the
building of more hospitals. In this case the provision of health care
was already primarily a public sector activity. And in anticipating future needs there was little or no consideration of private sector or market activity. Here then there was a close link between government provision, government coordination and non-market coordination; planning
was a method of balancing the two sides of the equation of needs and
services.

However, in general the word 'planning' is used in a wide variety of
ways. On a personal level we plan a holiday or plan our garden. Both
meanings imply a coordination of either physical things (as in the garden) or of activities (as in the holiday example). But as used here
planning refers to:

> A set of processes whereby decision makers engage in logical
> foresight before committing themselves. These include problem
> definition, problem analysis, goal and objective setting, fore-
> casting, problem projection, design of alternative solutions,
> evaluation of alternative solutions, decision processes, imple-
> mentation processes, monitoring, control and updating. Such
> processes are common to the planning of many public activities:
> defence, economic development, education, public order and
> welfare. Many of them are used in part, with different param-
> eters and with different objective functions, by large private
> corporations.

(Hall, 1980, pp. 1– 2)

This definition shows something of the complexity of the idea and
process of planning and its potential linkage to general bureaucratic coordination, in particular its reference to implementation, monitoring
and control. But as set out by Hall it is not specific to government action
and the hierarchical coordination that this may imply; indeed many
of the same processes can be found within large-scale private sector organizations. It is this linkage of planning to bureaucracy and specifically the government bureaucracy, its linkage to hierarchical coordination that I want to stress here.

One reason for this link between planning and government derives
from the responsibility that government now has for the overall supervision of economic activity. Sartori has commented that 'states have
always intervened in economic matters' but he suggests that limited

planning necessarily occurs because governments have targets which cannot be achieved through market mechanisms. Indeed, the dichotomy that he stresses — market or non-market — suggests both the reason for planning and its problems. 'The planning agency proposes development goals ... or equalization goals', but the system is 'monitored in part ... by a central agency that does not respond to market signals' and Sartori goes on to to suggest, the contradiction is that 'without a market system resources cannot be rationally or efficiently allocated' (see Sartori, 1991).

So why does planning still occur? The answer is that the state does not only have economic ends, government is not just interested in managing the economy. Governments have non-market political objectives — and so limited planning is inevitable. And this in turn necessarily leads on to a discussion of 'the planners' — they are either politicians or experts — which in its turn raises further questions of coherence and rationality, and of coordination within and between agencies. It also suggests that planning is carried out both by individuals and agencies, and so planning as a coordination mechanism, as 'an attempt at rationally calculated action to achieve a goal' is linked to hierarchies. The problems of planning overlap with the problems of bureaucratic coordination and because planning is a further strategy of hierarchical coordination it is linked to the role of government and its coordination of societal activities.

8 Recent changes in British government

These distinctions between market and non-market and the role of planning as a coordination mechanism echo some of the widespread criticisms of government bureaucracy. Many of the consequences follow from the suggestion that the basic problem with work in the civil service is the structure of individual incentives involved, or rather the lack of such incentives. So all bureaucratic decision making in government lacks a linkage to the efficient market allocation of resources. This should be contrasted with one of the justifications of the market which is that it provides incentives for individual actors that collectively provide socially desirable outcomes. Such criticisms have policy consequences. The Conservative government that was elected in 1979 wished to 'roll back the frontiers of the state'. It wished to do this by altering the balance between modes of coordination within British society as a whole, between market and non-market; it wished to alter the way in which Britain was managed. To alter this balance of coordination between hierarchical modes and others, it embarked on a programme of deregulation and of returning some areas of state activity to the private sector, together with a programme of reform within the civil service itself, such as *The Next Steps* initiative and the move to give some departments agency status.

The consequences of these policy decisions are discussed in more detail in other chapters but the rationale was to replace non-market criteria by market led ones. In bureaucratic/hierarchic terms the changes have been twofold. There has been a decline in the number of employees in the civil service since 1979, but in addition there have been attempts to alter the nature of the civil service radically. When these are fully in place they will change the nature of hierarchical coordination in government. Recent policy discussions of the nature of central government coordination have 'proposed that the civil service should be restructured so that as far as possible the delivery of services is separated from policy work and executed by agencies operating under a business style regime' (Flynn et al., 1990, p.159). It is too early to say how far such proposals will be extended and what their overall effect will be. But the recent changes in the balance between the use of different modes of coordination by central government must be seen, paradoxically, within a context of *increasing* hierarchical coordination.

This follows as a consequence of the transfer of some areas of state activity from the public to the private sector. Many of these activities were monopolies — gas, telephone and so on. Because there are inherent difficulties in the position of monopoly suppliers, at least as far as consumers are concerned, it was felt necessary to regulate the activities of these industries through independent regulatory agencies. 'The new regulatory offices have been endowed with elastic powers; the statutory language is general, designed to cover all contingencies. In principle, and in law, the electricity regulator could effect control of the generation and distribution of electricity in Great Britain; he could at least make a stab at planning it' (Walker, 1990, p. 153).

The transfer of some of these state industries to private ownership during the 1980s was part of the wider government programme which aimed to create a more competitive economic environment. However, as has been mentioned, some of the privatized industries were monopolies. The transfer of a monopoly from public to private sector creates problems. The government wished to create a competitive market place but monopolies are anti-competitive. So to try to prevent some of the undesirable consequences of such private monopolies these newly privatized industries operate within an environment which is regulated by a newly created government agency, they now operate in what we might call a modified market. Regulatory agencies such as the Office of Electricity Regulation or the Office of Telecommunications (Oftel) have a wide range of responsibilities. They monitor the performance of the industry concerned in terms of price, quality of service and overall performance. They are often consulted during the process of the negotiation of a rise in the cost to the consumer of the goods or services produced by a particular industry. They are also a channel for customer complaints and generally exist to limit anti-competitive policies. In short, they try to ensure that a particular industry operates with an approximation

of the benefits of the competitive market but without an actual competitive market structure. More importantly the price of the goods or services provided are not simply defined by market forces but are often influenced by decisions of government as well.

Thus the way privatization and deregulation seem to have worked in
the UK over the period from 1980 to the early 1990s was not to unam-
biguously increase competition and the market mechanism. Some re-
regulation has followed in the wake of this programme and this can be
viewed as an attempt at the renewal of forms of hierarchical control by
the public authorities. In addition, the large private companies that
were created in this process were themselves internally coordinated in
a hierarchical fashion. So we might see this change in the mode of
regulation as a modification in the link between hierarchy and the
market.

Similar comments could be made too about some of the external relationships in which the UK economy found itself in the early 1990s.
Britain joined the European Community in 1973, since when it has increasingly come under the influence of European institutional structures
of a hierarchical kind. As there is a deepening and widening of these
European institutional structures, the UK will find itself further constrained by a logic of coordination that is still essentially hierarchical
in character. But as in the case of the domestic privatization programme at the same time as this reinforcement of hierarchical relations is progressing, a new logic of integration through the market mode
is developing as the European Single Market programme itself matures.

9 Hierarchy, models and networks

However, although we have concentrated on hierarchy as a mechanism
for the coordination of processes and policies in large organizations,
particularly in relation to the activities of the state and the role of
government, they can also be identified in large-scale organizations in
the private sector or in voluntary organizations. But how does this
analysis of hierarchical coordination help us to understand the 'management of the country'? How many of the 'things managed' are done in
a purely hierarchical way? Perhaps a civil service department or an
industrial organization on its own can be understood in this way but
there is a major qualification — they are not isolated systems. They
are linked in the real world to other activities and other organizations,
and other modes of management and coordination.

How then are these 'other activities' run? Here we have an analytical problem. If we consider individual elements of this external world
— a single firm or a single interest group or a single voluntary association — then we may well find that such organizations exhibit hierarchical coordination to a greater or lesser extent in their internal workings. But if we consider the organization of the total set of firms, inter-

est groups or voluntary organizations, that total world may not be organized or coordinated hierarchically. Typically we might find that the
coordination mechanism for all firms is the market, or for a group of
voluntary organizations there might be a substantial element of network coordination involved.

This point is important. Partly it echoes other distinctions which we
have already discussed, such as that between state activity and the activities of firms or that between the public and private sectors. But it is
not just this. For economic agents some of the differences result from the
differences in ownership — and we saw that they may help to explain
differences between private and public organizations as Beetham suggests. These distinctions are important but they are not the point at issue here which is a very simple one: in analysing how the country is
run, either as a whole system, or in looking at one particular aspect of
it, we can disaggregate the total process into a set of linked and partially overlapping sub-processes. We can then look at the coordinating
mechanisms within these sub-processes in terms of the three models
discussed in this book. Consider how the television sector is managed in
Britain. Hierarchical coordination is involved through the government activity which structures and regulates television broadcasting.
Other elements of the industry, such as programme-making companies,
are coordinated by the market. Still other aspects — programme
content for example — are supervised by bodies such as the Broadcasting Standards Council. There is an industry network of institutions,
regulators and companies, and of individuals within these institutions,
which contributes to the overall coordination of the industry. In short,
we can explain how television is managed by using a combination of the
models of coordination, although individual aspects of the television
industry may be best understood by using one or other of the three
models on their own. This type of analysis can be represented
schematically as in Figure 1.6.

I am not saying that each of the three models is of equal importance
or equal weight in any or all particular processes. In some processes one
particular mode of coordination is more salient, in other processes one of
the other modes will itself contribute more to an understanding and de-

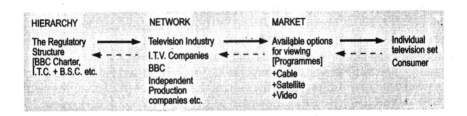

Figure 1.6   *The running of television*

scription of what is going on. The distinctions made are analytical distinctions, the models are more or less useful for understanding particular cases. In real life the way the country is managed may also be a good deal less clear cut than is suggested here. Markets, hierarchies and networks may blend into each other in a relatively seamless way. Coordination between hierarchical organizations may be achieved either through the market, or through networks, or indeed by some overarching hierarchical organization. What our distinctions between these separate processes provide is a way of analysing activities, a way of organizing our understanding. In the case studies in this book, the models of coordination are used to develop an analytical understanding of the process involved either by itself or in combination with other models.

References

Beetham, D. (1991) 'Bureaucracy' in Thompson et al. (eds.) (1991)

Dunleavy, P. (1990) 'Government at the centre' in Dunleavy, P., Gamble, A. and Peele, G. (eds.) *Developments in British Politics 3*, London, Macmillan.

Englefield, D. (ed.) (1984) *Today's Civil Service*, Harlow, Longman.

Flynn, A., Gray, A., and Jenkins, W. (1990) 'Taking the next steps: the changing management of government affairs', *Parliament Affairs*, vol. 43, no. 2, pp. 159–78.

Thompson, G., Frances, J., Levačić, R., and Mitchell, J. (eds.) (1991) *Markets, Hierarchies and Networks: The Coordination of Social Life*, London, Sage.

Hall, P. (1980) *Great Planning Disasters*, London, Weidenfeld.

Hennessy, P. (1989) *Whitehall*, London, Weidenfeld.

Parker, H.M.D. (1957) *Manpower*, London, HMSO.

Sartori, G. (1991) 'Market, capitalism, planning and technocracy' in Thompson, et al. (eds.) (1991).

Walker, D. (1990) 'Enter the regulators', *Parliamentary Affairs*, vol 43, no. 2, pp. 149–58.

CHAPTER 2:
MARKETS AS COORDINATIVE DEVICES

Rosalind Levačić

1 The market as a model of coordination

In this chapter I shall be examining the market as a method of coordinating the productive activities of individuals and organizations. As I am concerned with explaining the market as a *model of coordination* I shall not be attempting to describe in accurate detail the markets we observe in the complex world around us but rather I intend to provide an understanding of these market events and processes by focusing on their main features and attributes. To do this, I will address three key questions:

1   How does the market work as a coordinating mechanism?

2   What are the advantages and disadvantages of the market as a coordinating device?

3   What activities is it appropriate to coordinate using markets?

The questions follow logically one from the other. In examining the first question, it is emphasized that since the market is not a mechanical object, like an engine, there is no single accepted understanding of how it works. Different theoretical approaches offer somewhat different explanations of how the market works. I shall concentrate on two approaches, the neo-classical and the Austrian. The different explanations of how markets work provided by the neo-classical and Austrian approaches result in different answers to key questions 2 and 3 and provide a major focus for the chapter. The relative advantages and disadvantages of market coordination have always revolved round two main criteria — efficiency and equity. The market can be proposed or opposed on either criterion. While the Austrians sponsor the market as a superior coordination device to hierarchy and largely oppose state intervention in markets, the neo-classical tradition is much more even handed, providing an analysis of market failure which has been used· to justify a considerable degree of government intervention in the economy. In considering key question 3, I will focus in particular on two areas:

1   The appropriate allocation of activities between the public and private sectors.

2   Why a productive activity is coordinated within a firm or by the market.

A market is a forum in which buyers and sellers, even if very distant from each other, trade in a good or service for which a similar price is charged (allowing for differences in transport and handling costs). The prime feature of a market is that exchange takes place at a price — the good is bought and sold for money rather than being bartered. The ultimate buyers and sellers of the good usually do not trade directly with each other but through middle men — wholesalers and retailers. In a *perfect market* the good exchanges for the same price at the same time in every location where trade takes place. For this to occur each unit of the good must be identical to all the others. Examples of such goods are commodities, such as copper, coffee, oil or grain, which are graded according to their characteristics by the traders so that the commodity is homogenous within a given grade. Paper assets, such as currencies and securities are also homogenous.

In most cases the units of a good or service traded in a market are not identical but are differentiated. Often differentiation is caused by differences between suppliers and emphasized by brand names. If products are differentiated then, as they are not identical, they cannot be perfect substitutes. If units of the product are not perfect substitutes then it becomes more difficult to draw clear boundaries round a market to clearly delineate it from other markets.

There are many different kinds of markets, not only for goods but for different kinds of labour and for assets, both real assets like houses and factories and for paper assets or claims to real assets like company shares. An important feature of markets is that they are interrelated. For instance, the fortunes of the construction materials markets are closely linked to the state of the commercial and property markets, which in turn are linked to the market for shares in property companies. Because markets are so pervasive and interlinked they serve to coordinate a vast range of human activity.

2 The market as a coordination mechanism: the neo-classical approach

The neo-classical school of economics emerged in the last quarter of the nineteenth century and continues to dominate economics. Its chief hallmark is a highly systematized, formal and rigorous method of building models of economic behaviour derived from basic simplifying assumptions about the behaviour of 'economic agents' i.e. individuals and firms. Neo-classical models are based on the assumption that individual consumers choose goods so as to maximize satisfaction or utility. Firms are assumed to be motivated by profit maximization. Firms are purchasers of inputs to production in the form of materials and labour and are sellers of output. Households sell labour and obtain income from the ownership of assets which is then used to purchase consumption goods or further assets.

All these buying and selling activities take place in markets. A market brings together those demanding a good or service and those supplying it. The *demand* for a product is defined as the amount buyers wish to acquire by exchanging money for it at a given price. For demand to be registered in a market the desire to buy a certain quantity must be backed up by purchasing power. In a market, price is the pivotal coordinating device. It is generally the case that buyers will wish to purchase more of the good the lower its price while suppliers are willing to sell more the higher the price. The price at which the amount demanded and the amount supplied are equal or in balance is called *the equilibrium price*. Price thus performs the crucial coordinating function in the neo-classical market model: it provides the signal to which buyers and sellers react. A major feature which characterizes the neo-classical approach is the concept of *equilibrium*. When the market price is in equilibrium then there is nothing to cause either buyers and sellers to change their behaviour since they are both happy to trade the same quantity at the same price.

2.1 Coordinating across markets

But how does the market coordinate disturbances or changes to the conditions of demand and supply? What happens if a substitute product rises in price or is no longer favoured because of a health scare, or if the price of a raw material used in the product's manufacture falls? The answer to such questions, given by Alfred Marshall (1920), a major founder of neo-classical economics, is that:

> When demand and supply are in stable equilibrium, if any accident should remove the scale of production from its equilibrium position, there will be instantly brought into play forces tending to push it back to that position.
>
> *(Marshall, 1920; reproduced in Thompson et al., p. 30, 1991)*

So if a market is disturbed by some change the price will alter in order to bring the market back to equilibrium. For example, if a war in the Middle East reduces world supplies of oil, the first reaction is for oil suppliers to raise the price of oil because demand initially exceeds supply. The higher oil price will lead other producing countries to expand their production and oil refining companies to bring back mothballed refining capacity into use and invest in new capacity. But the higher price of oil will also reduce the demand for it. There will be a greater incentive for electricity generators to switch from oil to gas and coal, whose prices are therefore likely to rise because of extra demand. Higher fuel prices all round will encourage people to heat their homes less. Air fares rise and this will discourage holidays abroad. Higher petrol prices at the pumps may reduce the distances travelled by motorists and, in the longer term, increase the demand for more fuel-efficient cars. Thus the increase in oil prices serves to equilibrate the market by increasing supply and reducing demand. Any disturbance to markets in the neo-classical model gives rise to price changes and hence other responses which bring demand and supply back to equilibrium.

2.2 Market coordination as resource allocation

The whole complex of interrelated markets make up *the market system* which now links all countries to greater or lesser degrees into a global economy. The market system is the mode of coordination used for running the major part of the economy in countries such as Britain which are referred to as capitalist or market economies.

Any kind of society has to solve what is known as the 'economic problem'. This consists of deciding:

1   *What to produce*

   What kinds of goods and services to produce for consumption, e.g. more fish and less meat?

2   *How to produce*

   What kinds of production methods to use, e.g. oil, gas or coal fired electricity generating plants?

3   *For whom to produce*

   How much will each person get in income and wealth? This is the issue of distribution.

The market system is one type of allocative mechanism or coordinating device for solving the what, how and for whom questions. Two alternative allocative mechanisms are central economic planning and custom or rules determined by tradition. Central economic planning is a hierarchical and bureaucratic method of allocation. It has been attempted on an economy-wide basis in communist countries and, particularly in the immediate post-war period, to a limited extent in certain capitalist economies such as France and Japan. It also applies as a model to the non-market parts of the public sector such as health, defence, education and the transport infrastructure. In a central planning system coordination (i.e. allocation) is undertaken by a central unit at the top of the bureaucratic hierarchy which, by the promulgation of rules and the use of commands, seeks to get its plans implemented by the lower echelons of the hierarchy.

In contrast coordination in the market model is highly *decentralized*. Each economic agent decides how much it wants to buy or sell by comparing the price offered to the alternative benefits of not engaging in the exchange. There is no single agency coordinating the buying and selling plans of the individual agents in the market. Consumers respond to the price signal by deciding how many units to purchase at the going price. If demand exceeds supply at the going price, firms will discover they can charge more and still sell all they have. If profits now exceed costs, firms will be encouraged to invest in more plant or new firms are induced to enter the market. Supply is increased but in order to sell all the extra output firms have to lower the price. No one had told firms to increase supply — they responded to the signal emitted by price. Again, if cost had initially exceeded price some firms would cut production or leave (exit) the market. Supply would fall, excess demand materialize and price would rise.

A competitive market is completely decentralized. A *perfectly competitive market* exists if buyers and sellers are so numerous that their own purchases or sales are too small a proportion of the total to influence the market price.

At the other extreme is a market with very few buyers and sellers. One seller in a market is known as a *monopoly*, a handful as an *oligopoly*. A market dominated by a single buyer is a *monopsony*. There can be various permutations of many sellers and a few or a single buyer or many buyers and a handful of sellers. In a market with only a few buyers (or sellers) each can influence the price by the amount they choose to buy or sell and so are said to have *market power*. In such imperfectly competitive markets pricing decisions are not fully decentralized. A monopoly seller can decide what price to charge but then has to accept the quantity buyers will purchase at that price. Regulated private sector monopolies, such as British Telecom and British Gas, are constrained in the prices they charge by legislation on pricing rules and by an official regulator (OFTEL and OFGAS). Oligopolists may well collude over the prices they set, though this is illegal under competition law except in certain instances. When there are few buyers and sellers, as in many labour markets where a trade union bargains on behalf of its members with an employers' organization, then the price or wage is set by negotiation. In practice, markets vary from being highly competitive to strongly monopolized on both sides.

The market coordinates decisions about *what* to produce with those of *how* to produce and *for whom*. It does so because the markets for final (consumer) products are interlinked with those for inputs — for raw materials, capital and labour. If a product is in great demand it can sell at a high price and so, most likely, will be the inputs used to make it. The owners of these inputs will therefore receive high incomes for selling their factors of production. So someone with an ability at computer programming who has been trained at it can command a much higher salary, because there is a relative scarcity of computer analysts, than someone with few skills and little education. In a market economy individuals also own material assets, property, businesses or financial assets, the value of which depends on market forces and from which they receive an income. Thus market forces play a large part in determining the distribution of income and wealth which is highly unequal.

The great triumph of the market is seen to be its coordination of a highly diverse and dispersed complex of economic activity. One of the outstanding features of post-war economic development is that more countries and a higher proportion of their output have become integrated via markets into a global economy East European countries, which remained largely outside the world economic order, are now becoming or seeking to become better integrated. Price signals enable producers and consumers around the world to respond to information about the changing conditions of supply and demand for a complex chain of interrelated goods and services involving many national economies without their needing to know about the factors that caused these price changes. In the neo-classical view the market is an equilibrating coordination mechanism: it works to even out imbalances in demand and supply for final goods, for capital and even for labour since areas with low wages will attract capital investment because products can be made more cheaply there.

2.3 Efficient market allocation

The major claim made for market coordination in the neo-classical approach is that it promotes an *efficient allocation of resources*. Though efficiency is an everyday word and so seems to have a self-evident meaning, it is a rather tricky concept to come to grips with. In economics several kinds of efficiency are distinguished, of which the most important are *productive efficiency* and *allocative efficiency. Productive efficiency* corresponds to what normal people — other than economists — mean by efficiency. It is the least-cost way of producing something or achieving some specific end.

A competitive market in equilibrium is *productively efficient* because a profit maximizing firm will produce output as cheaply as possible given its production technology and the prices of inputs. When there is freedom of entry, which is an essential condition for a perfectly competitive market, any excess of price over the cost of a unit of output, where costs include the necessary market return on capital, will attract existing firms to expand capacity and new firms to enter until long-run equilibrium is achieved when price just equals the average cost of a unit of output. When price equals unit cost no more firms are induced to enter and expand supply and no firms are leaving as a result of making losses. Thus competition and the profit motive ensure that production costs are as low as possible and that the price of the product is driven into equality with its cost. Thus a key aspect of the efficiency of a perfectly competitive market is that the price consumers pay in equilibrium is equal to the cost of the resources used in making the product. Because of freedom of entry consumers need not pay a price in excess of the cost of the product.

A perfectly competitive market requires numerous buyers and sellers. If firms are to remain small when the industry is in equilibrium with no firms either entering or exiting, then it must be the case that the cost of each additional unit of output — the marginal cost — is rising as output expands. If marginal cost falls as the scale of production increases then the economic advantage lies with large firms. Successful firms then grow and the less successful leave the market so that the number of sellers diminishes and the market is not perfectly competitive.

The competitive market model assumes that firms maximize profits. It can be shown that in order to maximize profits a firm produces that level of output for which the marginal cost is equal to the price. To see why this is the case consider what would happen if marginal cost were less than price. In this case the firm could increase its profits by selling more output. This is because its revenue goes up by the price of a unit of output, but its total costs rise by the marginal cost of a unit of output, which is less than the price. Hence profits must increase as output expands so long as price exceeds marginal cost. Once the amount of output is reached at which marginal cost just equals price, then profits are at their maximum level.

If the firm expanded production when marginal cost exceeded price it would be adding more to costs than to revenues and would therefore reduce its profits.

Hence the condition for profit maximization in a perfectly competitive market is that marginal cost equals price. If all firms have marginal cost equal to price the market must be in equilibrium.

A further crucial deduction of neo-classical theory is that social welfare is maximized if prices equal marginal costs in all markets. The deduction goes roughly as follows. A consumer will reach a situation of maximum satisfaction when the last unit of a good gives just the same satisfaction as spending the same amount of money on an alternative good. If it didn't he or she would spend income differently. As equilibrium means no tendency to change, then in equilibrium consumers cannot be made better off, given their current income and the existing prices of goods, by changing their spending pattern. If prices in all markets equal marginal costs then consumers are achieving the maximum possible satisfaction from the way resources are allocated given the current distribution of income. Any reallocation — say producing less of one good and more of another, given tastes and production costs remain the same — would make at least one consumer worse off.

When an allocation of resources is achieved such that no reallocation could make anybody better off without making at least one other person worse off then resource allocation is allocatively efficient.

An alternative term for a situation where no one can be made better off without harming someone else is Pareto efficiency after the Italian economist Vilfredo Pareto (1848–1923).

The required condition for allocative efficiency in the neo-classical model is that prices in all markets equal marginal costs. This would be achieved if all markets were perfectly competitive and in long run equilibrium.

This is the theoretical core of the neo-classical conclusion that competitive markets are an efficient coordinating device. Consumer satisfaction is maximized and factors of production obtain the best possible return consistent with this.

3 Neo-classical and Keynesian analysis of market failure

There are three basic reasons why market coordination may fail to allocate resources efficiently. They are all conditions which would not enable the market to equilibrate at a price for the good which equals its marginal social cost of production. These are:

1   the absence of perfect competition;

2   externalities;

3   inability of markets to reach a 'market-clearing' equilibrium in which demand and supply are equal.

3.1 Imperfect competition.

The conditions for perfect competition are so restrictive that they exist in very few markets. When competition is not perfect because either buyers or sellers or both have market power, then prices will not be driven by competition into equality with marginal costs. The neo-classical approach has coped with this problem by arguing that less than perfect competition is adequate for promoting social welfare. Markets need to be *workably competitive* or *contestable* which means that new firms can enter the market if prices exceed marginal costs and drive down prices. This view justifies government intervention in the form of competition policy. This includes outlawing collusion between firms and various other uncompetitive practices, such as tie in sales and refusal to supply retailers who cut prices, and the prohibition of mergers which reduce competition. It also favours trade liberalization, that is the removal of import tariffs and quotas and other restrictions on imports. This has been the major economic purpose of the European Community and the international negotiations since the 1950s to liberalize international trade under the auspices of the General Agreement on Tariffs and Trade (GATT).

An alternative strand within neo-classical economics is to use the allocative efficiency criterion to specify conditions under which markets fail to be efficient and then argue for government intervention in order to replicate as far as possible the allocative efficiency condition of price equalling marginal cost. This argument was used to justify the state ownership of industries which are 'natural monopolies', like gas, water and electricity where it would be prohibitively expensive to have more than one supplier. The state owned company would then set prices equal to marginal costs to ensure it was allocatively efficient. One problem with this solution is the absence of any incentive for the state owned companies to keep costs down.

3.2 Externalities

Externalities are any costs or benefits arising from a transaction that do not affect the immediate parties engaging in the transaction and so are ignored by them and are therefore not reflected in market prices. A good example of an external cost is air pollution by motor vehicles. In the absence of laws restricting gas emissions a self-interested car user would have no incentive to buy an engine fitted with a catalytic converter. The only costs such a car user is prepared to pay are those necessary to secure the capital equipment, raw materials, components and labour required to manufacture the car. These costs are *private costs* since they are incurred by the producer and passed on to the consumer in the price of the product. The pollution costs due to gas emissions would be borne by the population in general, especially those living near busy roads.

Costs borne by others in society rather than by the consumer through paying the price of the product are known as *external costs*. The total of private and external costs are *social costs*. If the social costs of car use exceed private costs then the price of consuming the product is not conveying sufficient information to consumers. They are informed by the price mechanism that the use of cars is cheaper in terms of the resources sacrificed to make and run them than is really the case. Therefore more cars are consumed than is required for an efficient overall allocation of resources.

Externalities also exist when social benefits exceed private benefits, as for example immunization and health education programmes which reduce the incidence of contagious diseases.

The neo-classical analysis of market failure due to external costs and benefits supports government intervention to use laws, taxes and subsidies in order to reduce the consumption of goods for which the external costs exceed private costs and increase the consumption of goods which have external benefits in excess of private benefits.

3.3 Failure of markets to clear: Keynesian economics

Keynesian economics is in essence a critique of markets for failing to clear and getting stuck in an equilibrium where the labour market has excess supply. According to Keynes (1936) a generalized fall in demand in the economy will lead to fall in output and a rise in unemployment. Unlike the case of the single market, a fall in the general price level of goods will fail to stimulate aggregate demand sufficiently because such a generalized fall in prices would force employers to reduce workers' wages in order to maintain profits. With prices and wages falling proportionately, workers' real wages stay the same and so there could be no increase in aggregate demand from this source. Thus the economy will remain in depression with no natural equilibrating mechanism to restore full-employment equilibrium. Keynesians support government policy to stimulate aggregate demand to get an economy out of depression.

3.4 State intervention

It is often not appreciated how much support neo-classical economic theory has given to the case for government intervention and regulation in order to deal with inefficiencies arising from imperfect competition and externalities. The existence of these various forms of market failure provides a rationale for superimposing government hierarchical coordination on the market in order to improve allocative efficiency. In some instances state hierarchical coordination may replace the market entirely, as in the case of public sector provision of goods and services, such as electricity, water, rail travel, roads, medical services or education. In other cases the market is regulated, either through physical controls, or by altering prices by means of taxes and subsidies.

4 The market process of coordination: the Austrian approach

A quite different approach is that of Austrian economics which derives largely from the writings of von Mises and von Hayek who worked in pre-war Vienna. Von Hayek subsequently moved to London and then to the United States. Austrians emphasize the dynamic nature of markets and focus on the market as a process.

4.1 Austrian criticisms of neo-classical equilibrium economics

Austrian economists are highly critical of the neo-classical theory of the price mechanism for failing to provide an understanding of how markets actually work in the real world and therefore for providing misguided policy advice. Austrian fire is directed at two key assumptions of neo-classical price theory: the absence of real time and the assumption of perfect knowledge.

- *It is timeless*

  The absence of real time arises from the analytical device of a stationary state in which the market is in equilibrium until disturbed by some event, when it moves to another equilibrium.

There is no proper analysis of what happens to generate the movement from one equilibrium to another. But in the real world markets, even granted they tend towards equilibrium, are in continuous disequilibrium. The focus of a theory of markets should be the dynamics of market adjustments as they unfold through time, not a static equilibrium that is never attained.

- *Perfect knowledge*

   Neoclassical market theory (at least of the perfectly competitive market) assumes both buyers and sellers have complete information about the product. Producers are assumed to know the least cost way of producing output and whether it is appropriate to raise or lower price in order to maximize profit, while consumers know which is the best bargain. The state of technical knowledge is assumed given and fixed.

4.2 The market process

Austrians stress that the market has to be understood as a *process* whereby buyers and sellers seek out over time profitable opportunities for exchange. Market participants do not have complete and costless information. They have, in fact, only limited knowledge. The knowledge market participants act upon is their expectations about future events. For instance, producers engage in production and commit resources to it in the anticipation of profit, while consumers buy in the anticipation of satisfaction from consumption. Hence market information is subjective; it is not objective data externally given to market participants. The market functions as a coordinating mechanism precisely because it provides incentives for economic agents to seek out information upon which to base decisions to engage in market transactions which are anticipated to benefit them. By conducting market transactions, further information is generated upon which further actions are based.

An entrepreneur is anybody who seeks out and exploits market opportunities for gain. By exploiting opportunities for gain, entrepreneurs seek out and satisfy unmet consumer wants or discover and implement new and cheaper production methods. The great virtue of the market is that it is highly efficient in generating and transmitting information because it is decentralized. Each market participant need only possess sufficient information to apply his or her own skills to making saleable output or to purchasing goods and services.

Austrians maintain that by assuming complete knowledge the neoclassical model has removed the most important function of the market which is to generate and transmit information which gives incentives for mutually advantageous exchanges to take place. Because the market is a decentralized coordination mechanism it handles information much more efficiently than a centralized coordination agency could. If bureaucratic planning is to be as efficient as the market, then the central coordinating agency needs to acquire all the information about consumer preferences and production possibilities. With market coordination, each participant only needs a small amount of personally relevant knowledge. Competition then provides the incentive for a continual renewal of the search for mutually beneficial exchanges and so promotes innovation.

Because of the Austrians' rejection of static analysis and perfect information, the neo-classical analysis of market failure which relies upon these assumptions is also rejected. The neo-classical analysis of market failure makes efficiency judgements by attempting to compare the actual outcome of a coordination process to the ideal perfectly competitive outcome (at which marginal social cost equals price). Austrians reject this approach, arguing that it is the process of coordination itself that needs to be evaluated because static equilibrium is not attainable. Different institutional arrangements for achieving coordination should be evaluated and compared against the criterion of how well they coordinate. So, for example, one should compare a centrally planned health service with a private sector market system or one with managed internal markets by evaluating how they coordinate and not by attempting to assess their final outcomes in terms of net benefits and costs. A system of coordination is to be judged according to how well it enables participants to take account of all the information they need in order to make a decision. The more discoordination there is, the more participants would change their actions if they were aware of what others mean to do. A perfectly functioning coordinating mechanism would generate and transmit all the information needed for decision making so that participants would not change their decisions if further information were provided. So, for example, making producers 'more responsive to their clients' (an avowed objective of much recent government policy towards the public services) would be a criterion for a 'good' set of institutional coordination arrangements. Recent policies towards introducing more decentralized decision making about resource allocation in the local authority education and national health services can therefore be justified in terms of the Austrian approach.

The key differences between the neo-classical and Austrian models of market coordination are summarized in Table 2.1.

4.3 Policy implications of the Austrian approach

The Austrian approach is meant to be a strong defence of the market as the best coordinating mechanism available. In von Hayek's work (see Thompson et al., 1991, pp. 293–301) the market is integrated into a complete and elaborate view of the nature of social order. It is an example of what von Hayek terms 'a spontaneous social order' — one that arose out of the unplanned but purposeful activities of human beings to provide a stable framework for interaction and cooperation. Markets coordinate the diverse and often conflicting plans of individ-

Table 2.1 Contrasting Austrian and neo-classical theories of the market

Topic	Austrian	Neo-classical
Theoretical focus (with respect to equilibrium)	Disequilibrium — the competitive forces compelling change.	Pattern of prices and quantities established in equilibrium.
Assessment of efficiency	Reliability of market forces in generating spontaneous corrections to changes occurring in disequilibrium.	Optimal allocation of resources in static equilibrium given by marginal social cost = price.
Role of entrepreneur	Crucial — perceives and acts upon opportunities for gain in bringing together buyers and sellers. Has no owned resources.	Role given little significance. In equilibrium there is no function for the entrepreneur to perform since all mutually advantageous exchanges are taking place.
Nature of competition	Inseparable from entrepreneurship. Is the process of providing alternative and more attractive opportunities to buyers and sellers.	Defined in terms of structure — i.e. number of buyers and sellers — not process. Ceases to be an active force in equilibrium.
Information	Market participants start out ignorant. Gain information by participating in the market. The market process generates and transmits continually changing information. Is efficient because it is decentralized and so economizes on information.	Information given externally to consumers and producers. Latter know what consumers demand and what the least cost production methods are; consumers know prices and other attributes of products.
Monopoly	Distinguish between monopoly due to entrepreneurial activity and due to resource ownership. If due to former is because no other market participant is willing or able to supply the product. Former type should not be interfered with by government.	All monopolies regarded as allocatively inefficient and therefore socially undesirable because of focus on present outcome in which producer charges a price in excess of marginal cost.

uals without any single body having to reach and enforce agreement between participants. This, in von Hayek's view, underpins the superiority of the market because it coordinates while permitting and even promoting individual choice and freedom. In contrast state hierarchy as a coordination device is a deliberate and planned social order. It therefore restricts choice and fails to provide sufficient incentives for the generation of new information or for seizing opportunities for making transactions from which both parties benefit. In Austrian thinking the presumption is always in favour of market coordination and it is wary of government intervention. There is, however, a strong but more limited role for government in maintaining the framework within which the market can operate. This requires establishing rules for defining property rights and for exchanging them and, when necessary, enforcing contracts. There is also a role for the government in securing social justice by a more equal distribution of property rights prior to engaging in market transactions. Hence a state role in securing rights for all to the same educational opportunities is supported. If any further redistributions of income are favoured they should be in the form of cash, for example a national minimum social payment, rather than in kind in the form of free education and health services.

The Austrian view of the market process and the nature and role of competition and entrepreneurship leads to a very different stance towards monopoly and market power than that derived from neo-classical economics. In neo-classical analysis any deviation from perfectly competitive equilibrium is an instance of market failure and hence inefficiency in resource allocation. It therefore follows that the government should be active in preventing the build-up of monopoly power (e.g. by banning mergers which are deemed to reduce competition) and in regulating natural monopolies (when increasing the number of suppliers would raise costs). However, Austrians see such government activism as impeding the competitive process and reducing the efficiency of markets in the long run because entrepreneurs are impeded in seeking to innovate and attract more customers. Since the market process is only set in motion by entrepreneurs in search of profits, government action to deny entrepreneurs the fruits of entrepreneurship will weaken the competitive process and so retard economic development. Austrians are optimistic that so long as entry and exit into and out of markets remains unimpeded, any monopoly positions which can be challenged by rival producers will be competed away. Thus government action should be focused on maintaining free entry and exit, rather than protecting existing producers from competition, as governments have done on a wide scale through measures such as regulation, subsidies, favoured state purchasing arrangements and import restrictions.

4.4 Criticisms of the Austrian approach

The methods employed by Austrians in their work rely more on plausible deductions built up from propositions about human behaviour which Austrians see as self-evidently true (such as purposive human action and the continual striving for information on which to act for personal gain) than on empirical evidence. A major criticism of the Austrian approach is that it is too sanguine about the power of the market process to work in the beneficiently efficient manner presumed. Particularly subject to criticism is the Austrian denial of monopoly as a problem unless it stems from monopoly of resource ownership and their faith that monopoly power due to superior entrepreneurship will either be challenged by new entry or, if not challenged, be justified by its evident efficiency. Critics would argue that even if a position of market power were originally due to superior entrepreneurship, the resulting market power will be subsequently protected by the very fact that the successful firm was first off the mark and so can achieve lower costs through initial learning and larger scale, by building up dealer and customer loyalty and by raising barriers to entry against rivals.

Externalities are another aspect of market failure where the Austrian approach is too cavalier. Since Austrians are generally opposed to government intervention, their solution to the externality problem is to turn as many goods as possible into private goods, that is goods with property rights which can then be traded. So, for example, the government could issue property rights in the atmosphere which firms wishing to discharge noxious gases would have to buy before being entitled to emit pollutants. Similarly roads would be charged for by levying tolls. However, it is doubtful that property rights could be defined and traded for all potential markets affected by externalities without incurring high costs for transferring and enforcing property rights. For example, charging tolls on roads slows down traffic movement.

5 Markets and hierarchies: the coordination of firms

So far key questions 2 and 3 concerning the advantages and disadvantages of market coordination and its appropriate use have been examined in the context of the economy as a whole and in relation to government providing a corrective to market allocation through various aspects of hierarchical coordination. However, there is an increasingly important literature on the appropriate reliance of market and hierarchical coordination within firms and other types of organization. The central question being posed here is:

What determines whether a set of productive activities is undertaken by a number of independent firms and coordinated by the market, or is coordinated hierarchically within a single firm?

For instance, what determines whether a motor manufacturer buys in components from independent suppliers or makes them itself? Does it own its dealer network or not? These are all examples of vertical integration where the processes required at different stages to manufacture and sell a product are all undertaken by the same company. Horizontal integration occurs when two firms which are producing at the same stages of production merge, such as Ford's acquisition of Jaguar. A firm diversifies when it merges with another whose products are sold in entirely different markets, as for example British Aerospace's acquisition of Rover.

This question of what determines what is coordinated within a single firm rather than by the market was originally posed by Coase (1937). The answer he provided was that activities are coordinated within firms when the transactions cost of doing this are less than using market coordination. Transactions costs are all those costs that are incurred when undertaking an exchange. For example, if a car assembling firm buys its components from another firm it has to incur costs in obtaining information about the price and quality of the components and the delivery performance of the supplier. Then a market contract to purchase the components has to be negotiated. Once delivery starts, the car assembler has to monitor the contract and enforce the contract if the supplier fails to comply with it. The component supplier also incurs transaction costs in gathering information about the purchaser. If the component is being made to the unique specification of the purchaser, there is the risk that the investment in plant and machinery needed to produce this component will not obtain its expected return if the purchaser reneges on the contract. If the car assembler integrates vertically with the component producer and so coordinates the transaction within the firm, all these transactions costs are not eliminated since quality and delivery times have still to be ensured but the cost may well be lower.

Coase's ideas were later developed by Williamson (1975) in an influential book on industrial organization called *Markets and Hierarchies*. Williamson terms the coordination undertaken within firms 'hierarchy' in contrast to market coordination which takes place between firms. Firms rely upon rules and orders to coordinate activities within the organization. The rules and their interpretation set the framework for providing incentives for the firm's employees to act in the interests of the organization, rather than for their own or other organizations' interests as they would if outside the firm and engaging in market transactions. Williamson singles out three main reasons why internal hierarchical coordination is more efficient (that is it saves on transactions costs).

The first is 'bounded rationality'. This term means that decision makers do not have complete information and are limited in their capacity to process it. Therefore they have insufficient information to specify a market contract that will work satisfactorily as events unfold and the unexpected occurs. It is argued that hierarchical coordination, because it relies upon orders within a command structure rather than on a pre-specified contractual arrangement, is more flexible in responding to unfolding events.

The second reason is 'opportunism' or the guileful pursuit of self-interest. This behaviour means that parties to market contracts will try to take advantage of loopholes in the contract to pursue their own advantage at the expense of the other party. Assymetric information, which arises when one party to a transaction has more information about it than the other party, can also be exploited for personal gain. Williamson argues that internal hierarchy provides less incentive for opportunistic behaviour because its rewards cannot so easily come in monetary form and opportunistic behaviour can be better monitored within the firm. By internalizing the transaction the firm gains more information as well as reducing the scope for opportunistic behaviour which would exploit assymetric information.

The third factor is 'asset specificity'. This occurs when resources are committed to a particular activity but have very little value in any alternative use. A small number of buyers and sellers tends to increase asset specificity since it means that there are few alternative suppliers or customers to turn to and so each party can affect price. This makes market transactions vulnerable to opportunistic bargaining behaviour and engenders uncertainty. So a component supplier in this situation would charge a higher price to compensate for the riskiness of the investment. Internalization reduces risk and so lowers transactions costs.

Williamson (1985) proposed a framework, which is set out in Table 2.2, for relating the different kinds of coordinating mechanism that are most efficient (that is have lowest transactions costs) to the attributes of the contract or transaction. The attributes, as just explained, are bounded rationality, opportunism and asset specificity. Table 2.2 depicts four different situations in which transactions can occur. Each of the situations is defined by the presence or absence of the three attributes. In situation 1, bounded rationality and opportunism are present but asset specificity is absent. Williamson considers that market coordination is most efficient in these circumstances. Provided that there is no asset specificity then there is no loss to either party to the transaction if it breaks down. But if asset specificity is present as well (situation 2), then internal hierarchical coordination becomes more efficient than market coordination because it reduces transactions costs.

Table 2.2 Determinants of an efficient coordinating device

Situation	Bounded ra-tionality	Opportunism	Asset specificity	Efficient coordinating device
1	present	present	absent	market competition
2	present	present	present	internal hierarchy
3	absent	present	present	central economic planning
4	present	absent	present	networks

Source: Adapted from Williamson, 1985, p. 31

Situation 3 is characterized by the absence of bounded rationality and the presence of opportunism and asset specificity. In this case it would be possible to coordinate economic activity efficiently by means of central planning. In order to plan efficiently, central planners need access to huge amounts of information concerning both firms' production capabilities and consumers' wants. The difficulty of obtaining information of sufficient quality and quantity is now widely held to be one of the main reasons for the failure of central planning. In situation 4, networks can coordinate efficiently because opportunism is absent so that the parties to the transaction can trust each other.

The markets–hierarchies approach has much to offer in providing an analysis of why a particular coordination mechanism is superior to another in specific circumstances and hence why organizations may change the degree to which they rely on one mode of coordination relative to another.

Williamson treats market and internal hierarchical coordination as two discrete and mutually exclusive alternatives and used these ideas to explain the increasing size of firms attained through vertical integration and diversification into multiple product markets. However, since the 1970s the average size of industrial plants in terms of employees has been declining and large firms have ceased to gain an ever increasing share of their markets. Some recent research (reported in *The Economist*, 15–21 December 1990) proposes that this trend is due to the growth in information technology. In the 1950s it was predicted that IT in the form of main-frame computers would increase firm size by putting more information in the hands of top management. In fact the opposite has happened with firms decentralizing their operations, with more information being distributed amongst middle managers using personal computers. It has been shown that highly computerized firms are less vertically integrated and have narrowed the range of their activities. It is argued that computers encourage the substitution of hierarchies by markets because they reduce the cost of shopping around for market information. IT has led to decentralization of decision making because bounded rationality prevents top management making use of the vast quantity of information computers could now make available to them. Instead information and decision making based upon it has been dispersed through the firm and through market networks.

6 Critiques of market coordination

6.1 Social justice

Under the market system the amount a person can spend on goods and services depends on the value of goods and services he or she can exchange for money. This, in turn, depends on the quantities of goods, financial assets and labour services in which the individual has property rights and the prices at which these items will trade on their respective markets. So an individual with few claims to items which are valued by others in market exchanges will be poor.

Even if we imagined market exchange as a board game where everybody started out with the same number and value of counters, by the end of the game some players would have more counters than others. Depending on whether the game is ludo, Monopoly or chess, the outcome of the game is determined by some mixture of chance and individuals' skill in playing according to the rules.

The distributional outcome of market coordination is what individuals end up with. This depends on what individuals start out with (inherent abilities, acquired skills and material wealth) as well as chance events, the application of their skills and how much other players in the market value what they have to sell. Market coordination inevitably results in an unequal distribution of income and wealth even if people started out with equal amounts. When they don't the differential outcomes are much greater.

Social justice is a complex issue but two contrasting approaches to it can be distinguished.

* *Procedural justice*

   The classical liberal or modern libertarian tradition focuses on the initial state in which people come to the market. It would be socially just for everyone to enter the market on an equal footing, as far as this is possible given human differences. However, even if people start out equal, they will differ in effort, judgement and luck when operating on the market resulting in unequal outcomes. But provided the rules of the competitive market have been followed, the process has been procedurally just.

* *Distributive justice*

   Distributive justice focuses on the inequality of the outcomes of market transactions as being socially unjust. In this view it is the market process itself which is inherently unjust because it inevitably leads to unequal outcomes in terms of peoples' relative incomes and wealth.

A concern for distributive justice implies much greater diminution of the role of markets in order to reduce the inequalities of outcome produced by market coordination. An emphasis on procedural justice is used to justify the market process.

6.2 Socialist critiques of market coordination

In Marxist thought until recently there were no redeeming characteristics of markets. In the Marxist tradition, the market as a major social form is inextricably linked with capitalism. It is thus based on the class division between capitalists and workers and enables capitalists to exploit workers by buying their labour power for less than its value in terms of the products workers make. The market system is therefore condemned for alienating workers from the fruits of their labour. The notion of competitive markets is rejected as inapplicable in most sectors and Marxists argued that the long-term trend under capitalism was towards greater monopolization and concentrations of economic power.

Furthermore, markets are condemned for failing to coordinate. Shortages and surpluses continually reappear in particular markets and national economies (and the world economy) are subject to a succession of booms and slumps. This trade cycle demonstrates the chaotic nature of market coordination since the plans of consumers and producers are not coordinated. In a boom capitalists find they have insufficient productive capacity to fulfil demand and invest in more capacity only to find that a change in market expectations means they cannot sell all they had planned to. Cutting back on production leads to bankruptcies and higher unemployment. The chaotic nature of capitalist production is (or was) contrasted unfavourably with the rationality of socialist planning.

With the retreat from central planning in Eastern Europe, market socialists in both east and west are now searching for a workable model of limited markets. Market socialists advocate combining the decentralized freedom and efficiency of the price mechanism with state planning to achieve full employment, distributional justice and the eradication of private monopoly power.

7 Conclusion

Neo-classical theory emphasizes the role of price as the key signal by which the actions of consumers and producers in a vast complex of interrelated markets are coordinated. Austrians focus on the interlinkage between entrepreneurship and the competitive process as the key forces of coordination. As the neo-classical approach is the dominant one, it has tended to define the characteristics of efficiency and equity against which the market is evaluated. Austrians do not provide any critique of the market, but in their prescriptions for a well-ordered society Austrian thinkers point out that the market must be complemented by appropriate political and social processes. In particular the state needs a constitutional basis which enables society to reach collective agreement while protecting individual liberties. The state's prime task is to define and protect individuals' property rights and the means by which property rights are traded.

The neo-classical view is that public sector provision or government regulation of private sector production is justified when it is either more equitable on distributional grounds or more efficient. Austrian criticism of this policy recommendation has two main strands: an emphasis on procedural rather than distributional justice and rejection of market failure analysis.

The markets–hierarchies approach has been developed from within the neo-classical tradition. It pays much more attention to internal decision making in firms than did earlier neo-classical price theory. The markets–hierarchies approach has brought neo-classical and Austrian thinking closer as it emphasizes analysing a coordination mechanism in relation to its efficiency in coping with imperfect and costly information. A coordination mechanism is judged efficient depending on how well in given circumstances it resolves the problems of coordinating transactions which differ according to their degree of uncertainty, asset specificity and frequency, when humans are characterized by bounded rationality, opportunism and the need for 'dignity'. The richness of this approach is that it provides a common framework for evaluating markets, hierarchies and networks as coordination devices between and within all types of organization.

References

Coase, R. M. (1937) 'The nature of the firm', *Economica*, n.s., vol. 4, pp. 386–405.

Keynes, J.M. (1936) *The General Theory of Employment, Interest and Money*, Basingstoke, Macmillan.

Marshall, A. (1920) *Principles of Economics*, Basingstoke, Macmillan. Extracts reproduced in Thompson et al. (1991).

The Economist (1990) 'The incredible shrinking company', 15–21 December, pp. 89–90.

Thompson, G., Frances, J., Levačič, R., and Mitchell, J., (1991) *Markets, Hierarchies and Networks: The Coordination of Social Life*, London, Sage Publications Ltd.

Williamson, O. E. (1975) *Markets and Hierarchies: Analysis and Antitrust Implications*, New York, The Free Press.

Williamson, O. E. (1985) *The Economic Institutions of Capitalism*, New York, The Free Press.

CHAPTER 3:
NETWORK COORDINATION

Grahame Thompson

1 Introduction

Networks are increasingly popular as explanatory devices. The idea of networks has appeared as a driving motif for a good deal of recent intellectual work in the field of organization theory, and in adjacent discipline areas.[1] Although described in varying terms, that set of coordinative relationships that cannot be defined as either quintessentially market based on the one hand or as reducible to hierarchically based ones on the other has appeared as an attractive object of investigation by those attempting to come to terms with contemporary transformations in the structure of organizational arrangements and decision-making processes. The objective of this chapter is to bring into focus exactly what is involved in those mechanisms which can be called 'network forms of coordination'. For hierarchical forms of coordination the key features for governance are rule-bounded bureaucracy, authority, administration, and superordination and subordination, while for market forms the key features are price, self-interest, competition, and formal contracts. But what are the modes of governance that articulate network forms of coordination? These are explored below.

One problem in demarcating the specific boundary around the concept of networks is that any general definition of a network is often so all embracing that it encompasses both markets and hierarchies within it. Suppose we provide a preliminary formal definition of a network as *a specific set of relations making up an interconnected chain or system for a defined set of elements that forms a structure*. This is a loose definition designating nothing more than a set of interlinked elements which form a coordinating structure. As such it could quite easily embrace both market and hierarchical forms of organization. Indeed, when Knoke and Kuklinski (1990) provide a definition of 'network analysis' along these lines they include economic sales and purchases, and authority and power relations as types of networking relations. In addition, there is the so called 'Swedish' approach to modelling industrial systems, associated with the contrast between a network analysis and the transactions-cost analysis of Oliver Williamson, where each of these is making a claim to say how firms operate *within* market situations (Johanson and Mattsson, 1987). Some of the sets of relationships describing networks in the Swedish model are also perfectly compatible with what are usually thought of as hierarchical forms of organization.

Also, while sharing similar concerns, the analysis in this chapter should not be confused with a 'contract theory' approach to organizational coordination, one that brings together the transactions-cost approach with agency theory. For transaction-cost theory it is the properties of the transaction that determine the efficient governance structure. Agency theory is concerned with the question of how to align principal and agent interests. Both appeal to the notion of contracts as a solution to the twin problems of governance structure and interest alignment. Thus the firm, for instance, could be described as just a function of internal and external contracts (Reve, 1990), where such a 'nexus of treaties' acts akin to a network.

The problem with such a contract approach is, however, precisely that which the network form of governance outlined below is designed to address, that is, how organizational activity works that *cannot* be fully inscribed in, or proscribed by, formal contracts. It is well known, for instance, that all complex contracts are unavoidably incomplete. And without some other mechanism in the form of *credibility commitments*, contracts-as-promises are unsupportable. Thus the prime question becomes: 'What is the basis for those behavioural responses that make up the credibility commitments typifying the coordination through networks as opposed to other coordination mechanisms?' These I will call 'network attributes', and will analyse them in a moment.

1.1   Interlocking directorates as networks

One well researched example of an analysis involving the idea of networks concerns the relationships between firms and their owners and between these and the directors of companies. Although this has taken a number of forms in the literature (see for example Stokman, Ziegler and Scott 1985), for the purposes of this exposition we shall concentrate upon questions of company control and particularly on interlocking directorates between various commercial organizations (Scott and Griff, 1984).

The particular approach illustrated here revolves around the way directors of companies tend to 'interlock' between a number of different companies. Three main types of interlock were identified in a book analysing these relationships for the United Kingdom in 1976 (Scott and Griff 1984, p. 25-6). These are illustrated in Figure 3.1. The first — a *primary interlock* — occurs when an inside, executive director of company A, holds an outside, non-executive directorship in another company, B. Secondly, an *induced interlock* occurs as a consequence of the prior existence of two primary interlocks carried by one director. If an executive of company A holds outside directorships in companies B and C, then the primary interlocks A–B and A–C induce a loose interlock between companies B and C. Finally, a *secondary interlock* is totally unconnected with primary interlocks and exists where a person

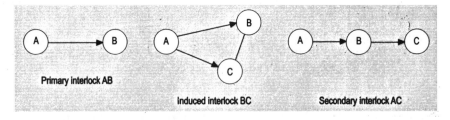

Figure 3.1 *Forms of interlock*

with a base outside the companies being sampled (for example a politician or personality) sits on two or more boards as an outside director. Thus, in this case that director can indirectly create a loose link between companies A and C. Added together, these connections could make up a network of contacts with considerable potential influence over commercial decisions.

The results of an analysis using this kind of a framework for the top 250 United Kingdom companies in 1976 is shown in Table 3.1.

Clearly, multiple directorships are a strong feature of the British commercial scene creating a network of contacts between 'the captains of industry'. In a later section we will return to some of the implications of this type of analysis. For instance, the directors of companies may in turn be linked in a network with political leaders thus creating a 'ruling elite' or oligarchy.

Table 3.1 **Interlocks and number of directorships, 1976**

No. of directorships held	% of interlocks generated		
	Primary	**Induced**	**Secondary**
2	19.0		14.0
3	14.9	7.4	8.1
4	7.1	7.1	2.5
5	5.4	8.1	1.7
6	0.8	1.7	2.5
Totals	47.2	24.4	28.4

Note: The total number of interlocks was 591. By definition, people with only two directorships can generate no induced interlocks.

Source: Scott and Friff, 1984, Table 5.1, p. 135

2 **Network attributes**

Any network involves a set of behavioural dispositions typifying the
agents implicated in it and a certain structural arrangement that sus-
tains those dispositions. This section elaborates what can be called
'network attributes'. Why should actors sustain a network, and what is
peculiar about network coordination as opposed to market or hierarchal
coordination? We will come back to a brief discussion of the differences
between markets, hierarchies and networks in a later section, but for
now it is sufficient to note the kinds of attributes that characterize a
cohesive network. These attributes can be considered as the forces that
articulate a network. Conceptually they occupy the gaps and distances
between network nodal points.

When discussing networks, in the first instance at least, it is probably
institutional arrangements like *informal* groups, *mutual-aid* organizations, *small-scale* and *local institutional* networks, *cooperative* forms of
social existence, *self-help* groups, and so on that come immediately to
mind. The words italicized indicate the key terms when discussing
these types of social relations. Another way of describing these kinds of
social arrangements is as 'flat' organizational forms. They seem to involve a kind of *equality of membership*, where *joint responsibility*
holds. One further term sometimes used to describe these contexts is
that of the 'collegiate' form. This is most often deployed where it is a
set of *professional* people that form the network. Thus it could be applied to the legal, medical, architectural or accounting professions, for
instance, which tend to organize and regulate themselves in a close
(and often clos*ed*) network context. Continuous coordination in these
types of situation outside the market or hierarchy could be predicated
upon a mixture of coexistent attributes such as sympathy, customary reciprocity, moral norms, common experience, trust, duty, obligation, and
similar virtues. What is needed, therefore, is to prise open these notions to see what they involve and how they operate. This is done as a
prelude to discussing the specifics of industrial and political network
governance later.

This section focuses on the terms *solidarity, altruism, loyalty, reciprocity* and *trust* which, it is suggested, are the attributes that best
summarize the reasons why networks exist and function.[2] It is these
terms that best differentiate the specific features of a network model
from either a hierarchical one or a market one.

2.1 Solidarity

How is solidarity formed? To a large extent this can be attributed to
the sharing of a common experience. Social classes, for instance, are often thought to form a solidaristic ethic because the people in them are
'objectively' placed in the same social or economic position and they

therefore experience the same kinds of pressures, cultural stimuli, work regimes, income consequences and so on. They 'stick together' as a result. Similarly, family groups, linguistic groups, ethnic groups, and the like, might also be thought to generate a solidaristic ethic for much the same reasons. The category *experience* is thus crucial to this type of explanation. It is peoples' common or shared experience that forges the solidarity between them.

In the history of the concept of solidarity a distinction is often drawn between 'mechanical solidarity', 'organic solidarity' and 'instrumental solidarity' (Durkheim, 1933). Mechanical solidarity typifies a segmentary community, often small in scale, in which there are clearly separated roles between its members and clear standards by which their behaviour can be assessed. This produces collective conscience in a 'mechanical' way as the members of the community interact along these strictly demarcated lines. People 'know their place' and then act accordingly. Tribal life is often thought to demonstrate this kind of solidarity.

Organic solidarity, on the other hand, refers to a functionally differentiated society of a more complex character. In this case solidarity is more difficult to generate. The complexity of the functions in a differentiated society imply a greater variability of social relations, where the social roles members are called upon to play are less clear-cut (and often multiple) and the behavioural norms associated with those roles equally complex. This leads to a more serious problem in forging the organic solidarity required to establish a collective consciousness. In these types of society self-interest, alienation and anomie can develop which hinder the formation of the necessary social consciousness (necessary for social order). The advanced industrial economies provide good examples of this form of organic solidarity.

Finally, we can point to what might be termed 'instrumental solidarity' as a specific response to the problem identified under the heading of organic solidarity just described. How can the pursuit of self-interest in a functionally differentiated society lead to a solidarity between its members? The generation of this, it is suggested, involves a certain calculus of the benefits and losses by individuals to determine whether, and under what circumstances, they would stand to achieve an overall gain in their welfare by cooperating. In this case then, solidarity would be instrumental to the calculation of individual *net* benefits. This kind of a conception thus shares an intellectual affinity with the neo-classical economic approach to the market. It is the interaction between welfare maximizing individuals in the context of the price system that produced an efficient market solution to the coordination problem. We return to this below.

Each of these forms of solidarity may have its place in explaining the existence of networks as we shall see later. But what they demonstrate is that explaining network solidarity is a *problem* in our type of complex society. How can a system in which individual calculation of benefit is central produce a network of solidaristic relationships? Is not this better understood as producing a market type set of relationships? We now move on to see how the other concepts might provide some further insights into this problem.

2.2 Altruism

Why do some people go to the help of others without any expected gain to themselves, indeed, sometimes even to sacrifice themselves? This is the problem the category altruism addresses, and it is clearly linked to the issue of the generation of solidarity between people. Strictly speaking altruism implies *selflessness*. Thus in being altruistic we expect no self gain to arise from our actions. We act solely in the interests of others. It certainly does not involve an instrumental act in the way the final form of solidarity was discussed above. Presumably, we display a kind of 'generalized benevolence' towards others. This could be in accordance with an ethical principle — 'love of humanity' or 'devotion to one's family' perhaps. Clearly, it could also constitute part of a feeling of solidarity in this sense.

Some have suggested that although altruism involves no calculation of a personal *material* gain it might be compatible with a feeling of internal well-being on the part of the initiator of the selfless action. As a result of introspection, it induces a positive feeling — having done some good. If this is socially recognized in some way — through explicit approval by others — a kind of 'psychical pleasure' might arise and encourage greater altruism.

But altruism should not be interpreted in the way just outlined. It must be totally non-selfish in character, even at the introspective level. One consequence of this is the need to recognize that although there may be individual acts of altruism in any society, to expect a society in general to run on altruistic lines is impossible. At a minimum, society must pay attention to the *rewards* (and penalties) for action. People will act on the basis of the incentives associated with rewards. Of course this does not imply simply material rewards. There may be a range of non-material rewards that will encourage individuals (or any social agent) to act — psychical pleasures, feelings of well-being, social recognition, etc.

2.3 Loyalty

Once a network is intact why should people remain committed to it, or how can 'repeated transactions' be guaranteed? To answer this question we need to examine loyalty. In his analysis of the way members of organizations react to disturbances in the operation of those organizations, Albert Hirshman suggests they have three strategies open to them: 'exit', 'voice' and 'loyalty' (Hirshman, 1970). First, to *exit* means that members simply decide to leave the organization to get on with its problems rather than try to help sort them out; they may take their custom elsewhere, they may retreat to some quiet corner, they may seek another job, or whatever. Secondly, members may stay and exercise their *voice*. In this case, they actively try to change things for the better as they see it. They may organize, petition, demonstrate, campaign, and so on — that is, voice their opposition or support for some change or action. Finally, they have the option of simply remaining *loyal* to the organization. In this case, they would very much 'carry on as before', perhaps in a rather passive way, supporting the organization and its leadership. In a network context, ties of personal and professional loyalty can be very important in securing a stable, robust set of enduring relationships, that are quite resistant to the temptations of voice or exit. Of course, in any real situation it is unlikely that network agents would only exercise one of these strategies exclusively. They are likely to be found in some combination, or in a sequence — voice *and* loyalty, voice *and* exit (but clearly not exit *and* loyalty!): or *first* loyalty, *then* voice, *then* exit.

To some extent it might seem loyalty is synonymous with a kind of indifference or acceptance. As long as things go reasonably well why bother to voice (loudly) or exit? But it really needs to be buttressed by some more positive attributes like *faith* in the ability (and loyalty) of others, *affection* for them, norms of *trust, duty* and *obligation*. Interestingly, these latter two 'norms' — duty and obligation — may not be secured just as 'social relations' but also as *symbolic relations*. Why are we prepared to do our duty and meet our obligations; to sacrifice our lives for Queen and country, say? The point here is that Queen and country have a symbolic significance — popularly represented by the crown and the flag. The emblemic character of ritual and the motifs of pomp and ceremony all serve to *symbolically* embed us in a loyalty. They thereby effect a *legitimation* of those practices and mechanisms of symbolic recognition that are so powerful in shaping many of the contours of contemporary social and political life. In fact, this is the site of a very important critique of 'coordination through networks of solidarity' which is pursued in a later section. Where does loyalty end and the manipulation and corruption it might engender or tolerate begin?

Finally in this subsection, we need to say a little more about the concept of voice. In its literal sense 'voice' has to do with the power of language. Thus one of the ways networks might be secured — one of the means by which they are organized — is through the activity of *argument, debate* and *persuasion*. This activity of argument, debate and persuasion is sometimes referred to as the 'art of rhetoric'. Networks can thus be articulated in a rhetorical or discursive fashion. In fact, this is an important way networks operate. Given that they are often informal, cooperative, local, small-scale, and the like, they are amenable to these kinds of devices. Given that they rely upon the at-

tributes of trust, affection, sympathy, and so on, consultation and negotiation are likely to be strongly present in the practices of networks.
Consultation and negotiation are nothing but the exercise of language
and rhetoric.

3.4   Reciprocity

One further way of stabilizing coordination in a network situation is
through the symmetry between giving and receiving. This also involves
the norm of obligation. When someone gives a gift, for instance, there is
not only an expectation that something will be given in return, perhaps
later, but also an obligation on the part of the receiver to reciprocate
(Mauss, 1970). A kind of moral sanction operates here, but this is not al-
truistically motivated. With altruistic behaviour there is *no* obligation expected or received. You give something when you genuinely expect nothing in return.

Written somewhat larger than just gift exchanging, the 'give and
take' of social interaction is an important contact building and sustaining mechanism. It implies the temporary foregoing of advantage by one
party, knowing that it can (and will) 'collect' later. But gift exchanging is important in illustrating one feature that pervades these kinds of
reciprocity relationships; their symbolic character. Just as in the case
of loyalty, reciprocity is not simply a social relation but also a symbolic
one. In the constant ritual of the exchange, deep obligations and duties
are established, symbolic statuses confirmed, metaphorical social references invoked.

The success of generalizing the expectation of reciprocation depends
on several factors: (1) it is easier in small collectivities; (2) it is easier
when the 'social distance' between actors is short, and chains of action
are not extended; (3) it is less difficult when the actors are homogeneous
in outlook, style of life, material circumstances, customs of action, etc.;
(4) in larger arenas, which are more heterogeneous with respect to actors and institutions, the generation of reciprocity is most successful
when differentiated (multiple) standards are developed by which different kinds of reciprocal expectation can be specified. Clearly, many of
these features required for reciprocity to work could also be duplicated
for the effective operation of networks more generally.

3.5   Trust

Finally, one other belief upon which cooperation is predicated is trust.
Cooperation is both a fragile and a vital relationship for networks, in
which trust plays a central organizing role. Clearly, if everybody behaved absolutely honestly there would be no need for trust. Trust appears as a category when there is an uncertainty about how people will
behave — a risk is always involved in relationship because of a poten-

tial for dishonesty, to which the notion of trust is the response. The more we trust people, the more honestly we expect them to behave, and vice versa.

Risk and uncertainty are endemic in a complex world. But the risks and uncertainties to which trust is the response are not those 'natural' risks and uncertainties imposed upon us by the vagrancies of fortune. They are, rather, the result of a potential opportunistic behaviour on the part of cooperating agents when such 'natural' events strike, as they are always threatening to do. Trust in our sense is a behavioural response to these kinds of events — we can 'bet against them' by building up trust, and its allied concepts of *reputation* and *consistency*. *Cooperation* is more secure and robust when agents have a *trust* because of the *reputation* of themselves and other agents in the network for *honesty* and *consistency*. Thus trust implies an expected action, to our benefit or not detrimental to it, which we cannot monitor in advance, or the circumstances associated with which we cannot directly control. It is a kind of device for coping with the freedoms of others. It minimizes the temptation to indulge in purely opportunistic behaviour (Gambetta, 1988). It is closely linked to loyalty.

Two important points concerning trust we will have to return to in a moment are posed by the above discussion. One is what comes first, trust or cooperation? And the second, related question, is how does trust/cooperation become established? Up till now we have rather presumed these to exist and gone about describing their characteristics. We return to these issues in a moment.

Clearly, these attributes of networks are not mutually exclusive. They overlap a good deal, complementing and reinforcing each other. Collectively they act to generate a *solidaristic-cooperative* behaviour between network agents. They do not guarantee it, of course — the social order marked out by networks may well break down and disintegrate; it may be replaced by hierarchy or the market. Solidaristic-cooperation can be interpreted very broadly to mean the set of rules or norms agreed to between agents which are then to be observed in the course of their interaction. These rules and norms constitute a kind of 'contract' between the agents (which could be individuals, firms or governments). Such agreements need not be formal and legally binding contracts, however (though they might be of this kind in part); they can be informal ones that have arisen implicitly in the course of the interaction, that need not be written down but established as a result of habit, prior successful experience, trial and error, and so on.

A major problem with cooperation is how to organize long-term agreement between the members of any group or club. This can become particularly acute in collegiate forms, or where there is a formal equality amongst those involved. No one single member has the power or authority to impose their own will on others. One strategy under these circumstances is to enter a bargaining arrangement. Diplomacy around a *quid pro quo* stance might be effective. Under these circumstances all the usual characteristics and caveats associated with bargaining become operative — careful deployment of arguments, persuasive skills, the revelation of only the most necessary information, deliberate concealment of objectives, even the possibility of downright dishonesty at times. Clearly, all the features of networks discussed in this section could be implicated here. But *if* the network is going to actually work and survive then a generalized trust, honesty and solidarity must transcend any minor negotiating infringements of these, and a shared common overriding objective be in place. These help produce those credibility commitments so necessary for network configurations.

One thing that is attractive about networks discussed in this manner is that they provide a set of *ethical virtues* at the same time as providing a realistic means to coordinate economic and social life. Thus trust, loyalty and cooperation — which might be said to arise 'spontaneously' in the context of network governance — take on a renewed significance.

3 Cooperation in practice

Trust and loyalty are intimately connected with cooperation, but so are reciprocity, solidarity and altruism. All these features mesh together as far as networks governance is concerned. This section concentrates upon the relationship between cooperation and trust in particular. Clearly, if distrust is complete cooperation will fail. History is legion with the consequences of such breakups of trust and cooperation. We could also enumerate cases where trust is very one-sided, which might also lead to a break up of cooperation. The extreme case of one-sided trust is where it is blind for one party. In this case, there is a clear incentive for the other party to engage in deception or to become opportunistic. However, repeated instances of deceit can only last for so long before they are uncovered, and cooperation undermined.

In fact, it is with the idea of repetition of actions and reactions that some of the issues associated with the establishment of trust and cooperation are usually explored. The most well known of these involves the so called 'prisoner's dilemma game' (PD). This is illustrated in Figure 3.2. It represents the following scenario. There are two players, Saddam and George. Saddam has invaded a small and helpless state while George has come to its rescue. George has decided upon two strategies in his attempt to persuade Saddam to leave the invaded state. The first involves the imposition of sanctions and a blockade of Saddam's country. The second is to threaten an all out air strike-led war against Saddam's country. In reaction to this, Saddam sees himself as faced with two options. He can either withdraw under these threats/actions, or he can stand firm against them. The pay-off matrix for this 'game' is sketched in the figure. The problem confronted here is

SADDAM

	Withdraw	Stay put
Blockade/ Sanctions	3,3 (mutual compromise)	1,4 (Saddam's victory)
Air strike	4,1 (George's victory)	0,0 (mutual destruction of forces)

GEORGE (to the left, spanning both rows)

Figure 3.2: Generating cooperation

one of the generation of trust and 'cooperation' between the two players whose interests seem so totally opposed.

The figures in this matrix (ordinal measures) are designed to represent a simple 'chicken game' which meets the rank order $T > R > S > P$.[3] Both sides wish to avoid an outright and devastating 'mutually assured destruction' of their forces, which is the least desirable outcome [0,0]. George would like to win a prestige victory on the account of his boldness in threatening and carrying out the air strike; on the other hand, Saddam would lose face if he withdrew under this threat. Thus for this outcome the pay-off values are [4,1]. But suppose that the blockade against Saddam was ineffective and he was able to maintain his position in the invaded country. Saddam would claim a stunning victory over George under these circumstances. George, on the other hand would be left with the cost of the ineffective blockade which he would consider a defeat. Thus the pay-off here is symmetrically the opposite of the previous case [1,4]. Finally, there is the possibility that George's blockade will be effective in forcing Saddam to withdraw. This 'compromise' outcome, while not so attractive to Saddam or George as an outright victory for either of them, is at least better than the mutually assured destruction of their respective forces. Thus for this outcome the pay-off value is [3,3].

This kind of a chicken game is one of a set of games of the PD type that do not have completely convincing rational (or equilibrium) solutions. For this they need a principle of choice based on collective interests. In its absence the temptation to 'go it alone' remains strong (thereby scoring 4 in the above pay-off matrix). The question asked of the chicken game is who will chicken out first? In the case of networks it would be a situation of which party withdrew from the network and for what reason. Clearly, there is no completely convincing rational solution to this kind of a dispute. What this highlights is the difficulty

of reaching a cooperative 'compromise' under the circumstances described. Without trust individual interests override collective ones.
But the collective outcome, the 'cooperative compromise' of a with-
drawal and no military victory or defeat for either, would give the
higher pay-off overall [6 > 5 > 0]. What this illustrates is the difficulty of generating a cooperative outcome, which would remain even if
both parties actually prefered the compromise anyway. But any condi-
tional cooperation that was forged amongst the players emerges solely
from a desire to maximize their individual long-term pay-offs. The
players are akin to neo-classical economic actors who act as rational
egotists, maximizing their expected individual utility functions. What
is more, these utility functions are quite independent of one another. In
this situation players do not care whether other players achieve or do
not achieve any gains from the cooperative relationship. Strictly
speaking, therefore, it rules out the analysis of situations characterized by common but mixed interests.[4] As was pointed out in the case of
the PD/chicken game above, the generation of cooperation under the
rules of game theory can be very difficult, relying upon quite restrictive
preconditions. But although the logic of self-interest might be thought
to mitigate against any motivation for solidarity and cooperation, that
is not necessarily the correct interpretation. Even on an individualistic
type calculation one of the cooperative strategies in the PD example
produces an *overall* higher benefit than the 'go it alone' options.[5]

However there is another important way to express the manner in
which cooperation could come about; it may *evolve* (Axelrod, 1990). In
Axelrod's examples cooperation emerges gradually as a result of a number of conditions; random signals and their interpretations; the testing
out of those interpretations to increase conviction and lessen misunder-
standings; the gradual learning of the rules and norms; and the solidifi-
cation of a mutual interest in cooperation as a result. The message of
this analysis is that cooperation does not necessarily have to be either
'taught' or 'imposed'. The crucial issue at stake is the need for a
'cooperative outlook' to be fostered. According to Axelrod, this can
come about if the game is played over and over again. If the expectation is that the players will have to deal with each other repeatedly
and frequently, this can counter the temptation to defect or counter-de-
fect. Thus from this perspective the foundation of cooperation is not
necessarily trust, but rather the durability of the relationships involved. It develops spontaneously (and possibly tacitly) between re-
ciprocating parties (as suggested above). The *reputation* of the parties
for cooperation rather than for competition becomes *expected* and
'socially embedded' as a result.[6]

These types of game situation — involving moral dilemmas and tacti-
cal choices — although rather artificially specified here, pervade a
good many real-life and more complex situations. Clearly, the outcomes crucially depend upon the pay-off figures given to the various ac-

tions of the players. Although illustrating the problem of generating cooperation in the context of game theory the point is that similar situations and problems can arise in a broader network context. The PD game raises subtle problems of trust and suspicion. A player who trusts the other to behave cooperatively has a reasonable justification for doing likewise, but one who suspects that the other may defect has himself or herself only one reasonable course of action, namely to defect also. For this reason, there is a tendency for pairs of players to adopt increasingly similar patterns of play when the game is repeated a number of times — if they have been faced with a similar situation before and acted cooperatively then. Thus if you start out with an initial (trusting) disposition to cooperate it is likely that you will actually end up cooperating, as the same situation repeats itself on a number of occasions. What it means, however, is that 'repeat transactions' — the repetition of day-to-day cooperative activity — tends to self-reinforce that very cooperation and secure it in a robust manner, even as it is based upon individualistic self-interested calculations.

An important feature of these models is that they begin from a position of non-trust/non-cooperation and ask how trust/cooperation can be generated. They begin with a set of already known interests and ask how these can be maximized, how they interact or how they might be modified in the process of that interaction. But there are a number of criticisms that can be levelled at this kind of a conception. First, why begin with a situation in which interests are already fully known before entering into any negotiation or relationship? It could be that the negotiation or relationship itself *establishes* those interests. Governments may not fully know their 'interests' before they enter into any negotiation. Similarly with members of networks. The activity engaged in will at least in part determine what are conceived to be the interests at stake and how they are made manifest.

Secondly, and in the same spirit, why should we begin by assuming a radical situation of non-trust/non-cooperation and ask how it can be generated from this absence? Suppose we begin from a slightly different starting point, accepting that trust/cooperation is already in existence or operative at some level. The point here is to recognize that cooperation and trust are a precondition for any form of collective existence. Thus at some level they must already exist. The analytical problem then becomes one of specifying the conditions in which, or under which, *greater trust* or *greater cooperation* can be generated, or different relations of cooperation/trust established. Alternatively it can be used to ask how relations can become more cooperative or more trusting (Sabel, 1990, p.4). How can governments or economic agents become more deserving of trust (more trustworthy) or more disposed to cooperate and more cooperative? In the main the game theory approaches discussed so far in this section are wedded to a conceptual framework that does not allow these more realistic problems to be either the most important ones or those foregrounded in the analytical situation. In a world of growing cooperative-integration we are in a world of already existing integrations and cooperations. The problem is not how to start integrative-cooperations — these already exist. Rather it is to encourage these to develop further in similar or different directions, in respect to different policy issues or areas, with respect to new arenas or economic groupings, etc. This would push the investigation into the complex institutional and historical conditions that have both characterized and fostered *more or less* trusting relationships.

Thirdly, the immediately preceding discussion concerns the underlying problem posed by the PD example; what is the *rationality* of cooperation? Note that rationality is posed in quite individualistic terms by the examples — as a means to a given end. The kind of rationality operating here is the instrumental calculative rationality already alluded to above when discussing instrumental solidarity as a response to the problem of organizing collective consciousness in an organic type society. This idea of rationality links objectives to actions by way of decisions about means to an end. It is individualistically rational and logical in these terms. But there are other quite legitimate descriptions of rational behaviour that do not operate in quite this manner. For instance, to recognize that there are all sorts of reasons why different types of social and economic agents make decisions, largely constrained by the conditions they face. In the case of human agents this is because of the activity of *thinking*, which may not be 'rationalistic' in a calculative ends/means sense. This particular approach does not necessarily rely upon an individualistic logic of utility calculation that assesses the costs and benefits of all options before making a decision based solely upon that logic. For instance, we have already seen that networks can be built on symbolic and discursive relations (rhetoric and persuasion) which may not be 'rational' in the sense just described. But that does not mean these are 'irrational' either. In addition, the very terms used to describe the means of network organization; trust, honesty, altruism, loyalty, solidarity and cooperation even, need not be thought of in rationalistic terms either. Trust, for instance, could simply describe a personality disposition; and a cooperative outlook a state of mind (Coleman, 1982; Lewis and Weigert, 1985). Supposing, then, that we assume from the outset that humans are naturally trusting rather than that trust is absent and that calculations of self-interest drive the motivation of social agents. Thus we might suggest that trust is a *precondition* for any form of *social* life.

4 Cooperation, trust and firm organization

This section examines the long-term relationships between main firms and their sub contractors and suppliers which is often characterized by authors as a network (for example see Lorenz, 1988). The relationships here tend to be informal and cooperative in form, relying on a trust between the main firm and its suppliers. They are neither straightforwardly hierarchically organized via orders and administrative edict, nor straightforwardly strict market relationships where the main firm continually searches for the least-cost supplier and only maintains a short-term arms length 'buyer/seller' relationship with its suppliers. The stimulus for this change comes from technological developments and the need to increase flexibility by the client firms. These are leading to the disintegration of their vertically hierarchical character as more and more of the production of manufactured parts needed for in-house assembly is located in subcontracting firms. This saves the main firms from investing in specialist machinery that they might not have been able to make full use of. The main firms often keep the design function in-house, however, using the subcontracting firms to produce to their specific plans.

To overcome the possibility of opportunism, trust between the companies is needed. In addition, and to create this trust at least in part, both the subcontracting and the client firms seek to diversify their client base in order to reduce the risk of dependency on any single main firm. All manner of mechanisms operate to secure the idea of a 'partnership' between the firms; mutual dependency and adaptation, discussion and negotiation, honesty, long-term commitments, quality control, common knowledge between them, etc. Two very important aspects of this are the exchange of *information* that the network encourages (and not just an exchange of information about prices), and the exchange of *personnel* between the client and the subcontracting firms, involving the mutual training in the practices of manufacturing. This reinforces a point from the PD situation in the previous section; there it was a lack of communication that threatened to undermine the fragile level of cooperation established. Cooperative networks thrive on communication and information exchange between their members. These new systems seem to work because they are the most *efficient* way of organizing the production of the particular range of products involved.

But according to writers such as Piore, Sable and Zeitlin these examples are not unique. These authors have argued that the changes just outlined are the tip of a major transformation in the organization of production that threatens to engulf much of the advanced industrial economies. They argue that we are experiencing a systemic transformation in the way industrial production is being organized. This is summed up under the terms 'mass production *versus* flexible specialization' (Piore and Sable, 1984; Hirst and Zeitlin, 1989). Mass production is giving way to a flexibly specialized technology and business strategy.

Flexible specialization involves the production of small batch outputs. It is niche-orientated and 'fashion' driven. It implies non-standardized and specialist demand from consumers. It calls for short production runs, requiring flexible machinery and a highly skilled and flexible labour force. Increasingly it is being undertaken in small- to medium-sized plants. As a result it can lead to the disintegration of the vertically integrated company and the refocusing of the horizontally diversified company. The most appropriate mechanism linking the kinds of firms that will produce most efficiently in this kind of an environment can be best described as the network type structure. Often this type of production takes place in highly integrated 'industrial districts' which might eventually expand into new regional economies.

Johnson and Lawrence (1988) describe these developments as the generation of 'value adding partnerships', seen as a network of interdependent and mutually supportive elements neither formally hierarchically organized nor simply articulated by price relationships. The need for greater flexibility is recognized as central to the reasons for the development of the extended partnership idea. New flexible technologies are seen as an important adjunct to, but not as the reason for, the changes in the production processes discussed. Along with these changes goes a redefinition of the management problem and outlook. But there is no single unambiguous 'model' that guarantees success of the trust forming and securing mechanism.

For Johnson and Lawrence these arrangements meet the implications of the change in economic climate and market structure for the types of products and services they consider. These relationships will be more efficient than the vertically or horizontally integrated firm. They may also be more profitable in the long run for all the elements concerned, although again, this is in no way guaranteed.

One additional point that should be noted from these examples is the way market type relationships, although not formally the object of the analyses, still remain at least partly present within the explanations of how the examples of networks operate. Thus we are dealing with an overlapping area when looking at these economic activities. Network and market relationships *coexist* (along with hierarchical ones), though it is the network type relationships that are highlighted as the most important and the ones that give the other coexisting relationships their particular specificity.

The above analysis concentrated on the nature of the relationships *between* firms in the newly evolving production environment. But it also involved some implications for how we might view the nature of the firm itself. We have already mentioned the case of vertical (dis)integration in the above discussion. According to Williamson's well-known theory about vertical integration, it developed (in a period of mass-production) to reap the scale economies to be had as transactions costs were eliminated with the successive integration of more and more production activity within the (expanding) boundaries of the master firm. The 'external costs' of market transactions were thereby eliminated·as these were 'internalized' under an increasingly hierarchical and bureaucratic coordinating mechanism. With the break up of mass-production, however, this process could be in reverse. But will it result in an increasing resort to purely market transactions?

Amongst others Sabel for one thinks not. He has suggested that one of the new organizational forms developing in the wake of the true mass-production firm could be termed a 'quasi-disintegrated firm' (Sabel in Hirst and Zeitlin, 1989). This acts as a systems integrator and specialization consortia within a collaborative manufacturing environment. His examples of this are taken from the reorganized European car manufacturing companies, particularly BMW, Fiat and Volkswagen (Sabel et al., 1990). A quasi-vertically disintegrated firm is one where an increasing range of part product processes are 'externalized' from the main firm, and located either in their own affiliated organizations or within separated supplier firms. The main firm may keep some of the overall design and R and D functions, but even these are increasingly being located in those organizational units with responsibility for the production of their own discrete part of the overall car manufacture. In this way, the functions of conception *and* execution are being remerged in the variable (sub-)units. These sub-units are also taking on more of the production process proper, with their own flexible process technologies. The main firm is thus able to hedge its technological bets under this kind of an arrangement for fear of getting burdened with a technology that quickly becomes outdated or redundant.

Under this kind of an arrangement the main firm must reorganize to cope with a 'snap-on' capital goods type production process, as the output elements from the related firms appear and are finally assembled. It also begins to appear as little more than an organizational, and possibly financial, centre for the extended network of suppliers and subcontractors. It becomes the systems integrator, organizing the specialist consortia of sub-units over which it has no direct control. But the manufacturing system becomes *collaborative* under these conditions. None of its elements can afford to completely go their own way, yet nor do they want to become totally dependent upon one single dominant firm. Thus increased trust and cooperation can be fostered by this kind of arrangement. The way this type of system operates is close to an 'internal network'. Indeed Sabel suggests it becomes difficult to specify a clear dividing line between where one firm ends and another one begins. There is no clear boundary around the firm; no internal network to pitch against an external one. It reminds one of a continual loop that has a twist in it, so that what is at one time the outside is at another the inside of the network.

Many of the attributes of networks operate and thrive in this kind of an environment. The relationships between the sub-units is too delicate to leave to market type arrangements, with their constant search for new cheaper suppliers or the ruthless attempt to reduce existing supplier output costs, Sabel suggests. In any case a long-term collaborative relationship needs to be forged, in which there is a constant exchange of ideas and personnel, requiring trust and loyalty *as well as competition*. The constant search for better process and product technologies forges a new common interest which is shared by all the members of the consortia. But it does not mean that a healthy rivalry between them is *necessarily* absent. It just means that competition is redefined — it is not necessarily strict market competition.

So much for the way the production process may be being reorganized in the context of network type arrangements. We can leave this now and look at another sphere where networks can provide a means of coordinating social activity, namely in the political arena. In this case another term will be introduced to describe a network type arrangement; 'associationalism'.

5 Political associations as networks?

The usual way of thinking about political representation in the kind of society in which we live is via the notion of a hierarchical set of layered governmental institutions culminating in the sovereignty of Parliament. Thus we have local government bodies of various types, each subordinate to some higher level. This is then overlayered by a set of central government apparatuses, administrative departments of the state, the government itself, the Cabinet, and finally the sovereignty of Parliament. These central government institutions are themselves also organized hierarchically, with sometimes complex relations of subordination and superordination between them, but with the final 'pinnacle of power' situated in a Parliament — the sovereignty of Parliament (that still shares some of its authority with residual and marginal power of the monarchy in our system). This downward flow of power is paralleled by an upward flow of representation, so that it is 'the people' that ultimately vest the democratically elected Parliament with its legitimacy to rule over it.

In democratic theory, then, the key concepts of representation and sovereignty go hand in hand. 'The people' are somehow divided into a constituency with an interest. This interest is then represented in the relevant legislative arena via the constituency representative. Political parties are the instruments of this representational mechanism. They mediate between the people, their interests (all political parties *claim* to represent an interest), the legislative arena, the government and the sovereignty of Parliament.

But against this orthodox conception can be posed a somewhat different and perhaps parallel mechanism that might be thought to capture another aspect of the way government is organized. This mobilizes the notions of 'elites', 'corporatism' and 'associationalism'. All these have at times been analysed as involving strong elements of networks, and that is why they are of interest here.

5.1 Elites

We have already come across this term earlier in the chapter in the context of the the discussion of interlocking directorates. This is a clear example of an elite group — a financial-industrial oligarchy some would say — whose activity is to manage a good deal of the economic resources of the country. Personal ties and a shared cultural outlook mean that they wield a great deal of power, perhaps unaccountable power. In addition, in as much as they share convictions and similar outlook with political elites, they can influence — some would say unduly influence — political processes as well.

It is this role of elites in the informal governance and coordination of power that explicitly raised the problem of the lack of accountability of that power within important areas of social life. Elites can serve to circumvent 'the proper conduct of democratic politics' (as seen from the point of view of the traditional sketch of politics that opened this section), by organizing influence behind the scenes, bringing their own interests to bear unduly on decisions, and so on. In these cases, the manner elites might be thought to work is via the notions that constitute networks as described earlier in the chapter. Elites combine a select and small-scale group, held together by reciprocal bonds of loyalty and trust.

Thus we can see that elite theories of politics would postulate another type of influence on the political arena which could largely escape the operation of the representation/sovereignty couple outlined above. This is also true of corporatist theories of government.

5.2 Corporatism

Corporatism is a political theory stressing the way large interest groups — the 'social partners' as they are sometimes referred to — combine informally in a cooperative manner to regulate and govern central aspects of social life. Thus we might see the government bargaining with the organizations of large and small industrialists, with agricultural interests, with the financial sector, and with organized labour, or some other important social groups like consumers or environmentalists, to establish a *modus vivendi* on an important social, political or economic issue. It generates cooperation by means of bargaining and negotiation.

Some analysts have seen whole countries partly governed along these lines, where these large social interest groups are integrated into an established regulatory order that smooths potential conflicts between them before they break out into a more open conflict or antagonism. In this way a consensus can be built up informally, and the business of government conducted in a more conciliatory manner as a result. The point here is that once again, this process tends to bypass the normal channels of political lobbying and representation. It operates a kind of large-scale network in the conduct of running a country.

5.3　Associationalism

The final form of this alternative political conception that is considered here is associationalism. This represents a more pluralistic version of corporatism (Philippe Schmitter is a contemporary representative author in this tradition — see Streeck and Schmitter, 1986). This particular approach stresses the myriad of political associations in which people invest their political energies and 'sovereign*ties*'. It challenges that there is a single dimension to sovereignty, organized along the hierarchical lines mentioned above. Rather it stresses the dispersion of this, and with it the representative mechanism that supports it. Thus from this perspective sovereignty is dispersed throughout the series of 'political' organizations to which one might owe an allegiance. These organizations go to govern the range of private interests existing in any society. There are thus a plurality of sites where the sovereignty of the people rests, some of which may not even be considered political in the usual sense, for example places of employment and social clubs.

In each of these sites a consensual, cooperative, or collaborative ethic *can* obtain (this is so in principle, though it might not always be there in practice). Thus again what we have here is a kind of elongated, 'flat' framework for political representation, working through a plurality of organizational forms, amounting to something akin to a network, that governs private interests.

In this section we have explored three alternative but connected approaches to the understanding of political organization, contrasting them to an 'orthodox' position. Each of these approaches displays some of the features of a network structure. Each of them also gives us some insight into the actual way politics works. Clearly, they do not exhaust the insights; the more orthodox position also has a lot to offer. Perhaps the best way of viewing the relationship between the two is as complementary. They run very much in parallel to each other, highlighting particular aspects of a complex whole.

6　An evaluation of networks

By way of conclusion I will step back a little from my presentation of the network model to critically evaluate it. A first point to ask is: Are networks essentially undemocratic? Clearly, they do not totally conform to traditional notions of 'representative democracy'. Elites, for instance, may become *cliques* — groups or bodies of partial and unrepresentative interests who, because they cooperate closely and share a common social or economic outlook, may exercise great power and influence. But that power and influence does not appear to be democratically accountable. Networks of interlocking directorates, for example, may weld together men and women of high finance and industrial muscle who decide matters between themselves informally. Those decisions then have a profound impact on the economy and beyond to affect us all. But how can we influence all this if the power so controlled is neither visible nor accountable? Indeed, how can our elected representatives properly conduct their own legitimate business if they face similar obstacles? The 'establishment' — operating as a network of influential opinion formers, agenda setters and decision takers with a shared social, educational and cultural background — may act to usurp and undermine genuine democratic government. If one happens to be in a network that may work to your advantage, but if you are one of those left out you may just have to lump it.

A second and related set of criticisms of networks focuses upon the 'informal rationality' that pervades these types of coordinating mechanisms. This is contrasted with the 'procedural rationality' that is thought to typify both the hierarchy and the market models. The advantage of procedural rationality is that it tends to be open, explicit and rule driven. It is either bureaucratic or contractual. Thus it is not so obviously open to possible manipulation and abuse as an informal rationality might be. Informal rationality relies much more upon the operation of *discretion*. It allows the agents in the network to decide as suits their purpose and whim. The fact that the network does rely more on discretion leads to the awkward problem of potential *corruption*. Who is to monitor and police informal networks? Of course, corruption and abuse are not immune from the market or hierarchy either, far from it. But there would seem to be more scope, in principle, for this to arise if discretion becomes the dominant form of network operation. For instance, in some ways the Mafia is the perfect network structure! It relies upon trust, loyalty, solidarity, etc. (but not honesty!), and would seem to operate with a wide scope for pragmatic discretion.

In fact we might well take this critique of networks even further. Above it was suggested that the attributes of a robust, cohesive and long-term network were to be found in the notions of trust, loyalty, honesty and the like. But one could point to networks where just the opposite characteristics were present. Thus some networks might work on the basis of *fear and suspicion*. This can be particularly the case if a group of otherwise competing 'insiders' are faced with an even greater threat from a group of 'outsiders'. In this case, the insiders can form a kind of (possibly only temporary) alliance in the form of a network, to try and deal with the threatening outsiders. Despite the mutual suspicions between them, it is the insiders' greater fear of the outsiders that leads them to establish and sustain a working network between themselves. Something along these lines led to the formation and sustaining of many lobbying networks of British firms when faced with the threat from foreign, particularly Japanese, suppliers in the 1970s.

Another possible criticism of the network model is rather method-ological in character. Is the network approach just an interesting de-scriptive device or idea with little analytical content? Is it not possi-ble (and tempting) to go around finding lots of networks without these being of great intellectual significance? Clearly, if we look hard enough we will find networks all over the place. Indeed, given the early definition of networks, more or less *all* forms of coordination could fall under its embrace, including hierarchy and market as we saw! In addition, does the network model have any predictive content? Can we delineate exactly when and where it will arise, and how it will shape the behaviour of the agents operating within it?

Clearly, if the network model can be found everywhere then it also operates nowhere. If it does not allow us to demarcate it from the mar-ket or hierarchy, say, then it is worthless as an analytical technique in its own right. But the analysis above has offered enough evidence to suggest that the network model does provide us with a genuine, useful and different analytical approach to social, political and economic re-ality. The key features of the network model elaborated here — as op-posed to a network approach that could include markets and hierar-chies — revolves around the notions of cooperation, loyalty, trust, re-ciprocity, solidarity and altruism that were analysed in the early sec-tions of this chapter. It is these categories describing how a certain range of social relations operate that specifies a network model of gov-ernance. These just do not operate, or operate in the same manner, for ei-ther hierarchy or markets.

Finally, does the network form of governance raise a new issue of 'cit-izenship'? Networks are regulative technologies that, though not nec-essarily 'rationally' conceived in a means-ends sense, are nonetheless imbued with their own rationalities. Thus they might imply a partic-ular vision of the active, social and moral citizen as a bearer of a 'regulated freedom', a particular form of what Foucault has termed 'governmentality'. They could open up a new 'fictive space' in which the active self-fulfilling subject engages with a particular field of eco-nomic choice. For instance, the newly flexible production systems dis-cussed above imply a set of techniques and workers that exercise their own discretion, delineating networks of activities where individual 'initiative', 'flexibility', 'judgement', and 'entreprenurialism' are cele-brated. Above all these processes, by splitting up the hierarchically organized firm, introduce a new emphasis of 'consumption' into the firm and between semi-autonomous organizational entities. Separate activ-ities consume costs, and the monitoring of these consumption-cost centres becomes the prime mode of network governance. The consumer as a per-sonage is also directly implicated in the organizational network of production as that production is increasingly subject to the dictates of marketing and consumption. This may be heralding a new, rather more general tryptic of *network-citizen-consumer* — recall the emphasis on the various Citizen's Charters so popular with the Conservative Government of John Major. However, as pointed out above, this also opens up a slightly different space of citizenship, one in which the behavioural and ethical virtues of loyalty, trust and cooperation can be celebrated. It is perhaps this idea of economic citizenry that becomes an attractive one in a period when both the market and hierarchy are loosing some of their attraction as coordinative mechanisms.

NOTES

1 Some of the recent overt deployments of the term within organizational theory can be found in Thompson, et al. (eds) 1991. As examples of its more implicit use adjacent to the discussion in this chapter, but set within more mainstream economics, see Aoki, Gustafsson and Williamson (1990) and Casson (1991). For the field of international relations the notion of 'epistemic communities' shares some of properties of networks as discussed in this chapter (International Organisation, 1992). On the sociological and political uses of networks see later in the main text.

2 Some of these notions are nicely posed in Kaufman et al. (1986).

3 T is the temptation to defect while the other player cooperates (4), R is the reward for mutual cooperation (3), S is the sucker's pay-off when the other player defects (1), and P is the punishment for defection (0).

4 These issues are discussed further in Thompson, 1993.

5 Cooperative solidarity as (the outcome of) a 'selfish' strategy will thus depend upon a number of conditions:
   (a) the relation between individual contributions and their expected benefits;
   (b) the probability of gaining the expected benefit even without cooperative endeavours and sacrifices;
   (c) the opportunity costs of the strategy. Solidarity will occur only if total benefits exceed total costs. If this produces a net benefit, the opportunity cost (the cost of the alternative forgone) of not cooperating will be negative, and 'rational' individuals would not decide on that option; and finally,
   (d) the ease of monitoring the other parties' actions, that is can non-cooperation and opportunism be detected?

6 One way this kind of evolved cooperation might be made manifest is through the notion of a 'regime'. A regime is the institutionalization of principles, norms, rules and decision-making procedures around specific policy areas where actor-expectations converge. Such regimes can assist the development of cooperation by improving the quality and flow of information, reducing uncertainty and the incentive for opportunist defection, and promoting mechanisms for monitoring compliance (Keohane, 1984).

References

Aoki, M., Gustfasson, B. and Williamson, O.E. (eds.) (1990) *The Firm as a Nexus of Treaties*, London, Sage.

Axelrod, R. (1984) *The Evolution of Cooperation*, New York, Basic Books.

Casson, M. (1991) *The Economics of Business Culture*, Oxford, Clarendon Press.

Coleman, J.S. (1982) 'Systems of trust', *Angewandte Sozialforschung*, vol. 10, pp. 277-300.

Durkheim, E. (1933) *The Division of Labour in Society*, New York, The Free Press (first published in 1893).

Gambetta, D. (ed.) (1988) *Trust: Making and Breaking Cooperative Relations*, Oxford, Blackwell.

Hirshman, A.O. (1970) *Exit, Voice and Loyalty*, Cambridge, Massachusetts, Harvard University Press.

Hirst, P.Q. and Zeitlin, J. (eds.) (1989) *Reversing Industrial Decline?*, Oxford, Berg.

International Organisation (1992) Special Issue on 'Epistemic communities', vol.64, no.1, Winter.

Johanson, J. and Mattsson, L-G. (1987) 'Interorganizational relations in industrial systems: a network approach compared with the transactions-cost approach', *International Studies of Management and Organisation*, 17(1), pp.34–48 (reprinted in Thompson et al. (eds),1991).

Johnston, R. and Lawrence, P.R. (1988) 'Beyond vertical integration — the rise of the value-adding partnership', *Harvard Business Review*, July-August, pp.94–101 (reprinted in Thompson et al. (eds), 1991).

Kaufman, F., Majone, G. and Ostrom, B. (eds.) (1986) *Guidance, Control and Evaluation in the Public Sector*, Berlin, de Gruyter.

Keohane, R.O. (1984) *After Hegemony: Cooperation and Discord in the World Political Economy*, Princeton, Princeton University Press.

Knoke, D. and Kuklinski, J.H. (1982) *Network Analysis*, Beverly Hills, Sage (reprinted in Thompson et al. (eds), 1991).

Lewis, J.D. and Weigert, A. (1985) 'Trust as a social reality', *Social Forces*, vol. 63, no. 4, pp. 476–85, June.

Lorenz, E.H. (1988) 'Neither friends nor strangers: informal networks of subcontracting in French industry' in Gambetta, D. (ed.), *op cit.* (reprinted in Thompson et al. (eds.), 1991).

Mauss, M. (1970) *The Gift*, London, Routledge and Keegan Paul.

Piore, M. and Sable, C. (1984) *The Second Industrial Divide*, New York, Basic Books.

Reve, T. (1990) 'The firm as a nexus of internal and external contracts' in Aoki, M. et al. (eds.), *op cit.*

Sabel, C. (1990) *Studied Trust: Building New Forms of Cooperation in a Volatile Economy*, Geneva, International Institute for Labor Studies.

Sabel, C., Herrigel, G. and Kern, H. (1990) 'Collaborative manufacturing' in Mendius, H.G. and Wendeling-Schröder, U. (eds.) *Zulieferer im Netz-Zwischen Abhängigkeit und Pärlnerschaft*, Köln, Bund Verlag.

Scott, J. and Griff, C. (1984) *Directors of Industry*, Cambridge, Polity Press.

Stockman, F.N., Ziegler, R. and Scott, J. (1985) *Networks of Corporate Power*, Cambridge, Polity Press.

Streeck, W. and Schmitter, P.C. (1985) 'Community, market, state and associations? The prospective contribution of interest governance to social order' in Streeck, W. and Schmitter, P.C. (eds.) *Private Interest Government: Beyond Market and State*, London, Sage (reprinted in Thompson et al. (eds.), 1991).

Thompson, G.F., Frances, J., Levacic, R. and Mitchell, J. (eds.) (1991) *Markets, Hierarchies and Networks: The Coordination of Social Life*, London, Sage.

Thompson, G.F. (1993) *The Economic Emergence·of a New Europe?: The Political Economy of Cooperation and Competition in the 1990s*, Cheltenham, Edward Elgar.

CHAPTER 4:
RUNNING TELEVISION

Richard Maidment

1 The political economy of British television

As the 1990s began, the public face of British broadcast television for most viewers was familiar, comfortable and reassuring. They received four channels, two of which were funded through a licence fee, while the other two were dependent on advertising for their income. Although Channel 4 was only created in the 1980s, the system that embraced both a publicly funded broadcasting organization and a commercial network, relatively insulated from the pressures of the market, was well established in the UK. It had been in place for over a quarter of a century and it was a system that appeared to work. It appeared to satisfy the demands of most British viewers. Moreover, these four channels collectively, according to many non-British observers, provided the best television service in the world. BBC1 and BBC2, ITV and Channel 4, broadcast a range, variety and quality of programming that few other national systems offered. The blend of entertainment, serious drama, news, sport, documentaries and current affairs, while not unique in the world, was nevertheless deemed to be of an especially high standard. Programmes with mass appeal coexisted with those that were designed with relatively small audiences in mind. British television by the end of the 1980s apparently had managed to achieve a wide popular appeal without sacrificing the ethic of public service broadcasting. It aroused the very real admiration of those in countries where television was driven entirely by commercial considerations or in other nations where a publicly-owned system provided a worthy but dull and rather pedestrian service.

Nevertheless, the four British channels did not provide as concentrated a diet of what most British viewers apparently wanted as did, for instance, the output of American television. This unwillingness to give viewers, who are a key component of the television market, what they wanted was, perhaps, one of the reasons why the structure of British television was altered radically by the late 1980s. The political agenda of the 1980s emphasized the primacy of the market, of consumer choice and of a multiplicity of suppliers. It was an agenda that had a profound effect on the television service.

A very striking change occurred in the reference and context of British political and economic discourse during the 1980s. Broadly speaking the Conservative government that was elected in 1979 entered office with the belief that large sections of the British economy were inefficient. Both the manufacturing and the service sector suffered from this deficiency, but perhaps the largest problem in the eyes of the government lay in what it claimed was an overly large and bureaucratic public sector. The government had several proposals for the elimination of inefficiency primarily through the 'discipline of the market'. The government wished to use the market as a mode of coordination for most industries and services. According to the government and those economists that supported this view, too many producers in Britain were insufficiently responsive to the demands of consumers, either in the United Kingdom or abroad. As a consequence they all too often produced goods and services that were inadequate; in terms of price, quality or speed of delivery. They lost customers, but they did not fully suffer the consequences of their inadequacy. They were protected usually through the willingness of virtually every post-war government, Labour and Conservative, to subsidize those industries that failed to compete in the market for goods and services that are traded internationally. Thus the steel industry was subsidized, as was the textile industry and several others, with the result, so the argument goes, that many of these British industries grew increasingly uncompetitive internationally, as they were allowed to ignore the 'discipline of the market'. There were different and harsh 'solutions' available with respect to the private sector. Large sections of an industry, if not the entire industry, could suffer the result of their inefficiency and during the deep recession of the early 1980s several major British companies, especially manufacturing companies, substantially diminished in size or went out of business entirely. They failed to compete successfully and the consequences of failing to do so were harsh but appropriate, according to those who believed that the market should resolve these issues. However, this 'solution' of letting the market decide who should survive and flourish was not as easily applied to the public sector.

The successive Conservative governments of the 1980s and 1990s sought to introduce the 'discipline of the market' to the public sector through a variety of innovative measures. The most striking of these was the policy of privatization, which was designed to end or diminish the public ownership of entire industries such as telecommunications and steel, or of those companies, like Rolls Royce, that found themselves in the public sector. Interestingly, television was not at the forefront of these attempts to make the public sector more accountable to the forces of the market. The government initially was more interested in other areas, but towards the end of the 1980s it decided that the existing arrangements of broadcast television needed to be reformed. Privatization was not felt to be an appropriate policy for the television industry, in part because the ITV network was already privately owned and there was no serious or concerted lobby to privatize the BBC. There was, however, a very serious and concerted attempt to make television more responsive to the forces of the market, which in the context of

British television meant viewers, advertisers, and producers of programming other than the BBC and the ITV network. It meant in practice diminishing the power and influence of the BBC and the ITV companies, providing more channels and increasing the role of independent producers. It also meant changing the regulatory framework of television and most significantly altering — if not reversing — the ethos that had governed British broadcasting since its inception.

1.1 The BBC monopoly: hierarchy and regulation

Although the structure and responsiveness of the British television service in the 1980s did not satisfy a government committed to introducing the 'discipline of the market', broadcasting had changed very substantially since the introduction of a radio service to the United Kingdom. The original organization of the industry, closely regulated by the government, reflected a hostility to the belief that the service should respond to the preferences of listeners and subsequently viewers, and was run in a very hierarchical manner. All of these characteristics were diluted in the seven decades after the formation of the BBC, although they have not entirely disappeared. Nevertheless the story of British broadcasting chronicles a gradual move away from these principles; a move that is due to a variety of reasons. However, in the 1920s the government was determined to control the nascent broadcasting industry.

In 1925 a Committee of Inquiry under the Earl of Crawford was formed to consider the state of the broadcasting service. The Crawford Committee produced a report that created the BBC as we currently know it. Crawford reached the following recommendations:

1   That broadcasting should be entrusted only to a public corporation.

2   That broadcasting should be organized as a monopoly, a legal monopoly and not the monopoly in effect that had been granted to the British Broadcasting Company.

3   That advertising should not be permitted.

4   That the source of revenue should be the licence fee.

5   That this new corporation should be protected from direct government interference in the production of its programmes, particularly news programmes. This was a departure from the rules that governed the British Broadcasting Company.

The government endorsed these conclusions and during 1926 created the British Broadcasting Corporation through a Royal Charter which was granted for a period of ten years from 1 January 1927. The charter, of course, was renewable.

One of the submissions to the Crawford Committee was made by John Reith. It offers a very clear indication of his beliefs that were imple-

mented during his term as Director-General and long after his resignation in 1938.

> Broadcasting must be conducted as a Public Service with defi-
> nite standards. The service must not be used for entertainment
> purposes alone ... to exploit so great and universal an agent in
> the pursuit of entertainment alone would have been not only an
> abdication of responsibility and a prostitution of its power, but
> also an insult to the intelligence of the public it serves. It is oc-
> casionally indicated to us that we are apparently setting out to
> give the public what we think they need — and not what they
> want, but few know what they want, and very few what they
> need. The preservation of a high moral tone is obviously of
> paramount importance.
>
> *(Briggs, 1979, p. 82)*

What is clear from these remarks is the central belief that broadcasting is a public service. It must maintain a 'high moral tone', instruct
and inform its audience and on occasion entertain it, which Reith did
accept was important. Nevertheless, in the Reithian outlook, those
who run broadcasting hold a public trust and it is their duty to provide
the programmes that the public require rather than that which they
want. Nothing could be further from the language of the market. It
was, however, the language of a British governing class that in the
1920s was unsure about the market, but very sure of its ability to rule.
After all, Britain still ruled an Empire on which the sun never set; it
continued to be a great power in all senses of the word. Reith reflected
this assurance; the assurance of those in the civil service, the City, the
military, and the ancient universities. These men were equally confident of their capacity to run broadcasting. They also had little doubt
that this new industry should transmit their values; values that included the Christian religion and moral uplift, but excluded jokes about
'drunkenness and mothers-in-law'. Equally there was no place for those
who 'countenance the doctrines of revolution', but neither was there
room for 'the school which interprets progress in terms of the profit for
the few and privation for the many.' Public service not private profit
was central to this governing class and it is precisely this sensibility
that Reith was articulating and applying to the new broadcasting service. Broadcasting must be protected from the interests of commerce, for
if it was not so protected it would succumb to providing the public with
what they wanted and not that which they needed. So how could this
best be achieved? The answer was through a public monopoly with the
'appropriate' personnel in charge, who would implement the values
that were cherished and would not be diverted by the attractions of
commerce.

1.2 The end of the monopoly: a move towards the market

The first moves towards the notion of a market in broadcasting occurred in 1954 when the BBC's monopoly was ended. However, it was only a tentative move. The creation of Independent Television did not arise from an overwhelming desire to introduce the disciplines of the market to broadcasting. Instead the government went to very considerable lengths to control the influence of both advertisers and viewers on the new channel. It wished to maintain the public service ethic, while offering a modicum of choice. The government sought to create, in effect, a BBC which was funded by advertising. In retrospect the creation of Independent Television might not have appeared to have altered significantly the landscape of British broadcasting, but at the time it was an extremely contentious issue. It certainly did not occur easily. Anthony Smith, one of the leading authorities on television in the United Kingdom, notes a paradox in that opposition to the broadcasting monopoly grew substantially after 1946 in spite of the fact that 'The BBC at the end of World War II was at the summit of its national and international esteem' (Smith, 1974). Certainly, the first reviews of broadcasting — the 1946 White Paper and the 1949 Beveridge Report — were firm in their desire to protect the BBC's monopoly. According to Beveridge, 'if broadcasting was to have any social purpose it had to be protected from any form of competition which brought about a degrading competition for numbers of listeners.' The United States was used as an illustration of the terrible impact of commercialism. The Beveridge Report helped to cement and reinforce the very considerable opposition both to ending the monopoly and to introducing the mechanisms of the market in broadcasting, which to many were synonymous. However the political climate of the early 1950s was appreciably different. The greatest change was that the Labour government had lost the general election of 1951. There was an influx of a new generation of MPs onto the Conservative benches after this election and from the one held the previous year which Labour had won but with a severely reduced majority. It was these Conservative MPs who provided the impetus and the leadership of the campaign for commercial television.

The Television Act of 1954 developed the framework within which ITV operated for the subsequent three and a half decades. The framework remained essentially unchanged until 1990 and the passage of the Broadcasting Act. The Television Act sought to diffuse the opposition to commercial television by locating responsibility for the new network in a newly created public corporation, the Independent Television Authority (ITA), subsequently named the Independent Broadcasting Authority (IBA) after the introduction of commercial radio in 1973. The ITA would own the transmitters for broadcasting the programmes on the ITV network but it would not produce the programmes to be broadcast.

The programmes would be produced by contractors, chosen by the ITA, and they would recoup their costs by the sale of advertising.

Each contractor was given an exclusive franchise to broadcast in one of the fifteen regions of the network, and it is these regional contractors who have provided the public face of ITV rather than the ITA. There are only two exceptions to this rule, Independent Television News (ITN) and GMTV — which replaced TV-AM in January 1993 to operate the breakfast television franchise — have no regional responsibilities. The five largest contractors in the ITV network in 1993 were London Weekend and Carlton in the London region, Granada in Manchester, Central in the Midlands and Yorkshire in Leeds. These five companies were substantial organizations, even by the standards of media organizations in other parts of the world. Unsurprisingly, because of their resources and the high costs of television production, they provided most of the programming output for the ITV network; often to the chagrin of the smaller contractors, most of which were broadcasting in the less populous and wealthy regions. Nevertheless all the ITV contractors, from the late 1950s until the end of the 1980s, operated within a more than satisfactory financial environment. Lord Thomson of Fleet, at the time in control of Scottish Television which had the franchise to broadcast to most of the Scottish population, described his franchise as 'a licence to print your own money'. It was a sentiment that the other contractors undoubtedly shared but wisely did not articulate. The profitability of the ITV companies was in part due to the procedures that had been created in the Television Act to limit and control the pressures of commerce and the influence of advertisers on the contractors.

Perhaps greatest control on the power of advertisers was the simple commercial fact that there was no alternative to ITV. If a company wished to advertise its products on television, ITV was the only game in town. The Television Act may have ended the BBC monopoly, but it had created a television advertising monopoly. As a result the influence of advertising was almost non-existent. The advertisers only threat was not to use the medium of television, which was not credible by the end of the 1950s when the success of television in selling consumer products was firmly established. The desire to protect ITV from the advertisers had left the television companies with all the cards in their hands, and they were not reluctant to play them. The results were evident in their profits, which grew so rapidly and to such an extent that during the 1960s the rules of taxation were altered and a special levy imposed on the television companies in order to limit their profitability. However, if by an unexpected and curious confluence of events advertisers were able to overcome the structural weakness of their position in relation to the ITV companies and sought to influence the process of programme making, the ITA had the power to intervene and prevent any such behaviour. The members of the ITA and subsequently the IBA, were a public body, appointed by the government and deliberately insulated from the marketplace. Their sympathies lay, in the main, with the contractors to whom they awarded the franchises and not the advertising agencies and their clients. The Television Act had created a commercial television network, which to a striking extent was able to distance itself from those who were providing the revenue for the service.

The same set of forces also provided the television companies with a degree of insulation from viewers. Although ITV was from the beginning concerned with obtaining a substantial percentage and preferably a majority of the audience, it never had the obsession with ratings of the American networks. In the United States the loss of viewers is directly translated into loss of revenue for the network. The revenue of the American networks has been, and continues to be, entirely dependent on their ability to provide programmes which are popular, particularly with relatively young and affluent consumers. The failure to do so will have the most profound consequences on their financial position. The ITV companies, at least until the 1990s, never had to be under these pressures. They never felt the relentless demand to obtain consistently high viewing figures. Their revenue was not tied to audience ratings. There have been periods when British advertising agencies have complained about the overall popularity of the network or the demographic profile of the audience, but while these views have not been ignored, they have not unnerved the ITV companies.

Of course, this was intended by those who drafted the 1954 Television Act. Certainly the Conservative government wished to end the BBC monopoly and permit advertising on television, but in doing so it did not fully reject the Reithian ethic. It did not reject the position, which had been made by Reith and others since the 1920s, that the principal constituent element of the market in the broadcast television industry, that is advertisers and viewers, could not be relied on to provide a satisfactory service. In particular if the public service ethic was to be maintained, then the preferences of the viewer and the advertiser had to be contained within a structure that placed them at a distance from the television companies. The structure that was formed by the Television Act did create such a buffer. It permitted the ITV network to operate in a manner similar to the BBC. On the whole the output of the ITV companies has obtained a higher share of the audience than BBC1, but the margin, at least since the early 1960s, has not been more than a few percentage points. Nor has its programming appeared significantly different from BBC1, covering approximately the same terrain of light entertainment, serious drama, news, current affairs, sport, etc., with roughly the same allocation of time. There are some commentators on the broadcast television industry who would claim that this is evidence that the BBC moved down the road of reducing its previously high standards, rather than an indication of ITV's commitment to public service broadcasting. However, this is a difficult argument to sustain. Some of the major achievements of British television in the 1980s were produced by the independent television companies. For instance, Granada produced two drama series, *Brideshead Revisited* and *The Jewel in the Crown*, which won international critical acclaim and were widely considered to be examples of British television at its best. The ITV network has provided a range of programming, of which a significant percentage has not sought nor obtained great viewer popularity. The overall output of the network over the first three and a half decades, on the whole, confirmed the belief that the principle of public service broadcasting could be maintained by a television system that ended the BBC monopoly and permitted advertising.

Nevertheless the creation of ITV did have a very significant impact on the British television system. It was not a clone of the early 1950s BBC. It introduced a variety of programmes that were not available to the BBC, quiz shows and a substantial number of American programmes, for instance, that proved to be very popular with British audiences. The initial impact of these new ITV programmes was to diminish the audience for the BBC. In 1957, the BBC obtained only a 28 per cent share of the overall audience, which was the low point reached by the Corporation in the competition between the two networks. However, by 1962 the BBC achieved parity with ITV and broadly this position has been maintained, although the situation was complicated by the advent of BBC2 in the mid 1960s, which gave the BBC a significant advantage until the appearance of Channel 4 in 1982. The BBC certainly altered its style to deal with the advent of commercial television. To some, as mentioned above, this resulted in the BBC lowering its standards. To most observers of the industry the BBC, in the 1960s in particular, became a far more creative and dynamic organization. 'The BBC responded to the competitive situation not by adopting the programmes or criteria of the commercial system but by acquiring a new impetus of its own ... producing an enormous flowering of talent and inventiveness which became the characteristic of broadcasting ... in the 1960s' (Smith, 1974). For most observers of British broadcasting ITV did not reduce the overall quality of the service but enhanced it, not only by its own contributions to the range of broadcasting in the UK, but also by the rejuvenation of the BBC that its presence had brought about.

As mentioned above, BBC2 commenced broadcasting in 1964. This channel was formed after a further review of the television service in the early 1960s by the Pilkington Committee, which reaffirmed the importance of the BBC's position in the overall structure, while not being quite as enthusiastic over the role of ITV. Pilkington urged the creation of BBC2 in order to protect the public service ethic, which it feared might be eroded through the competition with ITV. BBC2 was developed as a channel that catered primarily to minority tastes, which may not have received satisfactory attention from the two mainstream channels. It was the television equivalent of BBC Radio's Third Programme. On the whole BBC2 has fulfilled this remit, with a range of programmes that have been distinctive to the channel. It has sought to include within its broad output, programmes of a specialized interest and those which appealed to only a discrete element of the viewing audience. Nevertheless, BBC2 has consistently obtained approximately 10 per cent of the overall viewing audience. The possession of two channels also gave the BBC far greater flexibility over scheduling. It could and did schedule current affairs on one channel with, let us say, a light entertainment programme on the other. It allowed the BBC to offer viewers alternatives, without turning to ITV. The ITV companies found this increasingly difficult to deal with, which led to a campaign for a second commercial channel in the early 1970s. Certainly by the end of the 1970s, the pessimistic forecasts for both the BBC and the entire broadcasting service, made by the opponents of commercial television, were not realized and indeed the Corporation appeared to have been reinvigorated. The broadcasting service had both absorbed and responded to the introduction of commercial television.

1.3 Television in the 1980s: a market in broadcasting

The 1980s saw the most substantial changes in broadcasting since the BBC was created in the 1920s. By the end of the decade the government had effectively, if not abandoned, then severely modified its commitment to public service broadcasting. Even more interestingly it sought to create a genuine market in broadcasting through a series of measures. It sought to reduce the powers of the BBC and the ITV companies by insisting that 25 per cent of all the material they broadcast was not made within their respective organizations. Accordingly they encouraged the growth of an independent production sector. The government also sought to create further choices for viewers. They created a new terrestrial channel which would begin broadcasting in the 1990s. But perhaps most radically they permitted a new range of services to be provided for British viewers through the new technologies of direct broadcast by satellite (DBS) and cable. In other words the government created a range of new producers and suppliers for British broadcasting.

Initially television was not a priority of the first Thatcher administration. The government was beset by more pressing difficulties and as a result the structure of broadcast television was not high on the agenda of the government. Indeed, and somewhat ironically, the first major measure of the government appeared to endorse the broad consensus that had long been established over broadcasting. In 1982 the second commercial channel commenced broadcasting and the arrangements for Channel 4 appeared to suggest that despite its proclaimed beliefs, the government was not going to alter the ethos of British broadcasting. Channel 4 was placed under the aegis of the IBA and designed as the commercial counterpart of BBC2. The remit of this channel, as with BBC2, was to provide an alternative to the two principal channels and not to replicate their output. Channel 4 was intended to appeal to those minority interests that were not catered for satisfactorily by the ITV network. To ensure that Channel 4 fulfilled these intentions and did not succumb to commercial pressures and provide more mainstream programming, the government imposed an unusual form of financing. In the first ten years of the channel's existence its revenue was provided and guaranteed by the ITV companies, under a complicated system of financing. In return the ITV companies sold the advertising time on Channel 4 and retained the proceeds of the sale. The management of Channel 4 was independent and was protected from the influence of the ITV companies. Although there were fears that the new channel would be dominated by the major independent companies, the relationship that was created, if anything, placed the ITV companies in a potentially difficult position. They had to provide the revenue for a service over whose programming they had no control with no indication of its potential attractions to either viewers or advertisers. Understandably it was an arrangement that initially was not welcomed by the ITV companies. More importantly for our purposes, these arrangements indicated a continuing scepticism over the market. The channel required, if not insulation, then a very real distance between the management of Channel 4 and advertisers, otherwise it would not provide the service for which it was designed but go down the more conventional programming route of ITV. Evidently there was no confidence that such a service could be provided unless these arrangements were imposed by government. Presumably the government believed that a commercial television channel designed for minority interests could not attract sufficient viewers or advertising revenue. But as the market could not deliver, then the government was prepared to introduce a set of regulations that would provide such a service. It was not consistent with the government's constant reiterations of faith in the coordination of the market.

There was one further aspect of the formation of Channel 4 that is particularly interesting. Channel 4 did not produce its own programmes. It needed to purchase its entire output from external sources. Although the channel did buy programmes from the major ITV companies, it sought to obtain material from new sources. It commissioned programmes from new and/or small companies which were not used either by ITV or the BBC, who essentially provided their own programming needs 'in-house'. The commissioning policies of Channel 4 provided an enormous stimulus to the growth and development of these independent suppliers and by the end of the 1980s they were a significant part of the television industry. It was their success in providing the output for Channel 4 that led the government to examine the programming policies of both ITV and the BBC.

The primary characteristics of a sophisticated market in television requires a far greater number of channels than the UK had, even after the advent of Channel 4. It also required a reduction, if not the removal, of the very substantial barriers that had been erected around the broadcasters, in order to limit the influence of both viewers and advertisers. The market would most probably demand that the BBC and ITV companies did not produce most of their output 'in-house'. Channel 4 had fostered the development of the new independent production houses, but that was insufficient. In short, a market in British broadcasting depended on altering the rules and structures for both the BBC and the ITV companies, the very institutions which had created the reputation of British television around the world.

The government started this process of altering the environment in which television operated by permitting the creation of new services; services which were available because of new technology. One of the reasons why television has been very carefully regulated is that it is, or at least was, a scarce commodity in the UK. Until the early 1990s very few households received more than four channels. To some extent the desire for regulation was a consequence of this scarcity. If there could only be a few channels, then coordination by the market could not be risked. However, if there were far more than four channels, some of those fears and concerns might diminish and the market could then decide whether a particular channel should flourish. Success or failure in these circumstances could be left to viewers and advertisers. The demise of any one channel would not be a matter of public concern. Interestingly the technology of the industry permitted the potential expansion of the number of channels, and the government authorized the exploitation of this technology. The potential impact of cable television and direct broadcast by satellite (DBS) is considered below. It is too early to make a confident forecast about cable and DBS services that are already available, but what is clear is that British households will have the option to receive a far larger number of channels than they did during the 1980s. This alone will change the dynamics of British broadcasting in the 1990s.

The 1990 Broadcasting Act also reflected the government's desire to introduce the disciplines of the market into the broadcasting system. Even though the advent of cable and DBS services might well make a very real impact on the structure of the industry in the mid-1990s and beyond, for most viewers the reality of television at the start of the decade lay with the four terrestrial channels. The Broadcasting Act sought to reform certain aspects of these channels. It attempted to increase competition, make the BBC and the ITV companies more responsive to viewers and to the developments that were taking place in the industry. Firstly, it sought to lessen the power of the BBC and the ITV companies by requiring them to take 25 per cent of their output by 1993 from independent suppliers. They would be smaller organizations employing considerably fewer people. Secondly, it created a fifth channel, which is scheduled to commence broadcasting by the middle of the decade. Thirdly, it changed the system of allocating the franchises of the ITV companies to ensure that they are no longer a licence to print money. In 1991 the franchises were allocated by the newly created Independent Television Commission (ITC), the replacement for the IBA, on the basis of competitive bids; although the ITC also took into account the commitment of the bidder to providing viewers with quality programming.

Along with the Broadcasting Act the government also imposed a licence fee on the BBC until 1996, when the BBC Charter was to be reviewed, which would be adjusted in line with inflation as measured in the Retail Price Index. Unfortunately, for the BBC that is, inflation costs in the production of television programmes have been considerably higher than the Retail Price Index and are likely to continue to be; facts of which the government was aware. The intention, presumably, was to apply the same financial pressures to the BBC, which would also make the Corporation examine its costs and labour practices. The government's attitude to the BBC has never been entirely clear. Although it has stressed its commitment to the Corporation, relations between the successive Conservative governments and the BBC have never been satisfactory. Perhaps the most hostile act was the formation of the Peacock Committee with the unstated hope that it would advocate the introduction of advertising on the BBC. Although the Peacock Committee did not do so, it clearly considered the option and only rejected it on grounds of practicality, rather than out of commitment to the public service ethic of the BBC. To many observers it was the most accurate indication of the government's instincts towards the BBC and public service broadcasting.

Collectively these developments indicated the government's desire to see a change in the pattern of broadcasting. It clearly wished to diminish the role of the ITV companies and the BBC, allow the independent programme suppliers to flourish and see the introduction of a host of new channels which would be controlled by new broadcasting organizations. Clearly whatever the government claimed, it was less interested in public service broadcasting than its predecessors. It was far more committed to the introduction of market influences to an industry which it believed had been overly regulated and protected. Those who supported public service broadcasting, which included all the principal organizations of the broadcasting industry, objected to most of the above measures, with only a modicum of success. They did obtain certain concessions from the government, but in the main they were marginal. The central fact that the television industry had to confront was that for the first time a government did not endorse the long standing belief in public service broadcasting and did not reject the proposition that broadcasting should be coordinated by the market.

2 The impact of technology

The move towards a broadcasting market was not only due to the change in the political environment, advances in technology also played a very considerable role. The early 1980s already had seen the introduction of one major technological innovation, the domestic video-cassette recorder (VCR). By the start of the 1990s over 70 per cent of homes in the United Kingdom owned a VCR. This gave viewers the opportunity to rent or buy programmes, but it also provided the flexibility to create their own television schedules, viewing programmes at times that were convenient to them and not at the point of broadcast. This flexibility has certainly had an impact on ITV and Channel 4 in particular because it has had the effect of fragmenting the viewing audience. A programme will no longer be seen throughout the country at its time of broadcast: the consequence for advertisers of this development is that they can no longer be sure when and indeed if, their commercial will be seen. The impact of a television advertising campaign, which frequently requires an immediate and substantial audience, may well be diluted through the widespread use of the VCR and to some extent reduces the attractiveness of broadcast television as an advertising medium, given the very high costs of advertising on the ITV network and on Channel 4. However, this particular consequence of VCR ownership can be overstated, particularly when ITV and Channel 4 together possessed a monopoly of television advertising time in the UK. Advertisers effectively had nowhere else to go. However, other technological developments were about to erode this monopoly. Firstly, there was the introduction of a new and sophisticated cable technology; and secondly, the commencement of DBS, both of which very substantially increased the number of channels that are available to be received.

Interestingly cable is not a particularly new technology, at least in conception. It has been in use in the UK for some considerable time, primarily to provide or improve reception of the established broadcast channels. Cable had been introduced in the United States for the very same reasons. However, the development of the American cable industry took a very different path in the 1970s and 1980s. The industry was aware that the capacity of even the basic and unsophisticated cable system permitted a television set to receive far more than, for example, the seven channels that were available in New York during the 1960s. An advanced and sophisticated cable, known as multi-channel broad band cable, has the capacity to carry in the region of a hundred channels. As a result of this capacity an industry developed in the United States to provide programming for these channels that are delivered exclusively by the cable industry. The success of the American cable industry is evident from the statistic that over 60 per cent of all American households are connected to cable, and the percentage is rising. The consequence of the penetration of cable is that the three major American television networks, the American Broadcasting Corporation (ABC), the Columbia Broadcasting System (CBS) and the National Broadcasting· Corporation (NBC) no longer rule the airwaves in the United States. Before the advent of cable, approximately 95 per cent of the American viewing audience watched one of the three networks in prime time, the period between 7.00 pm and 11.00 pm. By 1992 that figure had been reduced to approximately 60 per cent and there was no indication that this reduction in audience share had come to an end. Indeed, there is every reason to believe that it will continue. Cable has created an enormous fragmentation of the American viewing audience. The networks are no longer as profitable as they once were and their straitened financial circumstances has in turn diminished their capacity to make the range and quality of programmes that they previously did. According to the networks they are no longer able to provide public service programming to the extent that they had once done. By contrast those organizations who have benefited from cable in the United States argue that the primary beneficiary of cable has been the viewer. The networks have indeed suffered but the viewer — the consumer — has gained. There is now a far greater number of channels available and a much wider range of programming. The cable channels, so their advocates proclaim, can focus on relatively small sectors of the national audience and satisfy their needs. If there is a demand for high quality drama or minority sports or documentaries, a cable channel dedicated to each of these areas can deliver the appropriate programmes. In other words American television in the 1990s is much more coordinated by the market. It has changed from a production driven system to one that is far more responsive to the preferences of the viewer. The question is: will this experience be repeated in the United Kingdom? The answer is still very much a matter for conjecture.

Modern cable systems arrived much later in the UK. By the start of the 1990s less than one million homes had been hooked to a cable system, and only a percentage of those were linked to a broad band multichannel system. Furthermore, there were indications that the cabling of Britain was going to be a far slower process than was envisaged during the 1980s. The cost of cabling in the major cities was higher than anticipated, primarily because the service had to be provided through an underground cable which had very high costs by comparison with the overhead cable provided in many American systems. Nevertheless, research conducted by the Cable Authority, the public body which regulates the industry, suggests that over eight million households would subscribe to a cable system should it become available. If these figures are borne out by the mid 1990s then cable will be a major force in the broadcasting industry.

The role and impact of DBS is equally a matter for conjecture. This service was the result of new technologies which allowed programmes to be received directly from satellites with low-powered transmitters. Those who wished to obtain the service had to install a dish aerial and decoding equipment. In addition they were required to pay a subscription fee for those channels which offered films within two years of their release in cinemas. Initially two competing DBS services were available, British Satellite Broadcasting and Sky Television, but they merged in 1990 with one of the organizations, Sky Television, emerging as the dominant partner in the newly merged company. Indeed, the merged company, known as British Sky Broadcasting, trades under the name of Sky Television. Half of the company's shares, an effective operating control, are in the hands of News International plc, a part of the global media company run by Rupert Murdoch.

The initial costs of running Sky Television were very considerable. News International had to accept an accumulative loss by 1990 of over £300m and the extent of this loss was no doubt one of the reasons for the merger. However, it has been Murdoch's view that DBS services in Britain will eventually be profitable and, although it is too early to judge, there are some indications that his belief has foundations. Surveys conducted by the Broadcasting Audience Research Board, which is jointly owned by the BBC and ITV companies, suggest that those households which receive Sky spent 44 per cent of their viewing time watching it. By contrast the figures for the two BBC channels was 24 per cent and for ITV and Channel 4, it was 32 per cent. Although too much significance can be read into this one survey, it is in line with several others, which suggests that there is a demand for DBS services. Presumably those who were surveyed were the most attracted to Sky and most predisposed to the programming offered by its four channels. Nevertheless while it is difficult at this stage to judge the overall viewer response and the commercial viability of DBS, there are reasons to believe these services will have an impact on British broadcasting.

If the American experience is replicated, the major impact will be on the ITV companies. The three American networks are no longer the profitable organizations they once were. Their profitability is closely tied to the audience for their programmes and as the number of viewers has declined so have their profits. The relationship between audience figures and revenue is not quite so explicit in Britain, although the principal protection that the ITV companies had was their possession of a television advertising monopoly until the arrival of Channel 4 in 1982 (and in any case they sold the advertising which appeared on Channel 4). Should cable and DBS services succeed to the extent that cable alone has in the United States, then the effective monopoly on television advertising will end, and that will have a severe impact on the ITV companies. They will lose their position of dominance with advertisers in the rates that they will be able to charge. More significantly if their revenue base is eroded, they will not be able to produce the range and quality of programmes that they have made over the past three and a half decades. The ITV companies have the most to lose in the event of the success of cable and DBS services.

The impact on the BBC will be less direct as the BBC is currently protected by the licence fee. The principal question mark hanging over the future concerns the continuing existence of the fee and its real value. Will governments wish to protect the licence fee and a service that is attracting a continually declining share of the audience? And if the licence fee is placed in jeopardy then what of public service broadcasting? The answers to these questions are not readily available.

3 The global environment

One of the most striking features of the British broadcast television industry is its intimate and close relationship to the global television industry. The forces that are structuring broadcast television in the UK are not solely domestic. The industry operates within a European and global environment and is profoundly affected by developments that take place beyond the shores of Britain. Of course, television has always been an international industry. Most national television systems have always imported a percentage of their broadcast output, and in this respect Britain has been no different. Both the ITV companies and the BBC have imported programmes, primarily from American production companies, although they have voluntarily limited these imports to approximately 15 per cent of their total output. In turn both the BBC and the major ITV companies have been very successful exporters throughout the world. So the international market in television programming has been long established, however, it is a marketplace that is undergoing some profound changes.

The changes are, in part, the result of the developments that have been described in the preceding sections. Britain is not the only country, outside the USA, to be in the throes of deregulation or to be affected by the advent of new technologies. France and Italy, to name just two, are also going through the same process and are experiencing the emergence of new channels and a restructuring of their industry. Moreover this phenomenon is not only restricted to Europe but is observable all over the globe. The result is a vast increase in demand for television programming to satisfy the requirements of all these new channels around the world. However the established broadcasting organizations, such as the three networks in the United States or the ITV companies, are not the beneficiaries of the new television landscape. They find themselves financially squeezed; a squeeze which is all the more awkward as the production costs of the television industry have increased disproportionately sharply throughout the 1980s. Accordingly, the established broadcasters have not been able to satisfy this demand, at least on their own. They have still to deal with this new configuration of increased costs and rising demand by pooling their resources into coproduction arrangements. Both the BBC and the ITV companies have developed several such arrangements with American and European companies. The experience of these co-productions has been mixed, they have been successful in the field of documentaries, particularly those that are not highly charged politically. However, their record in the field that is of most importance to broadcasters — drama or comedy, or entertainment generally — is much more varied. Coproductions apparently either satisfy the needs of only one of the partners or none of them. Very rarely are all of them satisfied. However, the financial advantages are so substantial that coproductions are firmly established in the international television market.

The second response to the changing terrain of the global television market has been the emergence of the integrated media corporation. The entertainment industry which includes television, motion pictures, book and magazine publishing, records, etc., has seen an unprecedented number of mergers and acquisitions in the latter half of the 1980s. It was estimated that well over US $80 billion was spent during this period and the process gives few signs of coming to an end. The result of this financial activity has seen the emergence of several large organizations which have an interest in most if not all of the above activities. It is noticeable that the two most powerful of these integrated media corporations, Time-Warner and News Corporation, are based in the United States, although News Corporation, in particular, has extensive interests outside the US, especially in the UK and Australia. The rationale for the emergence of these corporations is twofold. Firstly, it is believed that there are significant benefits from integration. News Corporation, for instance, owns the motion picture company Twentieth Century Fox, an American television network the Fox Network, and 50 per cent of British Sky Broadcasting in the UK. Accordingly, motion pictures produced by Twentieth Century Fox can be sold to the Fox Network in the USA and to Sky Television in Britain. News Corporation in addition owns book publishers whose titles could provide Twentieth Century Fox and its production subsidiary Fox Television with suitable material for motion pictures and television series. In the UK newspapers owned by News Corporation through its subsidiary News International plc carried special promotional advertising for Sky Television. The ability of the component elements of News Corporation to assist one another — to develop a synergy — is one of the principal rationales for the development of these integrated media corporations. In the case of Time-Warner, after the merger of Warner Brothers and the pay television (subscription) channel of Time, Home Box Office (HBO), agreed to let its programmes be marketed by Warner Brothers Video, one of the largest video distribution organizations in the world.

Secondly, another reason for the emergence of these corporations is size and prominence. News Corporation and Time-Warner simply have more power and influence than their competitors. They have access to greater resources. Sky Television, for instance, could not have survived in its initial years without the deep pockets of News Corporation. Time-Warner and News Corporation have the ability to attract actors, screenwriters, authors, singers, etc. who are most in demand, primarily because they have the resources to pay for their very expensive services. The advantages possessed by News Corporation and Time-Warner have not gone unnoticed and several other powerful integrated media corporations have been and are in the process of being formed. Interestingly most of them are not American owned, but they all have a major American presence. Sony, for example, has purchased Tristar and Columbia the motion picture companies as well as CBS records. Matsushita, another major Japanese electronics corporation, completed the purchase of MCA in late 1990, which includes Universal, the motion picture company. It appears that the globalization of the entertainment industry is proceeding apace. It is an industry which in 1989 had global revenues in the order of $150 billion with the expectation that it will continue to grow at an annual rate of 10–15 per cent. It also appears to be likely that this industry will be dominated by a relatively small group of very powerful media corporations.

These companies are likely to be the principal suppliers of the growing demand for television programming. They will own the motion picture studios and the television production companies. In addition they will own channels, especially in the United States, through which they will be able to distribute their programmes. Their presence in the American television market, the largest and wealthiest in the world, is of central importance because it allows them to recoup most of their production costs in the United States and then to sell their programmes overseas at extremely attractive prices. The potential impact on the television industry outside the United States is considerable.

In the United Kingdom, which may well have access to over 50 channels through a combination of DBS, cable and terrestrial broadcasting, the demand for television programming will have risen very considerably by the mid-1990s. It is extremely unlikely that the BBC, ITV companies or the independent sector will have the capacity to satisfy this demand. Coproduction and reliance on these large media corporations are likely to provide the solution. Consequently UK television programmes, which were primarily controlled by domestic producers until the 1990s, will have a different flavour as the decade draws to a close. British television will broadcast many more programmes designed primarily for the American market and with commercial objectives paramount. There are some indications from the early viewer responses to Sky Television that British audiences, or at least a percentage of them, may welcome this development. But whether it is welcomed or not the overall impact will be that the mix of British television will be fundamentally changed. The balance which has emerged over several decades between light entertainment and sport on the one hand and a commitment to serious drama, music, documentary and news on the other, will be altered. The commitment to public service broadcasting at best will be diluted. The British broadcasting organizations, which will be facing substantial and serious financial problems in the early 1990s, will be unable to compete with these powerful media corporations which have a global reach. If television in the UK during the 1990s is to be coordinated essentially by the market, then the integrated media corporations are likely to play a very substantial role in shaping the face of British television as the twentieth century draws to a close.

To a certain extent the UK can no longer insulate itself, because of its membership of the European Community. European programmes cannot be kept out of the UK. However, the global television market is dominated by English language producers, primarily from the United States, and their programmes could be excluded or limited. Indeed the BBC and ITV have had voluntary quotas over American programmes for some years, although these quotas are unlikely to continue. There was also a brief attempt by the European Community to place restrictions on American films and television programmes for the entire Community, but this was withdrawn after the threat of US retaliation on other products. Consequently insulation from this global market appears unlikely and indeed unwelcome as national markets would be cutting themselves off from one of the cheapest and most popular sources of programming.

4 Conclusion

In the 1980s the British government decided to restructure British broadcast television in a manner which would make it far less amenable to government and more responsive to the disciplines of the market. Although regulatory bodies would continue to monitor and control certain aspects of the industry in the 1990s, broadcast television, to a considerable extent, will be coordinated by the market as the twentieth century comes to a close. It will be driven by the demands of viewers and advertisers. There will be a considerable range of suppliers and a substantial number of broadcasters, all of whom will be dependent on advertising or subscription. Only the BBC will be publicly funded, at least until 1996 when its charter is due for renewal. The terrain of television will alter dramatically from that which existed as recently as the early 1980s.

The developments in the television industry, in many ways, reflects the changes that have occurred in the British economy and society. The movement from hierarchy and regulation to the market can be seen in several other industries and services. Hierarchical styles and management have been modified while the reliance of networks has grown. Heavily regulated environments have been progressively deregulated; a development that has occurred not only in the UK but in a host of other nations. The emergence of the market as a model of coordination in British broadcast television is not unique or distinct, but part of a much wider national and global development.

Another characteristic of this industry, which is part of a wider if not universal development, is the increasing integration of British television within the global industry. This phenomenon of globalization is evident in several of the industries and services examined in this book. If British television is to be coordinated by a global market, then some of the characteristics most identified with British television may well disappear. The commitment to public service broadcasting, in particular, may well be under threat and with it the range and quality of output which has earned British television its international reputation. Coordination by the market could well provide advertisers and viewers with what they want, but an essentially hierarchical and regulated industry produced an internationally highly regarded industry.

References

Briggs, A. (1979) *Governing the BBC*, London, BBC Publications.

Smith, A. (ed.) (1974) *British Broadcasting*, London, David and Charles.

CHAPTER 5:
RUNNING THE MOTOR INDUSTRY

PETER HAMILTON

1 Introduction

In this chapter, we shall be looking at the motor industry as an example of market-coordinated organizations, how these operate, and their relationship with other coordinating domains — principally hierarchy. To a very limited extent, we shall also look at both commercial vehicle manufacturers and component suppliers, but our main focus will be on car manufacturers. Our geographical focus is quite explicitly British, although we will, from time to time, bring in examples from and comparisons with Europe, the USA and Japan — because the motor industry is perhaps the most 'global' of all industries. The British motor industry has also been arguably more 'open' to global influences than many of its competitors. In this context we are concerned with the processes of change in the way car manufacturers organize their production and marketing activities.

The history of the British motor industry can be characterized as very much a history of the complex interplay of *state-sponsored hierarchically regulated* forces, such as government economic, regional, industrial and social policy, with *market-regulated* forces such as the strategies of motor manufacturers, the cost and supply of labour, and the demand for vehicles, which has determined the development and present composition of the industry. Overlaying the interplay of hierarchy and market is a more 'sociological' layer of social conflict, which can be broadly characterized as occurring between owners and managers of the industry and key groups of production-line workers, and has essentially been concerned with the 'right to manage' the enterprises concerned. At least some of this may be interpreted through the *networks* model, but it also relates very closely to 'Fordism'. We can also discern the growing importance of the networks model as a way of understanding how certain post-Fordist methods of organizing production in the motor industry have developed — especially those connected with Japanese firms.

It is not without some significance that the motor industry was the chosen site for a 'class struggle' by the post-1968 activists of the militant left. A large number of the students who graduated in the 1960s left university to become factory workers in the car plants of the western world (see, for accounts of this in France, Linhart, 1981; and in the UK, Beynon, 1973). As the militant-led disputes concerned various aspects of the design and organization of work within the industry, and given the numerical weight of motor industry workers within the labour force, not to mention the economic importance of the industry generally, it is not too surprising that the motor industry should become the arena in which many central issues about order and control in British society were transacted.

2 The firm and the market

In Chapter 2 economic theories of the market as a coordinating mechanism were discussed contrasting the 'neo-classical' and 'Austrian' approaches. As that chapter demonstrated quite clearly, there is no one generally accepted theoretical model of the market as a domain. Similarly, 'markets' as empirical entities vary very widely in how they function and in the consequences for the participants in their operation. As a result, when we come to look at how specific industries develop in the context of given markets we are faced with a classic problem of the social sciences: the sheer 'messiness' of actually observable human behaviour is often difficult to fit into the neat and logical models of the individual social sciences — economics, sociology, politics, etc. People — whether as producers or as consumers — do not always act exactly in ways which we might expect from the standpoint of theory.

2.1 Markets and models

In examining a case such as the motor industry, we must always be aware of the ways in which actual experience may diverge from the pure form of theoretical models. But this should not encourage the notion that abstract theoretical models are of no use in explaining 'real-life' processes. Models and theories are not, and can never be, exact replications of given, empirically observable situations: to believe otherwise is to give credence to a classical logical fallacy. A theory exists to help us think about and *understand* why the event or process has certain elements and consequences which we can observe.

In using the market models, we have to examine how the empirical markets in which motor firms exist actually operate, and then see how the theories of the market help us to understand their structure and consequences. In the simplest sense, motor industry firms must typically coordinate their internal functioning to take account of a market — the market for motor cars. (Of course they are also involved in a number of *other* contingent and interconnected markets, for example the labour market, the capital market, markets for components etc.) Their survival as corporate entities depends upon how effectively and profitably they can develop and sell cars in that market. However, the definition of a *market* in this context is very important, because we need to distinguish different socially and geographically defined markets, and also understand how market conditions themselves may be influenced by political or other non-market regulatory factors.

The market for cars depends upon the existence of consumers who wish to buy them. If all other things were equal, it would seem that the lowest cost producer would have the greatest share of any given market, since it can supply cars at the lowest price to consumers. It ought to follow that manufacturers will compete to produce the lowest-cost car, and that those whose costs mean that they cannot offer a competitively-priced vehicle will go out of business. Broadly speaking, the history of the industry is that of firms competing to make cars at the lowest cost: and the most successful appear to have been those able to sell high volumes at prices low enough to undercut the competition but which ensure they produce a profit. As the market for cars is essentially global, although in fact highly differentiated by particular national features and local preferences, the most successful companies (in terms of volumes sold) should, by this definition, be those able to operate at a global level, who can thus reduce their costs by huge economies of scale through the standardization of components and long production runs. On this logic the most profitable and successful companies should be the biggest mass-producers of standardized and low-cost cars operating at a global level. Now, as most readers will be aware, it is the Japanese car manufacturers such as Toyota, Nissan and Honda who are currently both the most profitable and the most successful manufacturers, both in terms of their productivity and in the quality and reliability of the cars they manufacture. The market share of individual car makers may vary quite widely. In the EEC Japanese cars, at the time of writing (in 1992), account for about 40 per cent of sales in Eire, but only 3 per cent in Italy. The differences are due almost entirely to local controls on imports of Japanese cars. What may come as the most surprising of all is that the Japanese have not achieved this position through the very high volume manufacture of a small range of highly standardized cars, but through relatively low sales volumes of a very wide range of markedly differentiated cars. By 1990, the sales of Japanese cars accounted for almost 30 per cent of total sales in the US car market. It has been argued that Toyota, about half the size in terms of volume of cars produced than General Motors (GM), nonetheless makes *more profitably* a wider range of cars (Womack et al., 1990, p. 64). And all this despite quotas on the sale of Japanese cars in both Europe and North America, which constitute artificial constraints on the car markets in those two regions.

2.2 Consumer-driven versus producer-driven markets

At first sight it might appear that the success of the Japanese car makers is due to the fact that here, as in many other areas of life, the formal laws of economics seem to break down. If the Japanese are not producing cars in the same numbers as their American competitors, and their access to car markets is restricted, how can they be reaping the economies of scale which would allow them to make higher profits on similarly priced products as compared to Ford, GM or Chrysler? To answer this question it is necessary first to explore some of the answer from the other side of the market fence, to move from producer to consumer.

Firstly, consumers in developed economies like the UK or the USA do not overwhelmingly demand the lowest-cost car — if they did, our roads would be full of the cheapest cars on the market — Ladas, Skodas, Yugos, Citroën 2CVs and Fiat Pandas. But they are not. This is because demand is highly differentiated, or *segmented*, into different market *sectors*. Within complex markets, economists would predict that consumers would favour the lowest-priced product conferring a given range of characteristics. In other words, they would expect consumer demand to be differentiated, but nonetheless to follow the basic laws of supply and demand which govern all markets. And consumer demand in a mature market like the UK is *highly* differentiated. Currently about 20 per cent of new cars sold are in the cheapest small car or 'supermini' sector; whilst another 33 per cent are 'lower medium' sized cars like Ford Escorts and Volkswagen Golfs; 'upper medium' sized cars like Ford Sierras and Vauxhall Cavaliers account for about 35 per cent of sales, and 'big' cars like Ford Scorpios, Volvo 740s, etc. make up about 9 per cent of sales. The remainder of the new cars sold (roughly 3 per cent of sales) are luxury and specialized vehicles such as Rolls-Royces, Porsches or Ferraris. Even within these 'market segments' it is possible to locate certain 'niche' markets for given types of vehicles — for example, four-wheel drive off-road cars; high-powered hatchbacks; estate cars; cabriolets; 'people carriers' (such as the Renault Espace); or open-top sports cars. And in developed or 'mature' markets like the USA and the UK, where large stocks of used cars ensure that acquiring a car need not be a costly investment, market segmentation is mushrooming as manufacturers seek new market niches to fill an ever-expanding consumer demand for new sorts of vehicles, and as households move from owning one to several cars.

Thus the market, from the consumer side, is organized in terms of a certain pattern of demand. Unless a car maker adjusts its model production policies so as to satisfy this demand pattern, it will not continue to operate profitably. In other words, the car manufacturer must adopt a business strategy which *positions* it effectively in terms of the pattern of consumer demand. Manufacturers invest heavily in the 'market positioning' of the range of cars which they produce, which means that they seek to establish their products quite clearly in the minds of potential consumers, to give their products clear attributes and values which mark them out or 'position' them *vis-à-vis* competitors.

Within the market for cars, *market positioning* of the individual models and their makers is of considerable importance because of the major impact it can have on demand, and as a result it may also influence the prices that a manufacturer can charge. A good example is Mercedes-Benz. Some Mercedes models are sold in their basic form as taxis in Germany, where they are made, and in other parts of Europe, at prices far below what they can be sold for in countries like the UK or the USA. Why? Because the *market positioning* of the Mercedes in the USA and the UK places it in the category of a luxury car of extremely high quality — hence it can be sold for a high price, even in its basic configuration. Mercedes however can produce these cars in quite large numbers (the company makes about 700,000 cars per year) because it is able to sell a given proportion as taxis at what is probably quite a low profit, and make very considerable profits on other model variants in export markets.

The business strategy adopted by the car maker thus involves decisions about market positioning as well as decisions about the model ranges which will be produced, for there has to be some connection between the two things: a Mercedes-type market positioning is simply not possible for a model range produced by Skoda, for example! This imposes a number of critical decisions on the car maker. Will it seek to offer a product for each major segment of consumer demand? What assumptions can it make about its ability to sell the number of cars needed to achieve a break-even point in terms of costs against revenue? As a result, and since the market is also constantly fragmenting into new 'niches', model-development policies must constantly evolve to match changing consumer demand. The car market, then could be said to be increasingly 'consumer driven' in the sense that the products offered by manufacturers must respond to consumer needs. This was not always the case: for example, even comparatively recently, in the immediate post-war period and up until the 1960s, when demand for cars was high because most households did not have one, manufacturers could decide what type of cars they could put on the market and how they would be equipped. They could even produce essentially the same car year in, year out, with very minor cosmetic changes and incite consumers to change their cars on almost a yearly basis because an old model was instantly recognizeable ('built-in obsolescence', as it came to be known in the USA in the 1950s and 1960s, when this form of marketing of cars was dominant). In such a context the market could be said to be *producer driven*. The shift from a pre-dominantly 'producer-driven' to a 'consumer-driven' car market since the early 1960s partly explains why Japanese firms have become globally dominant in car manufacture.

The perceived 'image' of a car for many consumers (but certainly not all) is thus paramount in their decision to purchase or choose it. (We should remember that in some markets new cars are bought by compa-nies as well as individuals: in the UK during the 1980s as many as 60 per cent or more of new cars were purchased by companies. A certain proportion of the three million or so company car users in the UK — who constitute another, segmented, 'market' in themselves — thus may be able to choose a car without bearing the cost of its purchase or maintenance and, as a result, its 'image' may be of greater importance to them than its functionality, reliability, resale value or running costs.) 'Image' — attributed prestige or status — is thus something that manufacturers also have to invest in — through advertising, public relations, and all of the ways in which they encounter the con-sumer. In economic terms, advertising to enhance a marque's prestige might be thought of as the building up of a stock of consumer goodwill towards the manufacturer's products.

Choices between products offered in the car market are frequently rationalized by consumers in terms of attributed benefits — for exam-ple, the 'solidity' of a Volkswagen (VW) or the 'quality' of a BMW may be cited as reasons for purchase, by people for whom neither as-pect is of major importance in terms of their use of the car. Finally, the purchase of a car may be more important for some consumers than for others, with the result that some people are willing to invest a much higher proportion of their disposable income in buying a car than others. Economists examining the car market have thus to take account of widely diversified — 'segmented' — consumer preferences.

The point of the above discussion is that the market for cars oper-ates in a highly complex way: the least-cost producer able to offer a 'good' car at a low price is not necessarily the most successful or most profitable manufacturer. This partly explains why the range of cars available to the consumer now is greater than at any time since the 1920s, and why small, medium and large firms continue to survive in the industry, when logic would seem to dictate that only large and profitable manufacturers reaping economies of scale advantages should succeed. Governments have intervened on a number of occa-sions over the years to prevent car firms going out of business, because in their view wider social or economic purposes were served by keep-ing the manufacturer in business. Rational economic behaviour is not always conducive to commercial success, and thus we may have to in-voke other theoretical models than those which explain the opera-tions of the market in order to understand why a particular firm op-erates in the way that it does.

3 Organizational characteristics of the motor industry

In looking at the role of the British car industry we also need to be aware of global industry-wide trends in the organization and development of motor car production. These can be 'stripped-down' into the oppositions between a number of business or 'corporate' strategies which car makers can adopt to the making and marketing of cars. These are, in essence, the key issues about manufacturing cars that all firms have had to face, and they provide the background against which we can understand what has happened to the UK industry. In the context of these trends, any manufacturing firm which intends to continue in the industry has to address, in strategic terms, how it should organize itself in order to survive.

In an important comparative study of the world automotive industry (Womack et al., 1990), three broad organizational forms in the development of car production are identified:

1   Craft production.
2   Mass-production (which is linked with 'Fordism').
3   'Lean-production' (which is linked to Flexible Specialization).

The first —*craft production* — is the type of system which was employed to produce cars during the early days of the industry. Essentially cars were built by hand by highly skilled craftsmen, it is a system which still survives today in the factories of specialist manufacturers like Rolls Royce, Aston Martin, Ferrari, and Lamborghini.

The second — *mass production* or 'Fordism' — is the type of volume production introduced originally by Henry Ford in his factories between 1908 and 1915, and then modified by such motor industry pioneers as Alfred P. Sloan of GM and André Citroën, in which standardized components are assembled on a production line by interchangeble semi-skilled operatives (and more recently by their automated, robotized equivalents).

The third — often referred to under the generic titles 'flexible manufacturing system' (FMS), or 'flexible specialization' (FS), and given the motor-industry specific name of *lean production* by Womack et al. — is the form of production introduced by the Japanese in the 1960s, whose characteristics will be explored in detail later. Its essential features include flexible production methods, the integration of suppliers and other aspects of the production system such as finance and marketing into a cooperative *network* with the manufacturer, rapid product development, short production cycles, and the systematic and effective targeting of differentiated or 'highly segmented' consumer demand.

In the 1970s and 1980s, the problems faced by both UK and multinational car companies with factories in Great Britain were (and for the foreseeable future will continue to be) first, the challenges posed by the decline of Fordism as a viable mode of corporate organization of the process technology of car manufacture; second, increased global market competition derived from the success of a new mode of corporate organization of the process technology of car manufacture, which is essentially Japanese in origin. As in the 1940s, 1950s and 1960s those companies which are likely to survive through the 1990s will be those best able to operate profitably in the prevailing market conditions. Since the 1970s, when they first proved competitive with domestic manufacturers, Japanese car makers have faced restrictive market barriers in most of Europe. During the 1990s these will be progressively reduced, and car makers in both the UK and the rest of the EEC will face almost unrestricted competition from Japanese car makers — of which most will have some sort of local (that is European) manufacturing facility, or what in car-industry terms is called a 'transplant'.

3.1 Craft production

When cars were first made at the end of the nineteenth century, they were produced for a small and wealthy clientele in very limited numbers. Because car manufacture was 'leading edge' technology, and because demand was limited, cars were made in small firms by highly-skilled craftsmen.

Craft production had the following characteristics:

A work force that was highly skilled in design, machine operations, and fitting. Most workers progressed through an apprenticeship to a full set of craft skills. Many could hope to run their own machine shops, becoming self-employed contractors to assembler firms.

Organizations that were extremely decentralized, although the vehicle's design came from small machine shops. The system was coordinated by an owner/entrepreneur in direct contact with everyone involved — customers, employers, and suppliers.

The use of general-purpose machine tools to perform drilling, grinding, and other operations on metal and wood.

A very low production volume — 1,000 or fewer automobiles a year, only a few of which (fifty or fewer) were built to the same design. And even among those fifty, no two were exactly alike since craft techniques inherently produced variations.

(*Womack et al., 1990, p. 24*)

In such a system, a great deal of control over production decisions was necessarily in the hands of the skilled craftsmen themselves.

The manager in such an enterprise has relatively little control over the production system ('the labour process'), and his or her role is confined to that of transmitting orders to the factory, assuring the supply of raw materials, bookkeeping and organizing the financing of the firm. (Design of the vehicle, typically another managerial function, also involves detailed cooperation with production workers, to introduce a manufacturable car.) Productivity in such a system is highly dependent upon the commitment and motivation of the workforce. Increasing output would have to be negotiated with the workers involved.

The craft-production system continues to the present day in the factories of the highly specialized makers of luxury and high performance cars. Their market 'niches' are protected by the fact that no mass producer would find it worthwhile to compete with them, as volumes are so small. The classic problem faced by luxury car manufacturers is that of pricing their product to balance supply and demand as they experience much more extreme cycles of fluctuating demand than mass producers. Peak demand, for example, may be 400 cars per year, whilst in a recession they may find it difficult to dispose of twenty-five cars per year. With obligatory crash tests and emission controls now required for such cars, the cost of developing new models has become very heavy in recent years, and now virtually all of the small luxury car makers have been taken over by mass producers who can supply the necessary type approval facilities — Ferrari is owned by Fiat, Aston Martin by Ford, Lamborghini by Chrysler, Lotus by GM. However, the Japanese car makers have shown that their 'lean' production methods are capable of attacking even these small 'niche' producers — Honda introduced in 1990 the NSX, a car very similar in concept and execution to a Ferrari, at a price about 40–50 per cent lower.

The introduction by Ford of mass-production techniques (he was until 1908 producing his cars essentially by craft methods) showed that the production and selling cost of cars could be dramatically reduced by a complete re-think of the economics, manufacturing and social organization of car production. In this process, virtually all of the aspects associated with car production in the 'craft' mode were changed.

3.2 Mass production and Fordism

The term 'Fordism' is employed in the social sciences (though not without some dispute as to its scope and meaning) to describe the mode of accumulation and mode of regulation which typified modern capitalist economies from 1945 to about 1975. In that context it has also come to mean a system of coordination of labour, capital and the state. In simple terms, Fordism describes not merely the organization of the factory as a production centre, but 'the relations'...(usually qualified by the adjective 'corporatist')...'between unions, management and the state, under which although conflicts existed there was general consensus on the state's task in managing the overall economic balance. The State was responsible for full-employment policies' (Harris, 1988, p. 33). We are going to look at a specific *domain* of the Fordist mode of accumulation and regulation, and examine the implications of the innovation and diffusion of what is a 'process technology', although we will not have the space to consider its wider implications.

Fordism (named of course after Henry Ford, who first introduced such a system to make cars at his Highland Park and River Rouge factories near Detroit) can also be used in a more narrow, industry-specific way. By Fordism I mean *a system of mass production of standardized commodities made in long runs on assembly lines, requiring massive investment in inflexible fixed plant.*

Ford's great innovation came in 1908, when he introduced the Model T, his twentieth design. He had realized that the market for cars was a truly mass one, in the sense that the manufacturer who produced cars for a mass-market of users, 'owner-drivers' rather than owners who employed chauffeur-mechanics, was the key to the future of the industry. But Ford's major innovation for the car industry was not the continuously moving assembly line, as many people believe, but the 'complete and consistent interchangeability of parts and the simplicity of attaching them to each other. Without such innovations the assembly line would not have been possible' (Womack et al., 1990, p. 27). Ford was in fact simply applying a principle already employed in other industries and known as 'dis-assembly' manufacture. The concept of 'dis-assembly' came from the food-processing industry, where it was applied to the dismemberment of animal carcasses, into their constituent elements. At the start of the twentieth century, the system was in the process of diffusing throughout industrial manufacture after its first successful large scale use during the American civil war, where it had been applied to the manufacture of rifles and pistols.

What Ford wanted to do was to use the 'dis-assembly' manufacturing system to 'de-skill' the assembly operation which, under craft production, required highly skilled operatives to make and fit parts to the vehicle. Ford's innovation in process technology was to fuse 'dis-assembly' manufacture with a principle of social order, and in so doing create a new system of labour control. In that sense he was not in fact a *technological* innovator at all: as Drucker pointed out, 'only (Ford's) concept of human organization for work was new' (Drucker, 1950, p. 19). Ford took many of his ideas from the 'systematic management' movement, of which F. H. Taylor is the best known exponent. Taylor's ideas were based on the notion that the average worker was both lazy and stupid, and that he or she therefore would never develop the best way, the 'scientific' way to do his or her job. Hence workers were essentially passive 'they should do what they are told to do promptly and without asking questions or making suggestions' (Littler, 1982, p. 51). In a craft production system, this is clearly impossible: and in nineteenth century America, there was a widespread populist tendency for workers to see themselves as the sole creative factor in production. Thus Taylor's ideas were part not simply of a system of management, but of an ideological movement designed to undermine the 'active' image of the worker in favour of this more passive role. Ford, who saw workers' partial autonomy in the production process as a hindrance to his plans to standardize the production processes, thus introduced a system which transposed Taylor's concepts of 'scientific management' to the car factory.

Taylor's approach involved a careful analysis of the production system and the division of labour, from which they could be 'decomposed' according to five principles which would deliver a systematic job analysis, from which production costs could be calculated, standard times for each task determined, and an associated incentive payment system drawn up.

Ford introduced most of Taylor's principles in his reorganization of his Highland Park factory. But he added to it two elements which Taylor had not specified: the continuous-flow assembly line and a new method of labour control.

In 1908, just before the Model T was introduced, it took some 514 minutes for the average Ford assembler to complete a work cycle. He (there were no women in Ford factories until the 1950s) would assemble a large part of the car before moving on to the next. He would have to get all the necessary parts, file them to fit and then assemble them all together. The first step in improving this was to bring all the parts to the worker. The second one, perfect interchangeability of parts, was achieved to fragment the tasks carried out by workers so that each carried out only one specialized task, moving around the assembly hall from vehicle to vehicle. By 1913 the task cycle had come down from 514 to 2.3 minutes.

Although task fragmentation had brought massive productivity advantages, it also had certain defects, the most important of which was the delay caused by workers walking from assembly stand to assembly stand, and jam-ups caused by some workers being faster than others. The continuous-flow assembly line solved all this, because it brought the car past the stationary worker. The cycle time came down from 2.3 to 1.19 minutes: and the pace of work was no longer determined by the worker, but by the assembly line.

The new system delivered both productivity increases and capital savings. The assembly line cost very little to install, but 'it speeded up production so dramatically that the savings (Ford) could realize from reducing the inventory of parts waiting to be assembled far exceeded this trivial outlay' (Womack et al., 1990, p. 29). The more cars produced the greater the savings, so that a car which was already cheaper than its rivals when introduced in 1908 was by the 1920s when two million had been made, 67 per cent cheaper still. The Model T would not have been a success, however, without a market to sell to: because Ford's manufacturing techniques allowed great interchangeability of parts, and the car was supplied with a detailed and simple set of instructions about how to make repairs, it appealed to a wide range of people, and particularly those in rural America. Ford even assumed the typical owner would be a farmer with a modest tool kit, able to repair farm machinery, and the instruction manual was written accordingly. The Model T is a classic example of a product designed for a relatively undifferentiated market: it assumes that what consumers want is a car ('you can have it in any colour as long as it's black'). Ford set out to make a car as cheaply and effectively as possible, on the assumption that all consumers wanted essentially the same set of product characteristics.

Ford's production system and the design of the Model T made Ford the world's largest car producer very quickly, and helped push most of the craft production companies out of business. There were some 100 car makers in the USA in 1914, but by the heyday of mass production in the mid-1950s three huge firms — Ford, GM and Chrysler — dominated the industry to the extent that they produced 95 per cent of all cars made in America. However, the human costs of his new system were such that Ford was soon forced to introduce a new method of labour control into his factories, to combat the high labour turnover which resulted. In 1913, for example, Ford required 13,000 workers at any one time to run the factory. In that year alone, 50,000 workers quit!

In making the assembly line worker 'interchangeable' through de-skilling, Ford also deprived such people of a career path — in Taylor's terminology Ford had created a regime of 'minimum interaction', in which they became simply extensions of a machine. The result was almost disastrous levels of labour turnover, which Ford attempted to reduce by instituting a high wage system combined with paternalistic controls. The 'Five-Dollar day' guaranteed a high wage, but only to those Ford workers who had six months continuous work with the firm, were over twenty-one, had satisfactory personal habits at home and work (cleanliness and prudence) and no consumption of alcohol or tobacco. A special department was even set up to check such matters – the 'sociological department'! (Littler, 1982, p. 51).

Ford's mass-production system has dominated the motor industry since the 1920s, although Ford's own version of it was not ultimately the most successful form. Ford's problem was that he wanted to be entirely independent of banks and outside suppliers: he was obsessed with the idea of autarchy (total self-reliance) which led him to vertically integrate the entire production system, from raw materials to distribution of his cars. Ford thought that everything could be made by mass-production techniques, from food, to tractors to aircraft, and that he could dramatically reduce the cost of everything, thus benefitting the welfare of the masses. All investment was internally financed because Ford did not trust banks. When his grandson Henry Ford II took over the company in 1945, he asked where the company's financial reserves were located: he was told that the $700m was all kept in cash in the company vault.

Ford wanted, and achieved, total centralized control of his companies: these were vast bureaucracies operated under hierarchical modes of regulation and control, with all the advantages and disadvantages inherent in such systems. His organizational model was a pyramid: all information about the company flowed up from the base to the top, whilst decisions flowed down from its apex — Ford himself. Such a form of organization is usually known as 'U-form.'

It was Ford's great competitor, General Motors, which was able to achieve the classic organizational form of the Fordist, mass-production system — the 'M-form' organization. GM was a conglomerate of twelve car companies put together by a financier: when it failed in 1919 because he was not able to manage it successfully, a specialist manager, Alfred P. Sloan, was put in charge by the group's bankers. Sloan saw that GM needed to resolve two key problems if it was going to be able to compete effectively with the Ford company, and manage the scale of the enterprises required by mass production effectively. These were:

1   How to introduce professional management of the enormous organizations necessitated and made possible by mass production.

2   How to develop differentiated product ranges which could, unlike Ford's one-model policy, 'serve every purse and purpose'. GM aspired to be a generalist manufacturer which was more 'market-driven' than Ford, for this appeared to offer a potentially more profitable business strategy in what was a rapidly segmenting market for cars.

Sloan's solutions were firstly to manage the factories and other operations in a decentralized way: he established divisions managed 'by the numbers' (that is using carefully controlled accounts of expenditure, production and revenue) from a small corporate headquarters.

Sloan's view was that the divisions (the legs of the M) should be allowed to get on with managing their operations. The centre's job was to ensure that the divisions were effectively managed by monitoring their performance, and that the financial resources they required were available.

Sloan's other innovation was to develop a five-model product range to satisfy the broad market GM wanted to serve: from cheap Chevrolets to expensive Cadillacs. The idea was to accomodate potential buyers of every income throughout their lives. He anticipated that the market for cars would be differentiated, and thus developed a model range to suit this differentiation. In order to allow model diversity to suit consumer demand whilst capitalizing on the production advantages of mass production, he standardized as many 'hidden' mechanical items as possible. In essence this modified Fordism provides the business strategy which 'generalist' car manufacturers have employed to this day.

Sloan made no changes, however, to the Fordist idea that the shop-floor workers were simply interchangeable parts of a big machine. For GM as for Ford, labour in Fordist mass production was seen as a *variable* cost: the motor industry then as now was subject to highly cyclical changes in demand, and workers were laid off at the first sign of recession. This created a union movement in the USA (with counterparts elsewhere) which sought an accomodation with management over the crucial issue of job-control — seniority became the criterion of who would go in a recession and who would stay, whilst it also determined who got the better production-line jobs. Whilst the situation in Europe differed in certain respects, the key problem of Fordism was universal and remained its use of labour as a variable cost, and its treatment of assembly line workers as essentially 'tainted by original sin and original stupidity.'

A final characteristic of Fordism is the increasing scale of mass-production enterprises. The logic of mass production calls for long production runs of standardized components, the car making firm will receive many advantages from multinational operation, essentially because of economies of scale benefits, as Table 5.1 indicates.

Most of the Fordist producers became multinationals — Ford and GM in the period from 1910 to 1940; British Motor Corporation (BMC), VW, Fiat, PSA, Renault, from the 1950s. In general the European manufacturers did not become fully Fordist until the post Second World War period, although innovators such as Agnelli (Fiat), Herbert Austin and Louis Renault had begun to set up Fordist factories to run alongside mixed Fordist-craft production facilities by the late 1930s.

To summarize, Fordism, as a corporate strategy for organizing car production, typically has four general characteristics:

1   Ford's factory organization principles.

2   Sloan's financial management and marketing techniques of decentralization (the M-form organization) and range differentiation.

3   Job-control labour organization, treating labour as a variable cost.

4   Multinational corporate structures.

Table 5.1 Optimum scale in various car-making activities

Process	Output per year (by volume)
Casting of engine block	1,000,000
Casting of various other parts	100,000–750,000
Power train (engine/transmission)	600,000
Pressing of various panels	1–2,000,000
Paint shop	250,000
Final assembly	250,000
Advertising	1,000,000
Sales	2,000,000
Risks	1,800,000
Finance	2,500,000
Research and development	5,000,000

Source: Tables 7 and 8, in Rhys, 1988, p.161

3.3 Flexible specialization and the crisis of mass production

What we describe here as *flexible specialization*, and Womack et al. terms 'lean production', is the production system which has enabled the Japanese car makers to become the major force in world car manufacture.

Michael Piore and Charles Sabel have argued in a very influential book, that a 'general crisis of the industrial system' occurred in the 1970s and early 1980s, due to the mass-production model of industrial development reaching its limits (Piore and Sabel, 1984, p. 165).

Their argument is that Fordist mass production, as we have described it in detail in the previous section using the example of car manufacture, is not simply a production system but is in fact a type of economic system where a particular form of production dominates an entire geographical area, regionally, nationally, or internationally.

For Piore and Sabel, the USA created a mass-production national economy led by key industries and especially car manufacture, which was successfully imitated by follower countries after 1945, as a result creating an international 'mass-production economy'.

The key industries in this international mass-production economy thus become those producing consumer durables (especially cars) and the other industries linked to the production of consumer durables such as steel, rubber and glass.

The main threats to the economic stability of this system, Piore and Sabel argue, come from the ever-present possibility of economic stagnation. Because mass-production systems can only progress through the capture of increasing economies of scale so as to reduce production costs and selling price, they are obliged to 'invest in increasingly costly production-specific equipment to turn out even larger volumes of standardized goods. If the market for these goods is depressed in any way as a result of an economic slowdown, then the manufacturer suffers the high fixed costs of an inflexible production system (ibid, 1984, pp. 52–4). Thus demand regulation, through Keynesian economic policies, to keep consumer demand at levels sufficient to absorb the products of mass-production industries is essential.

Mass-production economies operate most successfully when 'market stability is ensured' (ibid, 1984, p. 163), and as a result developed 'regulatory institutions' designed to secure a workable match between the production and consumption of goods. Such institutions are not however foolproof, and the economic crises experienced in both America and Europe in the 1890s and the 1930s, led to 'regulatory crises' — periods of innovation and reconstruction of the regulatory institutions. That of the 1930s was only resolved after the Second World War by the widespread use of Keynesian economic policies designed to maintain an adequate level of demand in the economy — these varied amongst different economies but often included high welfare spending, investment in arms production, and 'corporatist' arrangements between manufacturers, unions and the state, over full-employment and wage bargaining.

By the 1970s however, the mass-production economic system was experiencing a profound crisis. This came about, in Piore and Sabel's view, through a number of causes, chief amongst them being the breakdown of the post-war 'Bretton Woods' regime of fixed exchange rates, the two 'oil shocks' of 1973 and 1979, the saturation of the 'core markets' of mass-production economies, and a consequent fragmentation of the mass markets for standardized products. In addition, governments were not disposed to use Keynesian policies to stimulate demand, or to create the conditions under which the system would be reproduced at the levels seen in the 1950s and 1960s.

Mass production thus experienced crisis because of the 'saturation of industrial markets in the advanced economies' (Piore and Sabel, 1984, p. 187). Products were becoming more diversified on the supply side, whilst consumer tastes were becoming rapidly more sophisticated on the demand side: at the same time many protectionist developing economies closed off their internal markets, whilst a number of rapidly expanding Asian economies aggravated market congestion in the advanced countries by pursuing strategies of export-led growth (ibid, 1984, p. 189).

The outcome of this situation was a challenge to the dominance of Fordist organizational strategies for the mass production of consumer durables, and the provision of an opportunity for another economic-industrial system — flexible specialization — to become the dominant model of industrial organization. Nowhere is this clearer than in the rise of the Japanese car makers, who employ a particular variant of flexible specialization in the manufacture of their products. It has enabled them to surmount many of the structural problems of mass production.

Before turning to a more detailed examination of flexible specialization in the car industry, let us look at a schematic representation of some important differences (see Figure 5.1). These three characteristics are, according to Piore and Sabel, the main areas differentiating flexible specialization and mass production, and it is the advantages of flexible specialization which allow *relatively* low dedication of equipment (that is machine tools which can be used for more than one process), high product differentiation (that is the same plant can produce a number of different models or model variants); and significantly shorter production runs — so that scale economies are realized earlier in the production run than they would be for an equivalent product in mass production.

How and why did the Japanese car makers introduce flexible specialization? In a recent, and very detailed cross-national research study of the world motor industry, the background and history of the rise of a particular form of flexible specialization in the Toyota Motor Company is described in considerable detail. The authors of this study call the Toyota system, as it has been elaborated and developed by Toyota and the other Japanese producers, 'lean production'.

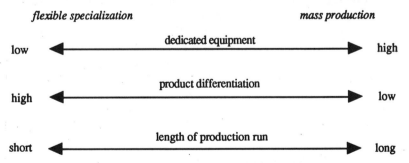

Figure 5.1 *Key characteristics of flexible specialization and mass production*
Source: Williams et al., 1987, p. 415.

As *The Machine that Changed the World* makes clear, the initial reasons for the development of the Toyota system were to get around certain indigenous problems associated with post-war economic development in Japan, and to improve upon certain central features of car production under Fordist systems.

Womack et al. describe how immediately after the Second World War, the occupying Americans imposed savage credit restrictions in an effort to contain inflation. The result was a recession combined with scarce bank loans and the Toyota car company found itself facing a collapse in sales and bankers unwilling to extend further loans.

Toyota responded to this situation by making a quarter of the work-force redundant and in turn this precipitated a workers' occupation of the factory and an all-out strike. So far it was an often-repeated tale in the history of mass production. What made it different was that the Japanese government had strengthened the power of the unions; firstly, by restricting the right of management to fire staff at will; and secondly, by strengthening the negotiating rights of the unions. Toyota knew that they would have to establish some sort of compromise with the workforce.

The compromise arrived at was for the workforce to accept flexible working practices and the redundancies in full in return for guaranteed job security for life for the remaining workforce. In addition, pay was to be linked to length of service to the company and to overall profitability. Thus was born the idea of the company as a community. Once a worker had been at Toyota for a number of years she or he would lose that part of their pay which was linked to length of service if they went to work for another company. Therefore almost all workers would remain with the company for their working life. Consequently, workers became valuable 'fixed assets' and not 'variable costs' to be tolerated until a machine could be found which could do the job better.

Why did these circumstances produce a system of production which was so superior to the existing processes? The answer lies in the lessons learned about the mass production of cars in the United States by Japanese management. A central figure in this is Toyota's Taiichi Ohno. He was a frequent visitor to Detroit after the war and what he learned there of mass-production techniques was to have a lasting effect. The car industry of Detroit had four identifiable areas of weakness. These were in the assembly process itself, in the supply of components, in the design of new products, and in customer relations. It is worthwhile looking briefly at these in turn.

In the car factories of Detroit there were many types of worker. There were housekeepers who cleaned, inspectors controlling quality, repairmen who fixed damaged tools, production-line workers, and utility men who could fill in for absentee workers. Workers were also divided between the production line and the rework area where errors were corrected. In each area, workers were controlled by foremen who gave instructions but did not do the work itself. The problem with this system was that once the production line was running it was crucial to keep it going as a delay at any one point would hold up the whole process. Therefore if mistakes were made they were generally ignored until the rework stage at the end of the line. One consequence of this was that production-line workers did not feel responsible for maintaining quality and nor was quality work rewarded. Furthermore inexpensive mistakes at an early stage in the line would be expensive to put right at the end — and some would not be discovered until after the car left the factory.

A second problem with the mass production system found in Detroit and elsewhere after the war lay in the supply of components. The production line only puts together the components of a car or truck. To a significant degree the efficiency of the whole depended upon the efficiency of component manufacturing yet this was seriously flawed. The flaw was that the car manufacturers would devise their own specifications for parts and then ask for tenders from both in-house producers and outside producers. Both were unsatisfactory; firstly, because the components manufacturers were told nothing about the problems and specifications of the whole car or truck (which were company secrets) and this lack of awareness could lead to mistakes. Secondly, the components designers were not involved at the design stage of the car. Therefore the components designers were unable to use their design skills to prevent problems arising later and nor were they fully aware of the overall nature of the car in which their components would be located.

A third problem lay with product development and engineering. In the car industry, which Ohno examined after the war, the development of a new product involved the creation of a very large team made up of individuals whose loyalty remained with their various departments rather than with the team. The membership of the team constantly changed as departments recalled individuals to deal with departmental problems. Problems of design, engineering, production and marketing were addressed sequentially rather than all of these being considered throughout the period of development. Finally, leaders were in a weak position both in relation to the members of the team and in relation to top level management. This was already a problem in the 1940s but as the market for cars and trucks became increasingly segmented and changeable, it created a very slow response time to changes in consumer demand.

The fourth and final problem was that relationships with the customer were mediated by a large number of small dealers who did not regard it as part of their function to provide the company with detailed information about changing consumer preferences and who gave a higher priority to short-term sales than to long-term customer loy-

alty. Up and down each country would be vast numbers of cars waiting to be sold which acted as a buffer between changing consumer
preferences and changes in production. This compounded the problems
caused by slow product development and distanced still further the
connection between changing consumer tastes and changes in cars in
the showroom.

What Ohno saw in the 1940s was an industry which just thirty
years earlier had pushed through an enormous increase in productivity by reorganizing craft production into continuous flow. The consequences of this reorganization were to continue to be felt up to the present day in some industries and in some nations. However, even then
it was clear that there were better ways of organizing production,
component supply, design and consumer relations. The significant
thing was that the domestic circumstances in Japan combined with
the understanding of managers such as Ohno to encourage the creation
of an altogether new solution to the problems of mass production.

Was this outcome inevitable? What was certainly inevitable was
that the problems associated with mass production would have piled
up until they became unmanageable and a period of intensive search
for alternatives would have arisen and it seems to me unlikely that
many of the techniques pioneered by Toyota would not have emerged
elsewhere. However, the precise form of lean production to emerge in
Japan was distinctive and owed much to the creativity with which
almost overwhelming problems in the Japanese car industry were ap-
proached. Having identified the context of lean production, let us
now look at it in more detail.

Lean production; was it new?

If we stay with the four problem areas identified above we can get a
good sense of the novelty of lean production. The responses developed
at Toyota and elsewhere did not emerge fully-formed from the womb
of mass production but as the result of trying out new ideas and seeing
what worked. The development of lean production took place over
time and, indeed, developments are still taking place. Nevertheless,
without ignoring the historical and developmental aspect of lean
production we can identify four distinct characteristics.

In the first place, Ohno reorganized the workers. This involved organizing workers into teams and each was given a section of the production line and encouraged to work together to come up with the best
way of doing things. Each team had a team leader who (unlike the
foreman in mass production) would also do assembly work and fill in
for any absentee workers. Then each team was given responsibility
for 'housekeeping', some tool repair, and quality control. Finally he
created regular meetings where the team could discuss with each
other and with the industrial engineers ways in which the process

could be improved still further. This process is known as 'quality circles' in Britain and the US and *kaizen* in Japan.

As an extension of this system of quality control, workers were encouraged to always trace back the causes of problems and to take steps to prevent them happening again. This limited the substantial wastage associated with mass production where mistakes were ignored and passed down the line to be sorted out at the end. In even sharper contrast was the instruction to stop the whole production line every time a fault is discovered. Initially this caused far more stoppages than on a mass-production line but once the problem-solving approach became fully applied it created both fewer stoppages and improved quality.

Not only was the workforce reorganized but so was the application of machinery. The essence of this was to allow a much shorter set-up time to facilitate much shorter runs of different models. In mass production the lines are very expensive to change and may take months to set up. In lean production, lines could be changed quickly and cheaply. (Perhaps the most important innovation lay in the creation of stamping presses with dies capable of being changed easily.)

All of these changes in the assembly process could only have had a limited impact on the efficiency of the whole process had it not been for improvements in the supply of components. In this second major area of change, Toyota and others sought to encourage the involvement of components producers in the design and problem-solving aspects of the whole process. Instead of merely being told what to produce, manufacturers were given the vehicle's performance specification and encouraged to come up with their own solution. Taking this a stage further, the main manufacturers were encouraged to discuss with each other their shared problems. Supplying these main manufacturers would be another tier of producers.

Toyota developed its relationships with its main suppliers in other ways, too. It holds shares in these companies and they hold shares in each other. Toyota also made senior members of staff available to its suppliers. This did not inhibit suppliers from trading elsewhere (indeed Toyota encouraged this) but it did create a close relationship amongst genuinely separate cost-centres. In turn this was to allow the famous *kanban* system of just-in-time production. If each supplier understood precisely what was happening, it should be possible to reduce stocks almost to zero and only produce components at the moment they were required. This is a fragile and complex system which requires considerable effort and trust to hold it together but is substantially more efficient than mass-production alternatives.

The third distinctive aspect of lean production lies in its product development and engineering. Basically, this involved strengthening the position of the leader of the product-development team, elevating the status of the team within the company, and making team members accountable to the team rather than to their own department. The outcome has a quicker response to consumer demand and yet a product which has the personality of the team (and the team leader in particular) stamped upon it. The advantages of this became even more apparent when information about consumer choice in a rapidly changing market became available. This characterizes the fourth area of lean production.

As the market for cars and trucks began to segment (that is as the market moved away from one basic family car and a couple of different truck sizes) Toyota, with its more flexible production system, was very well placed. It capitalized on this by maximizing the quantity and quality of information about both existing and potential Toyota users. They secured this through the network of distributors who were not only responsible for aggressively selling the product and developing a life-long relationship with consumers but were also responsible for generating information about fluctuations in demand and changes in consumer taste. Thus consumers were involved at the earliest stage in product development and were the first trigger in just-in-time production as the factories would know almost immediately of changes in demand for particular products.

Womack et al. provide an impressive list of factors which together help to explain the considerable success achieved by the Japanese car industry. Does this amount to a new system? It depends upon what is meant by 'a new system'. On the one hand, Ohno was clearly driven by the same desire to make profits under difficult circumstances which first motivated Henry Ford. On the other hand, it did offer a qualitatively novel response to what were to become increasingly difficult problems in the post-war system of mass production. Given its superiority as a system of production, it is interesting to speculate about its future. Will lean production go the same way as mass production? In a recent critical study which examines the Womack et al. research, Williams and his co-authors suggest that many of the advantages of the Japanese system were due to historically specific factors which allowed firms such as Toyota to reap the benefits of low-wage-cost component supply, and a lack of cyclicality in domestic demand, and to realize massive increases in productivity per worker through a factory regime which requires Japanese workers to work for longer periods and more intensively than their US or European counterparts (Williams et al., 1992). As such historical advantages reduce in significance, and their products encounter US and European patterns of market cyclicality, it is questionable whether the Japanese manufacturers will find their manufacturing systems facing the same constraints on growth that threatened Fordism.

4 Conclusion

The superiority of lean production over mass production was clear by the 1960s. As its leading practitioner, Japan was able to enjoy a substantial export-led boom until the end of the 1970s when the combination of a global recession and massive trade imbalances with North America and Europe forced some changes. Simultaneously, non-Japanese companies were absorbing the lessons from Japan and developing similar techniques. In response, Japanese companies have opted to directly invest in North America and Europe and in this way directly implant lean production methods in these countries. In the UK, Honda, Toyota and Nissan all have fully-fledged factories operating, whilst Isuzu has a joint operation with GM.

This has significant implications for the way in which the economy is likely to be run. On the one hand, it will bring with it changes in design, working practices and product development which will almost certainly enhance productive efficiency. On the other hand, will it bring with it an expanding market capable of absorbing these new products? Mass production brought with it many of the circumstances of mass consumption. Lean production may be forced to operate in limited and stagnant markets. If so, what does this imply? Only the lessons of the 1990s will tell us, but it is reasonable to suppose that the structure of the UK's motor industry will look markedly different in 1999 by comparison with 1989.

[NOTE: Peter Hamilton gratefully acknowledges the help of Tom Ling in the re-drafting of this material for publication.]

References

Beynon, H. (1973) *Working for Ford*, Harmondsworth, Penguin.

Drucker, P. F. (1950) *The New Society*, New York, Harper and Row.

Harris, L. (1988) 'The UK economy at a crossroads' in Allen, J. and Massey, D. (eds.) *The Economy in Question*, London, SAGE.

Linhart, R. (1978) *The Assembley Line*, London, John Calder.

Littler, C. R. (1982) *The Development of the Labour Process in Capitalist Societies*, London, Heinemann.

Piore, M. and Sabel, C. (1984) *The Second Industrial Divide: Possibilities for Prosperity*, New York: Basic Books.

Rhys, G. (1988) 'The economics of the motor industry', *Economics*, pp. 158–64.

Williams, J., Williams, K. and Haslam, C. (1987) 'The end of mass production?', *Economy and Society*, vol. 16, no. 3, pp. 404–39.

Williams, K., et al., (1992) 'Against lean production' in *Economy and Society*, vol. 21, no. 3, pp. 321–54

Womack, James P., Jones, D. T., Roos, D. (1990) 'The rise of lean production' in *The Machine that Changed the World*, New York, Rawson Associates.

CHAPTER 6:
A HIGH-TECH INDUSTRY: CONSUMER ELECTRONICS

Alan Cawson

1 Introduction

In this chapter I shall be analysing the evolution of the British consumer electronics (or 'brown goods') industry from the early 1970s to the present. I shall show how a market mode of coordinating the industry has given way to more visible network and hierarchical modes as a consequence of external and internal pressures for change. The most important of these in the 1980s were the need to adapt to a rapidly globalizing industry, the need to find new ways of competing with the innovative products of Japanese and other South East Asian consumer electronics producers, and the need to cope with the Single Market — to respond to the process of completing the internal market within the European Community.

We should see these changes in ways of coordinating the industry against the continual backdrop of technological change. With few exceptions, British firms have not been at the leading edge of new consumer technologies, and have experienced considerable difficulties in matching the relentless innovative challenge from Japan which began to be felt in the 1970s. The result has been that all but one of the major British firms left the industry, either closing down their factories or selling them to competitors from other European countries and the Far East. In Britain there *is* a successful consumer electronics industry but it is owned largely by the Japanese.

1.1 The industry in the 1970s

The main product of the big consumer electronics firms in the 1970s was colour television sets (CTVs), with such items as radios, hi-fi sets, and tape recorders either imported or, at the top end of the market, made by small firms. Table 6.1 shows the eight firms involved in CTV manufacture in 1973, together with an indication of their size in terms of market share. A small part of the market (10 per cent in 1973) was supplied by importers.

Governments had shown relatively little interest in consumer electronics manufacturing, but the decisions made concerning broadcasting (and especially the introduction of colour television in 1968) had a considerable effect on the fortunes of these firms. The success of CTV was

Table 6.1 Television manufacturers in Britain 1973

Firm	Ownership	Estimated market share per cent
Thorn	British	34
Philips/Pye	Dutch	18
Rank	British	11
GEC	British	10
Decca	British	7
ITT	American	4
Telefusion	British	3
Rediffusion	British	3
Imports		10

Source: Arnold, 1983, Table 4.4

something of a bonanza for them because the technology was European, and it was not initially available except to European firms. Moreover the price that the public was willing to pay for colour was such that very good profits could be made. When first introduced, a colour television set cost about the same as the cheapest car (£500). Now the cheapest car costs thirty times as much as the cheapest colour television set.

Almost all television (and other 'brown goods') manufacturers (but not importers) were members of the British Radio and Electronic Equipment Manufacturers' Association (BREMA). BREMA was neither formally nor informally a cartel (that is a group of firms which collude to control supply and prices in an industry). We can understand trade associations such as BREMA as a network of shared values and perceptions through which manufacturers can come to decisions about how they want to respond to market signals. Networks of this kind are essentially concerned with self-regulation; they provide a means for expressing the collective identity of a sector through which coordination takes place within the constraints of the market. The shared perceptions and informal monitoring of the market within BREMA led to a collective view in which the best outcome for member firms was to maintain high prices and margins through moderating competition between them. The incentive to seek improvements in the way in which their sets were manufactured, or innovations in the technology, was blunted as long as all producers took the same viewpoint. Such networks are social as well as business relationships; and are reinforced through regular meetings, conferences, annual dinners and the like. They maintain a sharp social distance between 'insiders' and 'outsiders' The extent to which members of such networks can themselves control or substitute for market forces varies considerably between industries, and they are more difficult to sustain when the final purchasers of their products are individuals rather than other firms. In the case of consumer electronics, the network promoted a false sense of security, and discouraged member firms from recognizing changes that were taking place in the industry outside Britain.

Two major events happened in the 1970s which transformed this brief honeymoon period after CTV was introduced. A Labour Government elected in 1974 decided to pursue an 'industrial strategy' through the medium of new 'Sector Working Parties' (SWPs) established by the National Economic Development Office (NEDO). The Electronic Consumer Goods SWP provided a different kind of network to that of BREMA — one in which government was involved and government intervention was firmly on the agenda. The second event, far more significant in retrospect, was the decision in 1972 by the Sony Corporation of Japan to build a brand new factory in south Wales to manufacture CTVs. As we shall see, inward investment by Japanese firms provided the main pressures for change in the industry.

By 1978 the SWP had begun to report on conditions in the consumer electronics industry, and had identified some of the major problems. The most immediate of these was the poor trade performance of the sector. Very few CTVs (or other brown goods) were exported from Britain, but increasingly, as British firms failed to keep pace with the boom in colour television, more and more sets were being imported, many from Germany, but most from Japan. Firms in those countries seemed to be able to produce higher quality sets than UK firms at comparable prices, and the view that prevailed within BREMA was that they were being 'dumped' at lower prices than in their home markets, or even lower than their cost of production and shipping. At this stage, however, British firms had very little knowledge of what was happening in the Japanese industry.

The Chairman and Secretary of the NEDO Working Party did not share this complacent view which prevailed in the industry, and believed that there was more to it than 'unfair competition'. Accordingly they persuaded the SWP to commission a respected American firm of consultants, the Boston Consulting Group (BCG) to prepare a report on the competitiveness of the British firms compared to their major competitors in Germany, South Korea and Japan. Half the £150,000 cost was met by the Department of Industry (DOI) and half, after considerable persuasion, by the British firms.

The conclusions of the BCG report were so explosive that each member of the SWP was sworn to secrecy, and not allowed to take away from the meeting the numbered copies of the document. The report showed that the Japanese firms were simply more efficient manufacturers than the British; they had invested in machinery to automate production, had produced new circuit designs to reduce the number of components in a set, and had developed effective measures to build quality controls into the manufacturing process. The Korean firms achieved their cost advantage by lower labour costs; the German firms faced roughly similar costs to the British, but made more reliable sets. In every case, the report argued, the British factories were too small to achieve the economies of scale required to compete effectively on world markets. The typical British firm made 250,000 sets a year compared to 500,000 in Germany and as many as one million sets a year at the biggest and most automated plants in Japan.

NEDO took this report very seriously, and persuaded the set makers that government action would be necessary for the industry to survive. NEDO's solution was for the government to finance a major programme of rationalization and modernization, which would halve the number of firms in the industry to five or six, and allow them to invest in the latest equipment for inserting components automatically. In return for the estimated £80 million of investment required, the Labour Government would have a major say in how the restructuring was to be achieved.

One such way was to control the entry of new Japanese firms into the industry to allow the British firms some 'breathing space' to get their house in order. Sony had quickly been followed into south Wales by Matsushita (Panasonic) and in 1977 Hitachi had announced its plan to build sets in the north-east using television tubes imported from its new automated plant in Finland. This was the last straw for the British firms, who quickly rallied behind the Philips subsidiary Mullard, which was the major supplier of tubes to the industry. So vociferous was the campaign against Hitachi, which evoked memories of the Second World War, that Hitachi decided to postpone its plans indefinitely.

The government was concerned to placate the British firms to some extent, but saw firms like Sony and Matsushita as models which the UK industry should emulate. The DOI did agree to persuade the Japanese to adhere to a voluntary code of practice drawn up by the SWP, but was determined to encourage the Japanese to locate in Britain, especially if the alternative was for them to go to Germany or France. Whilst agreeing that the Japanese should invest in existing plant rather than build their own 'greenfield factories' and should buy a minimum of 45 per cent of their components in the EC rather than operate 'screwdriver' plants which assembled components imported from Japan, the DOI nevertheless resisted the demands of the industry to exclude the Japanese altogether. Instead it persuaded (through large grants under the Industry Act of 1975) GEC to join forces with Hitachi in a new venture based at the GEC factory in south Wales, and Rank to join Toshiba to make televisions at the Rank Radio factory in Plymouth.

1.2 Changing modes of coordination

The setting up of the NEDO Sector Working Party can be seen as the establishment of a new network which eclipsed the BREMA network, partly because its quasi-governmental nature gave it privileged access to a Labour government prepared to invest in private industry, and partly because the member firms within the BREMA network had simply failed to analyse market conditions properly and respond to them effectively.

It tends to be market failures of this kind which lead to the search for new means of coordinating a sector. The preferred solution of the Labour government was for a form of corporatism which combined the models of hierarchy and network. The industry was to regulate itself (within the broad policy goals set by government in the Industrial Strategy) through the NEDO network, and implement the favoured policy (rationalization and modernization) through voluntary compliance by the firms 'policed' through the SWP. A more traditional Labour approach might have been to adopt a pure model hierarchical solution, in which the firms would have been taken into public ownership, and the state would have provided investment capital for modernization (as indeed happened in France with the major French CTV firm Thomson after the Mitterrand government came to power in 1981). A Conservative government might have adopted a pure model market solution, and let the inefficient firms go out of business, without worrying about whether the survivors were British (if indeed there were any survivors!). A pure network model would have been for the firms themselves to collaborate in restructuring, raise investment capital themselves, and perhaps form joint ventures to encourage research and technological development. It was a pure network model industry, acting on instructions from the Japanese government, which many in the industry believed, at least until they had visited the factories in Japan, accurately described how the Japanese consumer electronics firms coordinate their sector in Japan. The preferred British solution was a pragmatic hybrid: a looser mix of hierarchy and network which elsewhere I have called 'meso corporatism' (Cawson, 1985).

One of the problems with any network solution for sectoral coordination is whether the membership is the right one. In the case of the NEDO network Japanese firms were deliberately excluded from participation, because the market was seen as a struggle between British firms and Japanese firms (although ironically one major 'British' firm, ITT, had an American parent and another, Philips, was Dutch). BREMA faced a more difficult decision about whether to try to exclude

Japanese manufacturers with factories in Britain. Initially the British members (and Philips!) pressed for this, but eventually accepted the principle of Japanese membership in 1979. By the mid-1980s Japanese firms formed by far the largest group within BREMA.

For the purposes of trying to exclude competitors, and lobby for protection, NEDO was the right network. But to the extent that an industry flourishes through efficient firms regardless of national ownership, then the NEDO strategy was flawed. As we shall see, precisely the same dilemma faces the European Commission in organizing its own networks in the early 1990s. The strategy might have worked if public money had been used to protect British ownership, but, unfortunately for NEDO and the major British firms, the 1979 election was called before any support package could be agreed. Once the Thatcher government was installed the prospects for a meso-corporatist solution dimmed, and it was soon evident that market disciplines would be vigorously asserted.

2 'Japanization' and 'Europeanization'

In Chapter 5 the term 'Japanization' is used to refer to the adoption of ways of organizing manufacturing processes in the car industry which had been pioneered by Japanese firms. In the consumer electronics industry we find 'Japanization' of a rather different kind: the initiation of joint ventures between British and Japanese firms, with the subsequent takeover of the joint ventures by the Japanese, and the displacement of British firms in the industry by incoming Japanese firms. The result has been that what was once a 'British' industry is now almost entirely 'Japanese'.

After 1979 it became clear that the prospects of an industrial policy for the state subsidization of the rationalization of the British consumer electronics industry had disappeared. But we should recognize some important elements of continuity between the Labour and Conservative governments' policy towards the industry, despite the arrival of 'Thatcherism'. The policy of encouraging inward investment by Japanese firms was continued and, in very important ways, strengthened. Instead of providing a 'demonstration effect', incoming Japanese firms would be permitted to replace British firms if the latter were unable by themselves to become competitive. The policy guidelines forged by NEDO remained in place for the first few years of the Thatcher government, but since 1985 there has been no restriction on 'greenfield' investments.

The turning point came as it became clear that a competition was developing between European states and regions to attract the Japanese firms, who became the beneficiaries of an extraordinary auction in which higher and higher inducements were offered to potential entrants to the industry. In the new context of the early 1980s, restrictive guidelines were recognized as hindering the chances of Britain retaining its early lead as the most favoured nation for the Japanese. In 1984 Mrs Thatcher intervened personally on a visit to Tokyo, when she argued forcefully in favour of Britain as a site for the proposed investment in Europe by the Sharp Corporation. This was a forerunner of the much bigger prize of a Japanese car plant in the north east of England, where later Mrs Thatcher personally pleaded with the Nissan Corporation to choose Britain as the location for its European car plant. The remaining British and European firms complained bitterly that the Japanese were receiving unfair privileges, especially when in their view the Japanese market was effectively closed to European exports.

Figure 6.1 shows how British firms were gradually displaced by the Japanese in this period. The pace of Japanese inward investment in Britain, as well as in other parts of Europe, quickened with the stirrings of increasingly protectionist sentiments fostered by the European firms in the 1980s. It turned into a headlong rush at the end of the decade, when the Single Market programme became a major focus of international attention, and the fears of a 'Fortress Europe' spread to the United States and the Far East.

2.1 The arrival of the home video recorder

A second major factor accounting for the twin trends of Europeanization and Japanization was the introduction of a new consumer electronics product — the Video Cassette Recorder (VCR). Philips had been an early pioneer of this technology, but it was Japanese firms, led by Sony and a Matsushita subsidiary, the Japan Victor Company (JVC), which created a mass market for the product across the world. In Japan a number of different technologies for the domestic VCR emerged in the mid-1970s, but the Video Home System (VHS) format, invented by JVC, and Sony's Betamax format were the front runners. Sony, as we have seen, was the pioneer of inward investment in Europe, as it had been in the United States. Its approach to the European market was, as it had been with its proprietary television technology, Trinitron, to establish its own marketing and production facilities, although for VCR it chose Germany rather than Britain. JVC was a small company in the 1970s and was unable to adopt the same strategy. Instead it offered licences for the VHS system to the major competitor to Philips in each of the. major European markets. In Britain JVC signed a licensing deal with Thorn EMI Ferguson; in Germany with Telefunken and in France with Thomson. Each of these companies was permitted to market the VHS system under its own brand name, and each agreement contained a clause which allowed for European manufacturing of VCRs at a later date.

Philips was caught between VCR generations as the first Betamax and VHS machines began to find buyers in Europe. Its new machine, the

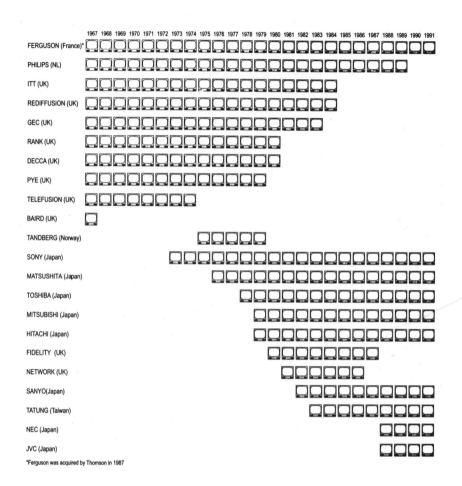

Figure 6.1 The displacement of British television manufacturers by the Japanese. (each box indicates production in that year)

V2000, was delayed by technical problems and the first supplies proved unreliable. Moreover, Philips took the view that the principal use for a domestic VCR would be time shifting: the recording of transmissions for later viewing. The company thought that consumers would invest in a second machine, the Laser Vision optical disc player, in order to view films and other programmes at home. The technical quality of the picture on both of these machines was excellent; arguably better than VHS or Betamax. Philips, however, misjudged the market and failed to anticipate consumer preferences. Partly because of its link with Thorn EMI, who also controlled the major television rental chains and had very strong music and film activities in Britain, the market leader for home VCRs, JVC, made no such mistakes. The Japanese-made Ferguson Videostar VCRs were widely available through rental chains, and maximum emphasis was given to persuading the film industry to release films on videocassette. Meanwhile Sony had declined to allow other companies to put their own brand names on Betamax machines, but a few other Japanese companies like Sanyo and Toshiba had adopted the Betamax format for their own VCRs.

The format battle between VHS, Betamax and V2000 was fought out in the early 1980s in Japan, Europe and the US. It was a crucial battle for the industry for several reasons. First, the VCR was a high value, high technology product which offered major opportunities to an industry facing the problems that I have examined in this chapter. Second, it was also a product that was difficult to manufacture; the precision engineering involved in the head, drum and tape transport mechanism was simply beyond the reach of all but the largest firms. Third, VCRs were small compared to CTVs, and cost rather less to ship from Japan. And since it was a brand new product there were fewer problems arising from established consumer tastes in different European countries. All of these conditions pointed towards a high level of penetration of European markets from Japan; JVC's system emerged as the format winner because of the exceptionally astute marketing strategy which exploited the divisions within the industry between Philips and its major competitors.

By the end of 1984 over seven million VCRs had been sold in Britain, which meant that there was a video recorder in more than one in three homes. It was clear by this time that the winner of the battle between the three video technologies was going to be VHS — 80 per cent of VCRs sold in Britain in 1984 were VHS machines. Although Sony's Betamax and the Philips V2000 formats had fared better in some other countries, by 1987 VHS had emerged as the worldwide standard for home video.

JVC had implemented the manufacturing clause in its VHS licensing agreement by offering Thorn, Telefunken and Thomson a stake in a joint venture to produce VCRs and later other video products such as cameras. The proposed J3T consortium shrank to J2T, however, after the French government vetoed Thomson's participation, preferring to encourage the firm to join Philips in promoting European technology. But after abortive negotiations to take over the ailing Grundig company, Thomson bought Telefunken and so gained access to J2T through the back door. Later still, in 1987, Thomson bought Ferguson from Thorn EMI, and with it the only British toehold on VCR manufacture, and thus became JVC's sole partner in Europe.

In 1983 it was already clear to Philips and its V2000 partner Grundig, that they were in danger of losing the format and market battles, and that the result would be very serious indeed for the economic fortunes of the firms. They filed an anti-dumping complaint with the European Commission against a small Japanese Betamax supplier (not Sony), which they claimed was selling VCRs at below manufacturing cost. Later on Philips and Grundig agreed to withdraw their action when it was announced that the EC's Industry Commissioner, Viscount Davignon, had reached a voluntary export restraint agreement (VER) with the Japanese Ministry of International Trade and Industry (MITI). The Japanese firms were given an annual ceiling for imports of VCRs into Europe (as a whole — there was no quota for each national market) and had to agree to keep prices above an agreed 'floor level'.

2.2 'Europrotectionism': the voluntary export restraint agreement (VER)

The VER was a protective device which was intended to safeguard European VCR technology by forcing the Japanese to charge more for their VCRs than they otherwise would have done. The floor price was geared to Philips' manufacturing costs, so that European consumers paid heavily and the more efficient Japanese manufacturers who had lower costs than Philips and Grundig were able to make very significant profits. What was more alarming for the Europeans was that in fixing the quotas they had assumed a rapidly expanding market for 1984, but in the event there was a temporary downturn in demand for VCRs which meant that Philips could not even sell all the V2000 machines it was allotted. The Japanese unexpectedly found their share generous, and were the clear and unintended beneficiaries of the VER. Before the agreement lapsed in 1986, Philips had decided to abandon the V2000 format and produce VHS machines under licence. As soon as they adopted the format, their VCR market share increased markedly. Eventually Sony also adopted VHS, which has become the *de facto* world standard for the domestic VCR.

The VCR story in Europe is important for a number of reasons. First, it demonstrated the shift of EC trade policy from national capitals to Brussels (Cawson et al., 1990). CTVs were still governed by pre-existing bilateral import quotas (especially in France and Italy) and (especially in Britain) a number of bilateral industry-to-industry agreements to restrict exports from the Far East. But for new products there were no such agreements and the EC was able to assert its powers. Second, it showed that the market mode of coordinating the sector, if not restrained, was likely to result in serious, if not terminal, difficulties for the European firms. Even Philips contemplated ceasing consumer electronics production in 1983, but shrank back. The established networks had also been transformed: in Britain BREMA's membership was changing rapidly as British firms withdrew from the sector and Japanese firms became members. The NEDO network was in disrepair: although it was possible for firms to use NEDO committees as a means of finding out about their competitors and the implications of technological changes, it was deficient as a mode of coordination as long as Japanese firms were excluded.

2.3 Parallel networks

The Japanese firms began to set up factories in Britain, but as 'outsiders' whose early moves had been opposed by the existing manufacturers in Britain, they needed to find their own ways of coordinating their activities. Although excluded from NEDO, the Japanese firms were admitted as members of the trade association, BREMA. But for them BREMA was of limited use as a coordinating mechanism or as a channel of influence to the government. The trade association was dominated by the strong voices of the representatives from Philips and Thorn EMI, whose views carried weight because they were speaking for respectively the biggest European firm and the major British firm. Moreover the voices spoke in unison: arguing that national governments and the European Commission should act to protect the indigenous industry (that is British, or European within Britain; European within Europe). It was not a simple split between native firms and inward investing firms, nor even European versus non-European firms, because (until it ceased production and left BREMA) the UK subsidiary of the American-owned multinational ITT was a member. It was a split between East and West, but perhaps more crucially a split between efficient newcomers and the longer standing and inefficient firms.

The Japanese firms (and the Taiwanese firm Tatung) wanted membership precisely because they were viewed as outsiders to the industry, and were charged with destabilizing it. The Japanese firms in particular wished to be seen as 'good corporate citizens' of the industry and the country, as responsible players, apparently sharing common concerns if not common interests. But interestingly, with almost no exceptions, the representatives of the firms sitting around the BREMA Council chamber were British, and for the most part had been recruited from the British firms which had left the industry. The fact that the Japanese firms sent British rather than Japanese managers to BREMA meetings suggests that here were 'outsider' firms seeking 'insider' status.

Status, however, is not power, and representation is not influence. The Japanese firms were powerful because they dominated the market, whereas they took care to be seen not to dominate the association. The efficiency of their manufacturing, their ability to persuade the British consumer to pay more for quality, and their strength arising from the sheer size and weight of their parent companies in the Japanese and US markets, assured them a receptive ear in Whitehall, Bonn and Brussels, if not at first in Paris where the French government was actively trying to protect the French market against Japanese imports, and was unwilling at first to permit Japanese firms to open factories there. They certainly did not need BREMA, either as a coordinating mechanism or a source of influence. As time and again BREMA members voted and pressed for protection against the Japanese firms, the representatives of the latter kept their heads firmly below the parapet. What they did need BREMA for was as a means of signalling their intentions to behave honourably as very long-term investors in Britain, both to the remaining non-Japanese firms but also to Whitehall and Brussels.

The Japanese firms coordinated their actions through the European organization of their parent trade association, the Electronic Industries Association of Japan (EIAJ). As long ago as 1962, eleven years before the first inward investment by a consumer electronics firm in Europe, the EIAJ decided that it would be helpful to its members to have an office in Europe. Exports to Europe were just beginning to build up, and the EIAJ could acquire and share expertise about the very different characteristics of each national market within Europe: their different laws, regulations and standards, and the contrasting public policies of the different national governments. European firms often complain that Japan is an impenetrable society and culture, conveniently forgetting that, from Japan, Europe must appear the same. The EIAJ chose to establish in Dusseldorf in northern Germany, not because Germany was the biggest consumer electronics market, but because the Japanese were uncertain of their welcome in Europe, and chose the country where memories of the Second World War would not present an immediate barrier to their acceptance.

The EIAJ is a highly organized and efficient trade association, which produces excellent statistics on almost every aspect of the industry in Japan at a formidable level of detail. The EIAJ does not itself conduct industrial research and development, but sees its role as a common resource for firms, helping them to compete more effectively against each other as well as against the non-Japanese firms in the industry. Like BREMA the EIAJ is not a cartel, but unlike BREMA it is a highly effective collective asset to its members, with valuable expertise built up over a very long period. There is also continuity of this expertise: in 1991 the Director had been twenty-seven years with the EIAJ in Europe, longer than any of the national civil servants or European bureaucrats with whom he came into contact. In the mid-1980s he was spending almost two weeks of every month travelling around the network of Japanese firms in Europe and visiting governments and the EC.

The EIAJ and BREMA offer the Japanese firms twin tracks of representation: the first offers political influence and knowledge; the second offers some legitimacy in the eyes of governments, if not the competitor firms. The EIAJ does not have formal meetings where firms are represented; it functions as a network with the EIAJ'S Dusseldorf office at the central node or hub. The Director and EIAJ staff can help firms to negotiate with national governments and the EC when setting up a new plant, for example. They can advise firms about the available grants and subsidies, and act as a broker in trying to get the best deal for the incoming firm. Such has been the effort put in to attract Japanese investment, the EIAJ did not have to discriminate between firms in supplying this brokerage service. This role has been highly effective, with the Japanese achieving very substantial subsidies from the British taxpayer. Even 23 per cent of the first investment, by Sony, was paid for by central and local government grants. Over a decade later Sharp was able to be a player in a very complex game, in effect holding an auction between several localities in several countries. The final subsidy, estimated at £5 million of a total initial investment of £9 million, amounted to over 50 per cent. In such complex games, the role played by the EIAJ is invaluable.

Firms have their own interests as competitors in a market, and share certain common interests as members of an 'industry' whose activities are affected by the policies of their own and foreign governments. Trade associations can be useful to firms in helping them to identify problems and opportunities, and in representing their interests when government policies are formulated. For inward investing firms, such as the Japanese consumer electronics producers in the 1970s and 1980s, largely political considerations led to their seeking membership of the British trade association BREMA, whereas the Japanese trade body the EIAJ was perhaps more important as a collective resource which briefed the firms about the opportunities and difficulties of operating in foreign markets.

What we have seen so far in this last section is that within an industry the nature of competition between firms has many different dimensions which go beyond a simple view of market competition. Firms form their judgements and make their commercial decisions on the basis of a view which takes into account the judgements made by other firms, and by governments. The incoming Japanese firms knew that they were likely to be the target of political campaigns mounted by the British firms, but also became aware that their presence could be useful to the government's policy of persuading British firms to become more efficient producers. This knowledge was important in bargaining with the government over regional aid and investment incentives for their new plants, and their trade association was an important intermediary in discussions with the government. But in order to present themselves as responsible investors, the firms found it very useful to become members of BREMA.

The British and European firms were acutely aware of the Japanese as efficient manufacturers, and tended to portray the threat facing them as coming from 'Japan Inc.' Many believed that the Japanese Ministry of International Trade and Industry (MITI) was the instrument through which the Japanese government coordinated the activities of the firms. They saw trade as 'unfair competition' because not only did the Japanese government sit at the apex of a hierarchically structured network of firms, its actions helped to prevent access to the Japanese market for the European firms. Some scholars, like the American Chalmers Johnson, had showed how in the 1950s MITI had used its control of licences for foreign technology as a means of insisting on its own investment priorities (Johnson, 1982). What that meant was MITI denied licences to some firms and gave them to others in order to build up certain industries which it saw as having a strong export potential. One of these industries was, indeed, consumer electronics, and MITI approved amongst other things the deal struck in 1951 between Matsushita and Philips, whereby Philips acquired a 50 per cent stake in a subsidiary of the parent Matsushita Electrical Industries in exchange for Philips' lighting technology. That stake remains to the present day, although now the subsidiary concentrates on semi-conductors.

What European managers and governments did was to misunderstand the essential elements of MITI's concern to focus its external trade strategy, that is, to pick key sectors for the future and help through licences and its famous 'administrative guidance' to ensure that those sectors flourished. The Europeans assumed that MITI orchestrated the policies of each firm, and failed early enough to detect a change in MITI's role in the 1970s and 1980s. 'MITI', when not a symbol for crude, racial, stereotyping of the 'yellow peril' kind, became a synonym for a state-directed cartelized industry, and the 'Japanese threat' was identified as a political and not principally a commercial problem. Thus they sought a 'level playing field' in which both European governments and the EC would act as a counterweight to the Japanese government and MITI. MITI's recent programmes, such as the 'Fifth Generation' computer programme, or its VLSI (Very Large-Scale Integration) semi-conductor project were taken as evidence of this. But in reality these were basic research and development programmes, which, whilst they did give the Japanese firms critical advantages in focusing and coordinating their own in-house R & D (Research and Development) programmes, did not amount to MITI coordinating the corporate strategies of the consumer electronics firms. Indeed the firms competed ferociously against each other for market share in Japan and the rest of the world.

3 European industry coordination: the case of High Definition Television

So far we have seen how the success of the Japanese firms in most consumer electronics products (home computers are the exception) led to the remaining European firms trying to protect their home market. Whereas in the 1970s most of the pressure was directed at national governments, in recent years the European Commission has taken a leading role in determining trade, competition and technology policies which affect the industry. During the same period, as British firms were leaving the industry and British consumer electronics was becoming 'Japanized', the industry in Western Europe was undergoing radical changes through mergers and acquisitions. At the time of writing, the three biggest European multinational companies are Philips of Holland, Thomson of France, and Nokia of Finland. Both Philips and

Thomson have important subsidiaries in the United States, and Nokia expanded from Scandinavia by acquiring firms based in Germany and France.

Philips and Thomson have been traditional rivals, struggling between them to take control of Grundig — a contest which Philips won. Despite pressure from the French government (which owns Thomson) to cooperate with Philips to protect European VCR technology in the early 1980s, the French firm preferred to collaborate with the Japanese, and Thomson and JVC are joint venture partners in Europe's largest VCR factory based in Berlin. In the mid-1980s, however, Philips and Thomson came to cooperate very closely, at the behest of the European Commission and national governments, in a project to develop a new high definition television (HDTV) technology in competition against the Japanese industry. HDTV promises to be the most important technology in consumer electronics in the near future, although as we shall see there is a considerable degree of uncertainty surrounding the technological choices which have to be made.

3.1 The background

What has brought these mutually suspicious firms into a very close relationship has been the race to develop a new world standard for HDTV. The race started with one runner, the Japanese State Broadcasting Company (NHK) in the 1970s, but behind NHK lay a coalition of electronics firms interested in R & D collaboration. The Japanese MUSE transmission standard offered the prospect of satellite-delivered HDTV pictures with double the number of horizontal lines displayed on a wide-screen cinema-style set. For the complete HDTV chain to be realized, the MUSE transmission system would need to be accompanied by completely new studio equipment and standards, and also by completely new domestic television receivers. Every link in the television chain would have to be renewed, which presupposed enormous investments by broadcasters as well as by consumers, since all the equipment would be far more expensive than existing terrestrial products, not least because expensive new satellites were necessary to carry the very large bandwidths needed to relay the amount of detail in high definition images. If the system had been adopted as a world standard by the international body responsible for radio and television transmissions, the CCIR, then it would have given the Japanese enormous advantages in their effort to dominate the world industry. It would have added patent protection to the existing commercial strengths of the major firms. Sony, in particular, had done most to develop studio equipment for HDTV, using their own HDVS brand, and had had some success in persuading professional broadcasters and film companies to try out the new medium. In the United States, Sony had cleverly lined up an important coalition of interests including deregulated cable operators and leading Hollywood production companies. All but one of the American-owned firms had pulled out of television manufacturing, and, as in Britain, the industry was in the hands of the Japanese firms, and Thomson and Philips. Since there was no longer an indigenous television manufacturing industry in the US, there was little American opposition to the Japanese HDTV proposals, and indeed the US had decided to support them at the CCIR meeting to be held in Dubrovnik in 1986.

The Japanese development of an entirely new HDTV television standard presented a major headache for the European firms who had faced earlier problems with new products like VCRs and CD players. By the mid 1980s the European-owned industry had become heavily concentrated into three major firm groupings, but even firms the size of Philips could not afford to develop new HDTV technologies by themselves. It is not at all surprising that they turned to the European Community and its member governments for help.

3.2 The European response to the Japanese HDTV proposal

The European response was to launch the Eureka–95 programme which has become, since 1986, the biggest collaborative effort ever mounted within the electronics industry. The HDTV project was approved by the Eureka committee of European governments (including non-EC governments) in June 1986, and the ambitious target was to have a fully functioning HDTV system to demonstrate to the CCIR at its 1990 meeting. The core firms comprised Philips (project leader), Thomson, Thorn EMI and Bosch. Twelve sub-projects were defined, including display technology, transmission, compression professional and consumer equipment. Each of these was led by one of the four core firms, although these became three rather than four when Thomson bought Ferguson in 1987. Also involved were the leading broadcasting organizations from the European countries, including the BBC and Independent Broadcasting Association (IBA).

The Eureka programme did not, of course, start from scratch, and the European firms have been relatively successful in pioneering television innovations such as teletext. In addition they had retained the lion's share of the European market for large screen televisions, so that it appeared plausible that they could defend the industry against this Japanese competitive threat. The Eureka team decided from the outset to make use of a new transmission technology being pioneered for satellite broadcasting by the IBA. This technology is known as MAC (Multiplex Analogue Component) and in 1987 the Commission issued the so-called MAC directive, which compelled EC member states to adopt one of the versions of MAC for new high power Direct Broadcast Satellites (DBS).

MAC offers a higher picture quality than the existing PAL/SECAM standard, but it is not HDTV in the sense that it uses the same number of horizontal lines (625 in Europe) as the present technology. The Eureka project's objectives were to further develop MAC into HD-MAC (High Definition MAC) and to offer to the broadcasting and consumer electronics manufacturing industries an incremental path through MAC to HD-MAC so that their investments could be staggered. Eureka firms made much of the fact that the Japanese MUSE system was a 'revolutionary' technology which would render existing equipment obsolete. This was a critical point in persuading the EC and member states to subsidize HD-MAC development.

At one technical level at least, Eureka has been a success. It has indeed produced a working HDTV system, and has been able successfully to demonstrate this to the industry, EC and governments, and in so doing has secured very large increases in promised support. Given the history of collaboration in consumer electronics between Philips and Thomson, this alone is a remarkable achievement. However, by 1991 there were considerable uncertainties in the HDTV project, which cast doubt on the effectiveness of state-sponsored inter-firm networks as a means of coordinating the introduction of new technologies on a large scale.

3.3 The uncertain future for HDTV

The major problem with HD-MAC is that it might become obsolete before it is perfected. Across the broad spectrum of electronics, the most significant trend since the 1970s has been digitalization through the use of semi-conductor and microprocessor technology. The computing world is based on an entirely digital technology; that is, information is coded in digital (1 or 0; + or −) form. The telecommunications industry has been rapidly moving to wholly digital technology since the 1970s with the development of computerized telephone exchanges, but the broadcasting industry is the odd man out. Most of the existing technology and hardware is analogue; that is, it captures and transmits audio and video information in analogue waveforms. But rapid advances in semiconductor technology and in techniques for compressing and decompressing video images have changed the basic assumption that television is analogue and will remain so for the foreseeable future. Digital audio has been a spectacular success in consumer electronics through Compact Discs, and has now appeared in consumer markets as Digital Compact Cassette (DCC). In the professional equipment field, digital video recording and other digital studio equipment is gaining ground. The present situation in broadcasting technology might best be described as digital islands in an analogue sea. But there seems little doubt that the islands are growing in size, and will eventually become a land mass.

The second aspect of technological uncertainty arises from the easily observable fact that technology never stands still. In the United States the Federal Communications Commission (FCC) has taken a different strategy from either Japan or Europe. It decided to permit satellite television stations to broadcast in any technology (HDTV or otherwise, including the Japanese system MUSE), and concentrate its efforts on moving to HDTV through terrestrial transmission. The FCC announced that it would be staging a competition and that afterwards it might adopt one of the HDTV systems. But there was a proviso: broadcasters would have to be able to transmit HDTV signals alongside ordinary NTSC signals (the American system) so that the same programmes would be available to everyone regardless of whether or not they bought an HDTV set. At the end of 1990, four of the five contenders were offering fully digitalized television systems. Philips and Thomson were trying to persuade the FCC that their all-digital system could be quickly introduced into the USA, while at the same time they were telling the European Commission that it ought to back the (hybrid) HD-MAC system in Europe.

It is probable that full HDTV may take several years to implement and there may be scope in the meantime for less radical improvements to television technology. Both in Japan and in Europe, and especially in the United States, there has been feverish activity in the last few years to develop improved picture quality through existing transmission technologies, thereby offering a truly incremental approach rather than an incremental second stage (MAC to HD-MAC) which assumes a big initial jump from PAL to MAC. In Europe Thomson and Philips, while still publicly committed to Eureka-95, were at the same time hedging their bets by developing the so-called 'PAL-Plus' system for market launch in 1995. There were also parallel developments in Japan ('ClearVision' as well as 'Hi-Vision') and the United States (but the FCC has in effect opted for a straight switch to digital technology). The essential principle underlying these 'enhanced definition' or EDTV technologies is the use of semiconductor storage and signal processing techniques within the receiver to offer a clearer and wider (cinema-style) picture. The information transmitted from the studio, via satellite, cable or ground transmitters, is captured in the set, stored, and reassembled to give the impression of 1,250 horizontal lines, although the signal itself only contains 625 lines (1,050 and 525 lines respectively in the case of the American NTSC system). The picture can be stretched to give a 16 x 9 'letterbox' image, or if only conventional 4 x 3 aspect ratio material is available, the remainder of the screen can be used to monitor what is on other channels.

The impetus behind PAL-Plus comes from public broadcasters, especially in Britain and Germany, who are afraid that improved widescreen television pictures on satellite channels will result in a loss of audience share for their own networks. These fears led to their opposition to the European Commission's proposals for a new directive on satellite broadcasting accompanied by a plan to subsidize the introduction of widescreen services in MAC. The directive, adopted by the Council of Ministers in May 1992, insists that new widescreen services use the MAC system, and requires widescreen television receivers to incorporate MAC circuitry. The directive restricts 'non fully digital' HDTV to the Eureka HD-MAC system, but in doing so leaves the door open for new fully digital HDTV technologies to challenge HD-MAC. This political compromise does little to resolve the uncertainty over the future of HDTV in Europe, and whilst at the time of writing (November 1992) the firms and the EC remain publicly committed to the Eureka-95 programme, the key industrial players are hedging their bets with parallel R & D on MAC, PAL-plus and digital technologies. In the face of opposition from the British government, the Council deferred a decision in November 1992 on an 'Action Plan' drawn up by the Commission which involved subsidizing broadcasters and producers with ECU 850 million over five years for the extra costs of making and broadcasting programmes in MAC. But even if the plan were adopted, there is so much uncertainty surrounding advanced television technologies that it is unlikely that the single route to high definition television envisaged in the Eureka project will be followed.

The consumer electronics industry is, as we have seen, increasingly governed by non-market means, such as state-producer networks and industry networks, and increasingly those hierarchical instruments of state influence are being refashioned at the European level. But it should not be forgotten that, compared to many other industries in which public purchasing and public regulation are involved, many consumer electronics products stand or fall in the market place according to the purchase decisions of consumers. There is no doubt that the Philips V2000 was technically more advanced than VHS or Betamax (although not more advanced than the subsequently developed 8mm, Super-VHS and Super-Betamax formats), but equally little doubt that it failed because Philips lost the battle in the marketplace and could not compensate for that by relatively weak political instruments such as the VER. Advanced television technology, and transmission technology in particular, brings the consumer electronics manufacturers directly onto the terrain of public broadcasting and public regulation.

Ultimately, however, it will be very difficult for national governments or the EC to distort the market to such an extent as to force market take off for HDTV, because that would have a knock-on effect on a much wider range of goods and services that the same body is trying to liberalize under the single market programme. Early market research appears to suggest that consumers may not easily perceive the benefits of HDTV in terms of a crisper picture, but may embrace more readily the idea of wide-screen pictures. The technology of television is sufficiently uncertain in the short run to cast doubt on the wisdom of going for the innovatory 'big bang' approach that characterizes the HD-MAC programme. Despite a sluggish start (but not sluggish if take-up rates of earlier technologies such as radio, monochrome and colour television are studied), B Sky B television has succeeded in building a large installed base. For the consumer the choice may be between more channels or clearer pictures, and it is not clear that the purchase decisions will turn out to be for clearer pictures. In the longer term, the technological trajectory seems to lead more certainly towards full digitalization. The fact that much of digital technology is common to the computer and telecoms industries, which can take advantage of large public and private markets to drive down production costs of key components like microchips, suggests that in the longer run alternative HDTV systems will be devised which will offer cheaper products based around standardized components and circuitry.

4 Conclusions

This chapter has traced the changes in the British consumer electronics industry in the period from the early 1970s to the early 1990s and has shown how the debate over the political issues surrounding the industry has shifted towards Brussels at the same time that control of the industry has largely passed into the hands of Japanese and a few large European multinational companies. A new kind of network of coordination is emerging in the set of relationships between the major firms, national governments and the European Commission, with the latter exerting a more and more important influence on policy.

The big firms use industrial policy arguments to try to persuade the European Commission and member states that the wider European interest lies in safeguarding key technologies and expertise. It is hard to disentangle the economic from the technological and from the political arguments, and the danger is that public support for major collaborative programmes like the Eureka-95 HDTV project becomes public support to maintain in existence those firms which are at present large firms. Given that consumer electronics is a global market, not confined to the borders even of a fortified European market, EC officials and politicians also have the unenviable task of evaluating the big firms' claim that protectionism in Japan prevents them competing for Far Eastern markets, whilst a competitive market offers very significant advantages to Japanese firms located in Europe.

It is difficult to read into the history of consumer electronics the proposition that it is the coordinating mechanism of government that makes the crucial difference. For consumer electronics, the most important factor seems to be the capacity of actors, whether individual marketing geniuses such as Amstrad's Alan Sugar, or creative geniuses such as Sony's Akio Morita, or more anonymous but efficiently organized follower firms such as Matsushita, to understand and act on market signals. The temptation, which has proved very strong very frequently, is for firms in market difficulties to conceive of political reasons for their market failures, and to seek political solutions to them. Hierarchy rather than market can be a fatal temptation for consumer goods producers, especially when it is coupled with political predispositions amongst governmental actors towards finding political solutions. That is the stark choice which Europeans face with respect to the HDTV programme: the danger that international and inter-firm collaboration on a epic scale may produce a Concorde, when the mass market and the paying customer are demanding Jumbo Jets.

References

Arnold, E. (1983) *Competition and Technological Change in the Television Industry*, D.Phil. thesis, University of Sussex.

Cawson, A. (1985) 'Introduction' in Cawson, A. (ed.) *Organized Interests and the State: Studies in Meso-Corporatism*, London, Sage Publications.

Cawson, A., Morgan, K., Webber, D., Holmes, P. and Stevens, A. (1990) *Hostile Brothers: Competition and Closure in the European Electronics Industry*, Oxford, Clarendon Press.

Johnson, C. (1982) *MITI and the Japanese Miracle*, Stanford, California, Stanford University Press.

CHAPTER 7:
RUNNING HOUSING POLICY AND THE BRITISH HOUSING SYSTEM

CHRIS HAMNETT

1 Introduction

At the time of writing (March 1993) the home-ownership market in Britain is in the depth of the worst slump since the 1920s. Prices have fallen sharply, particularly in southern Britain, and the number of sales are down 40 per cent from their peak in 1988. One and a half million owners who bought since 1987 now own houses worth not only less than they paid for them but less than the outstanding mortgage. Hundreds of thousands of home owners are more than three months behind with their mortgage payments, and 180,000 owners have been repossessed by lenders since 1989. This is an appalling, and admittedly unusual situation.

The quantity, quality, organization and cost of housing is also a continuing political issue. For over 150 years, successive governments have intervened in the market to regulate minimum housing and sanitary standards and, for over seventy years, governments have attempted, to greater or lesser extent, and with greater or lesser success, to influence the quantity, quality and price of housing. At certain times, general elections have been won or lost to a large extent on the 'housing question'. Last, but not least, there has been continuing political controversy over the most appropriate form and organization of housing provision. Much of this controversy has revolved around the most appropriate balance between public and private provision, and the scale and form of housing subsidies. Put simply, the controversy focuses on the relative importance of state versus market forms of provision.

This debate has been going on for over a hundred years, but as we will argue later in the chapter, it achieved a greater prominence during the 1980s with the emergence of a radical right government committed to 'rolling back the frontiers of the state', expanding private provision and private choice, and moving towards a market form of housing provision across the board. The issue of 'running housing' became very important during the 1980s.

I will argue in this chapter that the British housing system has always been market dominated in terms of its production and ownership structure. Most housing (public and private) is privately built for profit, and the owner-occupied and privately rented sectors are sold, exchanged and let on the private market. But within each sector there

MIRAS

is a network of builders, local authorities and landlords — such as the House Builders' Federation, The British Property Federation, the Small Landlords' Association, the Association of District Councils, the Association of Metropolitan Authorities, and the Building Societies' Association who represent their interests to central government and to society at large. And local authority and housing associations let and manage their properties on a combination of hierarchical and network lines.

Last, but not least, central government has exercised a strong degree of hierarchical control over the structure and running of the housing system from the late nineteenth century onwards. This control has tended to increase over time, and it will be argued that the hierarchical control of central government in the housing system has increased sharply since 1979. We thus have the seeming paradox of a government advocating greater consumer choice, and a greater role for markets, placing major restrictions on the state sector in order to achieve this goal.

Later sections of this chapter focus on the radical changes in the government housing policy in Britain since 1979. But in order to fully appreciate the significance of these changes for the way housing in Britain is run (and the debate over the way it should be run) it is first necessary to look at the changing structure of housing tenure in Britain over the last seventy years. This has provided the context to the Conservatives' desire to cut back the size and role of the council sector and replace it with a more market-orientated system of housing provision.

2   The changing structure of the British housing system

Tables 7.1 and 7.2 show that the tenure structure of the British housing system has undergone a profound transformation during the course of the last seventy years, and the pace of this transformation has been particularly rapid since the end of the Second World War.

During the nineteenth and early twentieth centuries, the great majority of housing was provided by private landlords. There were a variety of reasons for this, notably the absence of any form of state provision, the primitive development of building societies and finance markets, and generally low or irregular incomes which prevented most people buying their own home. On the other hand, private landlordism was a major outlet for small investors and it was commonly seen to be 'As safe as houses'. It is generally accepted that in 1914 no fewer than 90 per cent of households in Britain rented privately, council housing scarcely existed and home ownership accounted for only 10 per cent. But three things changed this situation by the end of the 1930s. The first was the emergence of directly state-subsidized council housing in 1919 which began to errode the market for renting. The second was the declining profitability of private renting, which was compounded by the

Table 7.1 The changing tenure structure of Great Britain: 1919–1991 (in percentages)

	Owner occupied %	Council rented %	Private rented %	Housing associations %
1914	10	0	90	
1945	26	12	62	
1951	29	18	53	
1961	43	27	31	
1971	50	31	19	
1981	56	31	12	1
1986	63	27	8	2
1991	68	22	7	3

Table 7.2 Changing tenure structure of dwellings in Great Britain, 1919–1991 (millions)

	Owner occupied	Council rented	Private rented	Total
1914*	0.8	-	7.1	7.9
1938*	3.7	1.1	6.6	11.4
1950	4.0	2.5	7.4	13.9
1961	6.9	4.2	5.2	16.3
1971	9.6	5.8	3.6	19.0
1980	11.8	6.5	2.7	21.0
1988	14.7	5.6	2.2	22.5
1991	15.6	5.0	2.4	23.0C

Note: Figures for 1914 and 1938 are for England and Wales only.

Source: DoE (1976) *Housing Policy, Technical Volume 1*, Table 1.23 and Building Societies Association (1989) *Housing in Britain*, Table 1.2

introduction of rent controls in 1915, and the third was the rapid development of the building societies and the growth of home ownership in the 1930s. Money flowed into the building societies between the wars and they were able to lend at 5 per cent interest. Also, falling wages and building costs meant that houses were cheap to build during the 1930s. The 1930s saw a major boom in building for home ownership with over three million new houses. As a result, the tenure structure changed considerably by 1939. Private renting accounted for 62 per cent of households, while the council sector had grown rapidly to 12 per cent and owner occupation to 26 per cent.

The post-war period saw the intensification of these trends. By 1971 owner occupation reached the 50 per cent mark, and council housing reached 31 per cent. The next 20 years reinforced the domination of owner occupation. By 1991, aided by over 1.5 million council house sales since 1979 and a sharp fall in new council building, owner occupation accounted for two-thirds (68 per cent) of households, council renting for 23 per cent, and private renting and housing associations for less than 10 per cent. The size of the owner-occupied sector grew by over 60 per cent between 1971 and 1991: from 9.6 million to 15.6 million dwellings. To summarize, the past seventy years have seen the almost complete reversal of the position of private renting and home ownership. From being a nation of private renters, Britain has been transformed into a nation of home owners with a large but declining minority of council tenants.

Sections 4, 5 and 6 of this chapter examine the nature and causes of some of these changes paying particular attention to developments since 1979. But before we look at government housing policy it is important to examine the structure, organization and financing of the owner-occupied sector which accounts for two-thirds of all households in Britain.

3   Owner occupation: coordination through the market

3.1   The structure of the house-building industry

Housing production in Britain has been almost completely dominated by the private sector. Apart from a few direct labour organizations, building directly for local authorities, almost all housing in Britain has been built by the private building industry. Where council houses are concerned, competitive tendering by builders for contracts was generally the rule, and in the private sector most building is carried out on a speculative basis by builder-developers for sale to home owners. The number of houses built in any year reflects builders' estimation of the likely market and the numbers they can profitably sell.

Because houses can take anything up to two years to complete from scratch, there are inevitable delays in increasing house-building production. Equally, it is difficult to cut production quickly in response to falling demand or rising interest rates. As a result, the house-building industry is very cyclical with booms and busts. During the last twenty years these have generally been triggered by changes in mortgage availability and mortgage interest rates which have in turn been influenced by changes in government macro economic policy. This sets the context within which private house builders operate. The 'loose money' policy operated in the early 1970s and the mid-1980s led to rapid house price inflation and a major boom in new housing starts. Thus, from 1970–73 house prices rose rapidly and house builders responded by increasing the number of housing starts. Unfortunately, just as new completions were rising rapidly at the end of 1973, the government increased interest rates by 4 per cent in one jump — from 7.5 to 11.5 per cent in an effort to bring the money supply and inflation under control; the house price boom and the owner-occupied housing market collapsed almost immediately, leaving thousands of new houses unsold.

This cycle was repeated in the 1980s. House prices rose rapidly between 1983 and 1988, particularly in the South East, and private house-building starts rose from a low of 99,000 in 1979 to a high of 221,000 in 1988. But from autumn 1988 interest rates were raised very sharply, the house price boom faltered and stopped, and new starts fell to 170,000 in 1989 — and to 135,000 in 1990 and 1991. Builders profits fell sharply from the record levels of 1988, and they have responded to the slump by cutting output, dropping prices and offering a variety of incentives to buyers to maintain sales and cash flow.

Council house building provided a major source of work until the late 1970s. But with the cut-back in public-sector building under the Conservatives, public-sector starts fell from 174,000 in 1975 to 81,000 in 1979 and 25,000 in 1991. As a result, the proportion of public sector starts fell from 54 per cent in 1975 to 12 per cent in 1988. This has meant that public-sector building has not been able to act as a counter cyclical regulator to offset slumps in private house building.

3.2 Owner-occupied housing finance

The great majority of owner-occupied houses are purchased through the market with mortgages from banks or building societies. This seems normal, but it has not always been so. The building society as we know it today developed from nineteenth century working men's building clubs and 'terminating' building societies. These gradually evolved into 'permanent' building societies and then through expansion and amalgamation into the present 'national' building societies, although a few small local societies remain. A rapid process of concentration took place between 1960 and 1991, the number of societies falling from 726 in 1960 to 273 in 1980 and to 110 in 1991. A number which is likely to shrink further still.

Because easily available mortgage finance is a necessary pre-requisite for mass home ownership, the growth of the building societies between the wars provided the key to the growth of home ownership in Britain. Until the early 1980s mortgages were almost exclusively the preserve of the building societies who accounted for 85 per cent of the market. Until this time the building societies obtained virtually all their money from individual depositors and interest rates, which were below market rates, were controlled by a cartel. Thus, when demand for mortgages was greater than the available cash for lending the only way the societies could ration mortgages was via a queuing system. Borrowers needed to have had an account with a society for one or two years, and they sometimes needed to wait for another year or two before they were offered a mortgage. Lending criteria were generally conservative and in the 1970s the traditional rule of thumb was that the loan should not exceed 2 or 2.5 times male income plus a wife's income where applicable. Lending to women or to unrelated individuals was viewed with considerable suspicion and women often found it very difficult to get a mortgage.

The major change came when the Bank of England relaxed lending controls on the banks in the early 1980s. The banks had burnt their fingers with Third World debt, and the domestic mortgage market seemed to offer a relatively safe and profitable outlet for their capital. By the mid-1980s they had taken 35 per cent of new lending and at one stage this rose to almost 50 per cent. But the advent of the banks into the market forced the building societies to change their lending policies and procedures in an attempt to regain market share. Restrictions on new lending were greatly relaxed and 90 per cent and 100 per cent mortgages became much more common with subsequent disastrous consequences for lenders and borrowers alike. Since 1986 building societies have also been able to borrow cash in the money markets at market rates of interest. As a result, there are no longer mortgage shortages, and interest rates reflect the market rate. The late 1980s also saw the emergence of a new group of specialist mortgage lenders such as the Mortgage Corporation who get all their money on the wholesale money markets and relend it. During the 1980s the separate circuit of mortgage capital was partly absorbed into more general circuits of financial flows and the mortgage finance industry has become much more market orientated. But, as the rise in mortgage rates in 1989 and 1990 shows, mortgage interest rates are now strongly influenced by the bank rate.

Finally, it is necessary to mention the fiscal regime for owner occupation. Mortgage interest tax relief for home owners has been in force for many years, but it was partly offset by Schedule A tax on imputed rents which was abolished in 1963. When tax relief on interest charges was abolished in 1974, mortgage interest tax relief (£25,000) was left intact. This was later raised to £30,000 in 1983 but it has not been increased subsequently and its value in real terms has fallen considerably, partly as a result of the cut in basic tax rate to 25 per cent. In the 1991 Budget, the benefit to higher rate tax payers who could offset mortgage interest at a 40 per cent rate was abolished. In addition, there is no capital gains tax on a main residence. As a result, home ownership has been uniquely privileged in tax terms, and the cost of the tax foregone from mortgage interest relief has risen steadily to reach £7,000 million in

1991. When exemption from capital gains tax on a main residence is added, it can be argued that the free market for home owners is heavily subsidized and underpinned by tax incentives. These subsidies are seen as a considerable distortion of the market by both the left and the radical right. Government policy thus sets the financial context within which the market operates.

3.3 The owner-occupied housing market: access and affordability

The owner-occupied housing market is an unusual one in economic terms in that the overwhelming majority of houses which come on the market are second hand ones. In 1988 the building societies made 1,230,000 new mortgage advances. Of these, only 116,000 were for new houses. The other 1,112,000 were for existing dwellings — a ratio of about 10:1. The banks made about 300,000 new advances. The total owner-occupied housing stock in Britain in 1988 was 14.7 million. But only 200,000 new private houses were built in 1988 (the peak year of the 1980s) about 1.3 per cent of the existing stock. This is a very small annual addition to the stock which is more or less fixed in the short term. Consequently, although there is some academic dispute about this, the price of houses is largely determined through the balance of demand and the supply of existing dwellings. As a result, any sharp increase in demand will increase prices very rapidly as it is impossible to increase supply quickly.

Access to the private housing market in market economies is controlled through the price mechanism. Housing is a scarce and expensive commodity for which buyers compete in the market. Those with more money find it easier to buy, or to afford more expensive houses than those on low incomes. When demand rises relative to supply (which is fixed in the short term) prices rise, and lower income buyers are squeezed out of the market. Conversely, when demand falls prices fall (or rise less rapidly), and lower income buyers find it easier to enter the market. From 1982 to 1989 national average house prices increased from £25,500 to £62,000 — an increase of 144 per cent in cash terms. Not surprisingly, there was growing concern that housing was becoming less affordable and that large numbers of potential first time buyers were priced out of the market.

If initial repayments are calculated as a proportion of average male incomes, one finds that from a low of about 21 per cent in 1983–1984 they rose to 31 per cent in 1989 and thence to a staggering 41 per cent in 1991. This compares to a rise of between 14 per cent and 15 per cent in the late 1960s (Council of Mortgage Lenders, 1990). On this basis, house purchase clearly became far more difficult during the late 1980s. Another method of measuring affordability involves house price income ratios. If the average house price is divided by average income, we obtain a house price/income ratio.

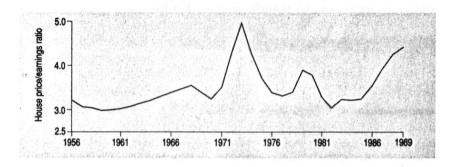

Figure 7.1   *House price/income ratios 1969–89.*

Source: *Housing Finance*, no.7, August 1990, Council of Mortgage Lenders.

The house price/income ratio can rise fast during periods of rapid
house price inflation but it cannot keep rising indefinitely as households simply cannot afford to pay ever higher multiples of earnings.
The mortgage repayments quickly become unaffordable. Consequently,
when the ratio rises sharply to 4.5:1 or over as it did in the early 1970s
and the late 1980s a growing number of potential buyers are priced out of
the market, the rate of price increase slows down, and may stop or even
go into reverse as occurred in 1990, 1991 and 1992. As incomes rise and
house prices mark time the ratio is gradually restored to its 'normal'
level of about 3.5:1. But, as an increasing number of households include
two earners, the potential to bid up the price of houses is growing, and
the long-term house price/income ratio is rising if male earnings are
taken as the basis of calculation. However, if household earnings were
the basis this would be less marked.

3.4 Home ownership, wealth, consumption and macro-economic policy

As home ownership has grown and house prices have risen post-war,
home owning became a major source of wealth accumulation for many
households. Someone who bought a house in 1970 at the then national
average price of £5,000 is now likely to own an asset worth £55,000. As
the mortgage outstanding is likely to be minimal — perhaps £2,000 or
less, the owner will have equity of £50,000 plus, possibly far more than
savings from earned income over the same period. As a result, residential property has taken a larger share of personal wealth holdings in
Britain (from 17 per cent in 1960 to 48 per cent in 1986), and the distribution of personal wealth has widened slightly within the top 50 per cent
of wealth owners.

This is clearly a positive benefit, but as home ownership and house
prices have risen, so the amount of mortgage finance needed to keep the

owner-occupied housing market afloat has grown very rapidly. Gross advances increased from £3.5 billion in 1973 to £49.4 billion in 1988, the peak year of the 1980s housing boom. Repayments of interest and principal also increased rapidly, but net advances rose from £716 million to £7.8 billion — a tenfold increase in fifteen years. This has led to arguments that the massive demand for housing finance makes less money available for other key sectors of the economy (such as loans to industry), but this has not been proved.

Home ownership has come to play an important role in macro-economic management. Mortgage loans now account for about 80 per cent of personal sector debt, and house price booms such as occurred in the late 1980s are an important factor in increasing the money supply. The late 1980s credit boom which followed Nigel Lawson's 1989 budget and the cuts in higher rate taxation for the better off, was partly reinforced by the housing market. The rapid increase of housing equity provided a base to borrow against and allowed home owners to reduce savings or to increase debt. The late 1980s saw a massive surge in the value of what is termed 'equity release', as home owners took out larger mortgages than strictly necessary and used the surplus for consumer spending or investment. The effect was to increase consumer demand and some economists now believe that the late 1980s consumer spending boom was achieved partly on the back of rising house prices and housing wealth.

One reason Nigel Lawson increased interest rates rapidly from the autumn of 1988 to 1989 was that he was concerned to halt the housing related consumer boom. Now that the controls on mortgage lending have largely been abolished, and mortgage finance has been integrated into the wider financial circuits, so it becomes a growing problem for the management of the economy.

3.5 The crisis in the home ownership market in Britain

At the time of writing (March 1993), the home ownership market in Britain is in the throes of its deepest and most severe crisis since the 1920s. From the peak of the boom in southern Britain in 1988, the annual number of sales has slumped by 40 per cent, and national average prices have fallen by nearly 20 per cent. In southern Britain the fall in real prices has been nearer 30 per cent.

As a consequence of rising unemployment and inability to meet mortgage repayments combined with falling prices and inability to sell, mortgage repossessions have soared. In 1991 there were some 75,000 repossessions: a fivefold increase over the 15,800 in 1989. In addition, nearly 1 per cent of all mortgages — 91,700 — were 12 months or more behind with payments in 1992 and 183,600 (2 per cent) were six to twelve months behind. A total of 590,000 mortgages (6 per cent) were three months or more behind with payments. This rapid rise in mortgage arrears is partly a product of rising unemployment in the early 1990s with its associated financial problems for unemployed house-holds. The rise in repossessions has led to losses for lenders and insur-ers, and has depressed prices as repossessed properties are sold for whatever the lenders can get.

But falling prices have created another problem known as *negative equity*. In mid 1992 it was estimated (Bank of England, 1992; Dorling, Gentle and Cornford, 1992) that approximately one million mortgagees had bought houses which were now worth less than the value of the outstanding mortgages owing on them. It was estimated that by Decem-ber 1992 the number would have risen to 1.5 million or one in seven mort-gagees. These buyers almost all of whom bought after 1987 — often on 90 per cent or even 100 per cent mortgages — are generally unable to sell or move. They are concentrated in the south of Britain where price falls have been most severe. In Greater London an estimated 40 per cent of recent buyers have negative equity compared to just one per cent in Scotland. National average negative equity in late 1992 was estimated at £4,400 per affected household but in the South East it was higher.

The crisis has led to frequent calls for government intervention (just as there were calls in the late 1980s for government to control the adverse effects of the house price boom) on the grounds that the slump in the housing market has reinforced the severity of the recession. Home owners with large mortgages are cutting back on consumer spending in an effort to rebuild their savings or cut debt levels. It is also argued, with strong evidence, that a fall in the volume of house puchases causes a sharp fall in purchases of new consumer goods as well as a sharp decline in new house building and has knock on effects on the building supply industry. Action to date has been limited, however, partly because of the belief that intervention in a fiee market is unnecessary and unde-sirable.

In late 1991 the government announced a plan to reduce the effect of repossessions by encouraging housing associations to take over repos-sessed dwellings and rent them to affected households. To date, how-ever, hardly any housholds have been helped by the plan. In April 1992 the government temporarily abolished stamp duty on purchases under £250,000 but the effects were minimal and buyer confidence is still very weak. In late 1992 the government gave an extra £700m to housing associations to enable them to buy up to 20,000 new unsold houses for rent. Mortgage lenders have argued for a doubling of mortgage interest tax relief to stimulate the market, and there have been calls for the government to subsidize owners with negative equity in an effort to get sales going again. If the home ownership market did not show signs of recovery by the Spring of 1993, it was thought the Conservatives might possibly overcome their ideological antipathy to intervention as eco-nomic and political considerations became paramount.

4 The development of hierarchical coordination?: state housing policy 1919–1979

In Section 3 I examined the structure and operation of owner occupation in Britain. It was argued that the market model of coordination was dominant, although the market was underpinned and supported by very favourable tax treatment of home ownership. In this section, and the next one, I shall examine the evolution of state housing policy in Britain, particularly as it effects council housing. As housing policy in Britain is conceived and legislated by central government (though implimented by local government), I will argue that this is partly an example of hierarchical coordination, and that the degree of hierarchical control has increased during the 1980s and 1990s, though under the guise of breaking up council 'monopolies' and encouraging a greater variety of social housing landlords and more consumer choice.

Although local government possesses certain powers of its own and has a degree of autonomy, its duties, powers and autonomy are determined in the final analysis by central government. Local government can only undertake activities specified by legislation and central government can, by legislation, compel local authorities to carry out certain tasks (such as the sale of council housing to tenants or the establishment of compulsory tendering for services). And at the end of the day, if local governments refuse to undertake such tasks or duties, they can be taken to court, or even dissolved as in the case of the GLC and ILEA. Additionally, central government can remove powers from local authorities and grant them to other bodies such as Urban Development Corporations. It is also possible for central government to design financial regulations and controls which effectively compel local authorities to do their bidding.

There are, to be sure, several cases of local government refusal to impliment central government housing policy but, at the risk of over-simplification, I would argue that these rebellions have generally fizzled out or been crushed in the courts. At the end of the day, central government controls the purse-strings and has legal power to compel local authorities to carry out its policies. They design and structure the framework in which housing policies are locally conducted.

The focus on the discussion in Section 5 of the chapter is on the radical changes in housing policy introduced by the Conservative government since 1979 but, in order to fully appreciate these and place them in context, it is necessary to look at the evolution of government housing policy over a longer time span. Accordingly, the rest of this section gives an overview of the evolution of housing policy from the late nineteenth century onwards, paying most attention to the development of policy from 1945 to 1979. First however it is necessary to look briefly at the allocation and distribution of council housing.

4.1 The allocation and distribution of council housing

Unlike owner occupation which is allocated through the market on the
basis of ability to pay, council housing is bureaucratically allocated by
local authorities primarily on the basis of perceived need. This is a
difficult concept to define, but in practice households have to register
their names on a waiting list and they are then give 'points' to reflect
their situation. Different local authorities operate different schemes,
but generally points are awarded for length of time on the waiting list,
poor housing conditions, overcrowding, number of children, medical
complaints and so on. When households have accumulated enough
points, and get to the top of the waiting list they may be offered a
house or flat of a size corresponding to their requirements if one is
available. This is an important caveat, because the whole system is
predicated on scarcity. There are usually more people on the waiting
list than there are houses for allocation and *rationing is partly by time
and perceived need rather than price*. Although a larger or better quality property generally has a higher rent than a smaller property, rents
are often subsidized and are lower than they would be if the property
were let on the open market on a 'for profit' basis.

4.2 Government housing policy until 1945

The prevailing ethos during the nineteenth century was *laissez faire*,
and state intervention in housing was gradual and reluctant. The early
legislation was primarily for public health rather than housing reasons, and most of it was permissive or enabling — rather than compulsory. Local autonomy was considerable. Slum clearance was permitted
by Acts of 1868 and 1875, but councils were not permitted to build replacement housing until The Housing of the Working Classes Act of
1890. Rate fund subsidies were not permitted, and only about 1,000
houses per year were built between 1890 and 1919, most by the old London County Council in its pioneering slum rehousing schemes.

There was strong opposition to the idea of subsidizing housing for the
working class which, it was believed would lead to fecklessness and
improvidence. Things did not change significantly until the First
World War when concentration of munitions workers into the already
overcrowded cities, led to a growing housing shortage, rising rents and
widespread social unrest. As a result the government reluctantly introduced the 1915 Rent Act to control rents as a war-time emergency measure (Englander, 1983).

Social unrest continued throughout the war and in 1919 Lloyd George
announced his 'Homes fit for Heroes' policy (Merrett, 1979; Swenerton,
1981). This Act marked the effective start of large scale council-hous-
ing building.

Although the Act imposed a duty on local authorities (as the agents
of government policy) to survey their local housing needs and build ac-

cordingly, it was up to the local councils to draw up plans and submit them for approval. Few did so until the government conceded to their demand that the financial burden on them should not exceed a 1p rate. Costs over and above this were to be borne by central government. Needless to say, the Treasury were strongly opposed to such an open-ended subsidy and, as building costs rose after the war, there was considerable pressure to end it.

The commitment to build half a million 'homes for heroes' was quickly abandoned, with 170,000 built, and the 1923 Act which followed introduced a fixed subsidy of £6 per house per year for twenty years. This enabled the government to control the level of housing expenditure much more closely and this form of subsidy dominated for the next forty years.

The 1930s saw a huge boom in house building for owner occupation (a reassertion of the market) but, despite the ups and downs of policy between the wars and a shift towards council slum clearance and redevelopment rather than 'general needs' building, nearly 1.5 million council houses were built between 1919 and 1939. State landlordism was here to stay.

4.3 Housing policy 1945–1979

In 1945 a reforming Labour government came to power committed to the creation of a Welfare State. The housing situation at the time was grim and the state sector was chosen as the main instrument of policy on the grounds that resources were scarce, and that housing output should be directed to those in greatest need. Speculative building was to make up no more than one-fifth of the housing output in each local authority and, given the shortages of building materials, new private dwellings had to be licensed. This reflected a strong degree of central coordination. As Nye Bevan put it: 'If we are to plan we have to plan with plannable instruments, and the speculative builder, by his very nature, is not a plannable instrument'.

Labour support for council housing has traditionally been stronger than that of the Conservatives, who have generally viewed state housing with some suspicion as a necessary, if rather undesirable social expedient. But when the Conservatives took power in 1951 (with Harold Macmillan as Minister of Housing) they built more council houses in the mid-1950s (180,000 a year between 1951 and 1957) than any government before or since in an attempt to beat the post-war housing shortage. When the worst shortages appeared to be over in the mid-1950s, the Conservatives switched to the encouragement of private building, with local authority building focusing on slum clearance. This parallelled the policy shift during the interwar years.

The twenty years from 1953 to 1972 saw an emerging consensus advocating a dominant role for owner occupation with a subsidiary, but still important, role for council housing. The main competition was over the number of houses built each year. The pattern of energetic post-war council building followed by a switch to slum clearance and a reversion to private enterprise when the economy recovered, and the worst of the shortages were over, was essentially a re-run of the interwar period. It appears that while governments are willing to tolerate the rapid growth of state housing in periods of acute shortage, they revert to private provision as soon as conditions have returned to normal, and the worst of the shortages seem to be over.

Conservative opposition to the cost of council housing, which was believed to be expensive and inefficient, began to harden in the early 1970s. The Conservatives outlined a radical new policy in their 1971 White Paper *Fair Deal for Housing* which was designed to raise council house rents towards 'fair market' levels, target subsidies to the lower paid and to reduce Exchequer subsidies to council housing. The 1972 Housing Finance Act which followed was the first move towards market rents and away from universal to targeted housing subsidies. It marked the breakdown of the post-war political consensus on council housing.

The 1974 Labour government repealed the 1972 Housing Finance Act and replaced it with the Housing Rents and Subsidies Act, 1975. But the 1972 Act showed how the Conservatives intended to proceed, and during the 1970s the seeds were sown for the even more radical Conservative policies of the 1980s.

5 Housing policy under the Conservatives. 1979–1990: a new era for council housing

It can be argued that the importance of council housing has been in decline since the 1950s when the worst of the post-war shortage was over (Figure 7.2). This may be true, but it is also true that the return of the Conservatives to power in 1979 marked the beginning of a radical break with previous policies towards council housing which cannot be interpreted just in terms of a continuation or intensification of previous policies. While governments from 1919 to 1979 accepted, with varying degrees of enthusiasm or reluctance, the importance of council housing, subsequent Conservative governments rejected this consensus in favour of a radically new approach to the organization of housing provision and finance in Britain.

Conservative housing policy has been innovative, radical and far reaching. Its main thrust is simple to summarize. It has been to greatly reduce the size and cost of the council sector, to expand home ownership and, more recently, to revitalize private renting and to encourage the growth of alternative landlords. Put simply its aim has been to sharply reduce and replace council housing in Britain with a more market orientated system. As such Malpass (1990) has argued that it is more of

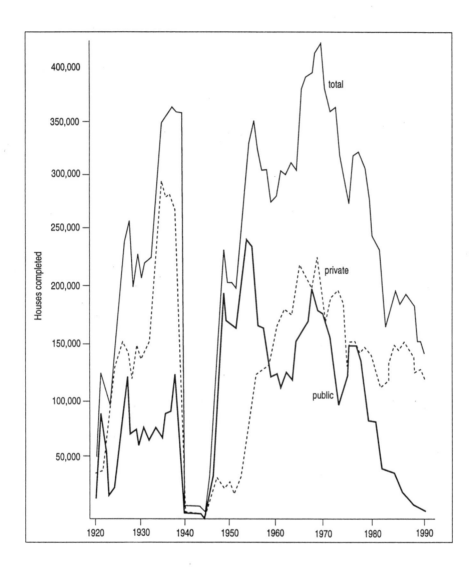

Figure 7.2   *Annual housing completions 1919–1989*

Source: Boleat, M., 1989, Table 1.2.

a *tenure policy* than a housing policy. There is a good deal of truth in this observation, but the policy changes have been many and complex, and it is necessary to examine these in detail if we are to understand how the housing system in Britain has changed since 1979.

5.1   The first phase of Conservative housing policy: 1979–1986.

The first phase of Conservative housing policy, between 1979 and 1986 had *four* main elements. The *first* policy change was incorporated in the Housing Act 1980 and involved the introduction of a 'right to buy' for all council tenants. Council housing had previously been sold to tenants on a small scale, particularly in Conservative-controlled authorities, but sales were voluntary and unsubsidized. The 1980 Act gave most council tenants a statutory right to buy with discounts of up to 50 per cent on the official valuation after twenty years residence.

The right to buy was initially resisted by some Labour-controlled councils, but opposition faded and sales in England and Wales rose to a peak of 202,000 in 1982. Sales then declined which led the government to raise the maximum discount to 60 per cent in 1984 after thirty years and to 70 per cent (on flats) after fifteen years in 1986. The minimum discount was also raised in 1986 from 33 per cent after three years residence to 45 per cent. By 1990 over a million council houses had been sold — over 16 per cent of stock (Forrest and Murie, 1987; 1988). Council house sales had the great advantage of killing two birds with one stone. They reduced the size of the council sector and increased home ownership. They also provided a massive boost to the Exchequer through sale proceeds which until recently have exceeded the income from all other privatizations combined (Forrest and Murie, 1987). Given Conservative commitment to a reduction of the Public Sector Borrowing Requirement (PSBR), the right to buy has been a popular policy with government.

The *second* prong of the assault on council housing consisted of a dramatic cut in the level of capital expenditure on new council house building. This was cut from £5.3 billion in 1979–80 to £2.8 billion in 1983–1984. Out of a 4 per cent overall cut in public expenditure, no less than 92 per cent of total savings were from housing, the great majority from council housing (Forrest and Murie, 1987). The results were predictable. New council housing starts fell from of 107,000 in 1978 to 37,000 in 1981 — a fifth of the level in 1975, and the lowest peacetime level since the 1930s. By 1989 new council starts had fallen to just 16,000 (Figure 7.2).

The *third* prong is the most difficult to comprehend, involving as it does, fundamental changes in the structure of local government finance. In 1979, just prior to the general election, Labour had formulated a new flexible housing subsidy system to replace the existing fixed sum per dwelling. It involved a 'deficit subsidy' which would be paid to local authorities on the basis of the difference between their housing expenditure and rent income. A central objective of this scheme was to reduce the overall subsidy levels and target it more effectively.

The Conservative 1980 Housing Act contained three key differences from the 1979 Labour bill. First, there was no provision for rent increases to be kept in line with earnings Second, they allowed central government to calculate subsidy entitlement on the basis of *assumed* rather than actual changes in costs and income in individual local authorities. Third, fundamental changes were made to the financial rules governing local authority housing revenue accounts (HRAs).

For sixty years, from 1919 to 1979 it had been assumed that council housing necessarily required central government subsidy. The 1980 Act dispelled that idea. By enabling local authorities to run a surplus (but not a loss) on their HRAs it implied that council housing could be operated at a profit without government subsidy.

The government rapidly implimented large assumed rent increases. Taking the government's first term as a whole, council rents rose by 119 per cent compared to a rise of 55 per cent in the retail price index. As a result, total subsidies fell rapidly — and a majority of councils got no subsidy at all. In addition, the abolition of the no profit rule for HRAs meant that a growing number of authorities were able to transfer surpluses from the HRAs to the general rate fund. This represents a remarkable transformation. In some authorities council housing was used to subsidize the rates, rather than vice versa.

The *fourth* policy change involved housing benefit. Before 1982, low-income tenants could receive help with housing costs via rent and rate rebates or allowances administered by local authorities or via supplementary benefit, administered by the DHSS. But the rise in unemployment and rent levels since 1979 had led to a rapid growth in the number of council tenants claiming assistance with housing costs. In 1982 the government introduced housing benefit (HB) which was administered by local authorities, but financed by the DHSS. This is a form of income support which is part of a general policy to replace universal housing subsidies with higher rents and means-tested income subsidies.

5.2 Conservative housing policy 1987 onwards: the final solution? Large scale disposal of council housing

In their first two terms of office the Conservatives had been primarily concerned with the 'right to buy' and the growth of home ownership as part of their goal of fostering a property-owning democracy. But in the 1987 White Paper on housing policy, *Housing: The Government's Proposals*, there was a shift of focus away from the 'right to buy' scheme and towards the *de-municipalization* of council rented housing provision across the board. The market form of provision and coordination was to be introduced en masse.

One reason was that the number of right to buy sales to sitting tenants had fallen from a peak of 200,000 in 1982 to 84,000 in 1986. And the sale of flats remained very low. They accounted for 30 per cent of the stock but only 3 per cent of sales, despite an increase in the maximum level of discount on flats to 70 per cent in 1986. It became apparent that there were limits to the growth of 'right to buy' sales, and the idea of selling entire estates to other landlords was a logical next step if the privatization drive was to be maintained. 'If the tenants could not afford to, or did not want to, buy their homes then other purchasers would have to be found' (Kemp, 1990, p.797).

The first step was estate sales to private developers. A number of authorities had already started selling vacant houses or estates to private developers after 1979, but the numbers were quite small. The process was greatly assisted by Section 9 of the Housing and Planning Act 1986 which enabled local authorities to re-possess property from tenants where they wished to dispose of properties for re-development subject to alternative accommodation being provided. Between 1981–1987 around 30,000 dwellings in 150 estates were sold to private developers (Usher, 1988) but it was clear that estate sales did not have the potential to significantly reduce the size of the council sector.

Council housing versus the market.

Consequently, in the aftermath of the 1987 General Election, the Conservatives initiated more comprehensive and far-reaching policies for de-municipalization. These policies were linked to what Kemp (1990) has termed 'a sustained ideological assault' on the alleged inefficiency and bureaucratic nature of municipal provision. This was contrasted to the perceived virtues of a market form of provision and coordination.

John Patten, then Minister of Housing, stated in early 1987 that: 'we should get rid of these monoliths', and transfer council housing to other agencies 'who will be closer in touch with the needs and aspirations of individual tenants'. And Nicholas Ridley, ex-Secretary of State for Environment, said in 1988 that a key objective of the White Paper was 'the breaking up of the local authority monopoly in social rented housing'.

The assault was continued in the 1987 housing policy White Paper, *Housing: The Government's Proposals,* where it was argued that in many large cities local authorities operate on such a large scale that they 'inevitably risk becoming distant and bureaucratic' (p.2). The White Paper said it was 'not healthy' for the public sector to dominate rented housing and argued that, at the local level:

> ...short term political factors can override efficient and economic management of housing in the long term, leading to unrealistically low rents and wholly inadequate standards of maintainence. Local authority housing allocation methods can easily result in inefficiences and bureaucracy, producing queuing and lack of choice for the tenant... A more pluralist and more market-orientated system will ensure that housing supply can

respond more flexibly to demand, will give the tenant wider choice over his housing and will allow greater scope for private investment and more effective use of public sector money.

(DoE, 1987, p.3).

More generally, the then Minister of Housing, William Waldegrave, stated in a policy document that he could:

...see no arguments for generalised new build by councils, now or in the future... It is an oddity confined largely to Britain amongst European countries that the state goes on landlording on this scale. The next great push after the Right to Buy should be to get rid of the state as a big landlord and bring housing back to the community... the landlords should be the type of social housing organizations we see overseas.

(Waldegrave, 1987)

The role envisaged for councils is clear. It is as organizers, regulators and enablers; not as providers of housing or large scale landlords. This is seen as inappropriate for local authorities despite, or perhaps because of, the fact that for sixty years they have been the major social landlords, and housed up to 30 per cent of households in Britain in 1981.

Why are the Conservatives so keen to dispense with councils as major providers of rented housing? I shall consider this question in Section 6. First it is important to look at some of the policies put forward by the Conservatives to demunicipalize council housing and create a commercially viable climate for private rented housing.

The de-municipalization of social housing

The *first* new element in the Conservative policy of de-municipalizing of social housing was specifically aimed at run-down inner urban areas with major social and environmental problems In these areas, the 1988 Housing Act proposed establishing Housing Action Trusts (HATs) which would take over responsibility for managing and improving the housing after which they would be handed over to other unspecified owners. Not surprisingly, the few HATs which have been proposed have not proved popular with their potential tenants who are fearful of what the future may hold and have voted against designation (Woodward, 1991). Some HATs have now been approved however.

Second, the 1988 Housing Act also gave prospective landlords the right to bid for the ownership of council properties. Although this new scheme is called 'Tenant's Choice' by the government, this is something of a misnomer as the right of transfer is given to the landlord not to tenants. These bids (at the market value of properties, subject to tenancy and less the cost of necessary improvements) are subject to a ballot in which at least 50 per cent of eligible tenants must have taken part. But, in order for a sale *not to proceed*, at least 50 per cent of eligible tenants must vote against the proposals. Thus, if only 60 per cent of tenants voted, and 80 per cent of them voted against, the sale would go ahead as only 48 per cent (80 per cent x 60 per cent) of eligible tenants would have voted against. Not surprisingly, this method of voting aroused considerable critical comment.

The *third* initiative has come not from government but from the local authorities themselves, a number of whom have attempted to transfer their entire stock to other landlords, generally either existing housing associations or new ones specifically established for the purpose. The government has welcomed this initiative, but has laid down guidelines for transfers as it does not wish to see the continuation of municipal housing under a new name. What is remarkable about wholesale transfers is that they are not subject to the Tenant's Choice scheme but can be carried out under earlier legislation irrespective of the tenant's wishes.

The encouragement of alternative landlords.

The Conservative government's plans to replace councils with other landlords have been paralleled by policies to encourage other landlords to expand their sphere of activities. In many ways these policies can be seen as an acceptance of the fact that it is impossible to get most council tenants to buy their own homes. The government has recognized that there are limits to the growth of ownership, and that a large rented sector is both inevitable and necessary. But it will not be a predominantly municipal rented sector.

The 1986 Building Societies Act gave the societies permission to own land and property. This measure, which was part of a wider de-regulation of the societies was aimed in particular at encouraging the societies to enter the market for rented housing, both in new build and council estates. Thus far few building societies have shown interest, but the Nationwide through its subsidiary Quality Street aims to buy or develop several thousand houses for rent. Perhaps more importantly the 1988 Housing Act contained measures to de-regulate private renting and to radically change the financial regime for housing associations.

The Conservatives first attempted to partly de-regulate private rented housing in 1980 when they introduced shorthold and assured tenancies which were designed to offer landlords either higher rents or a reduction in tenant's security of tenure on approved new lettings. Neither of these measures were very effective, and the 1988 Housing Act de-regulated all new lettings. Landlords are allowed to charge a market rent and tenant security of tenure was weakened. The rationale behind these changes is the belief that rent controls have been the main reason for the decline of the private rented sector. In addition, the Government extended the Business Expansion Scheme (BES) in the 1988 Budget to allow new residential property companies to provide housing to let at market rents. They have attracted considerable interest from investors and seem to have generated a mini-boom in rental investment.

Finally, the government has strengthened its support for housing associations. The status of housing associations has always been an ambiguous one, intermediate between public and private sector, and different governments have supported them for very different reasons. The housing associations have been the chameleons of housing provision. Labour supported them because they saw them as quasi-public, while the Conservatives supported them because they saw them as quasi-private and non-municipal (Back and Hamnett, 1985). They are crucial to the Government's strategy because the BES schemes are unlikely to produce sufficient housing to replace the role of local authorities and private landlords are unlikely to attempt large scale take-overs of tenants council estates.

The most recent element of Conservative policy to dismantle the council sector and to convert council tenants to owners or tenants of social or private landlords is the 'Rent into Mortgages' scheme which treats rent as mortgage payments and is designed to enable lower income tenants to buy their homes. But, as tenants on housing benefit are unlikely to be able to enter the scheme, a large proportion of tenants will be excluded, and some critics have argued that the policy is likely to prove a damp squib. Indeed, the recent collapse in the home-ownership market points to the need for a mortgage to rent policy rather than a rent into mortgage policy.

6 Why has Conservative housing policy radically changed since 1979?

6.1 Introduction

In previous sections of the chapter I examined some of the radical changes in Conservative housing policy since 1979. In this section I want to look at the question of *why* the Conservatives made such radical changes. What were the objectives of the policies they have pursued so vigorously? and Why were they undertaken in the 1980s rather than the 1950s, 1960s or 1970s?

To try to comprehensively explain why Conservative housing policy has changed so radically from what had gone before would need an analysis of the development of state housing and social policy in general. I do not have the space to do all that here. Instead, I shall briefly summarize some key explanations starting with what can be termed the *historical or stage theory* of council housing provision. From this perspective, the Conservatives are simply the agents of an inevitable long-term historical transformation in the role of council housing.

Saunders (1984) suggests that over the last 150 years there has been a shift from what he terms a 'market' form of consumption during the nineteenth and early twentieth centuries, to a 'socialized' form which gradually grew in importance from 1919 onwards and reached its peak in the early post-war period. Finally, we have seen the rise of a 'reprivatized' form of consumption. Saunders argues that the problem of reconciling low wages and the provision of adequate housing in the market was initially resolved via the emergence of subsidized housing and growing state intervention in the market. But in the 1960s and 1970s the growing cost of welfare provision created a further problem for rapidly growing state expenditure.

This problem was increasingly marked and was only resolved through re-privatization, which was dependent on rising incomes to enable households to meet the costs of buying services in the market. Socialized housing provision, says Saunders, is not a permanent feature of advanced capitalism, but is a historically specific phenomenon which, in retrospect, may come to be seen as a 'holding' operation during which the 're-emergence of a dominant market mode has become both possible and attractive for an increasingly large proportion of the population'. Viewed in these terms, state housing has had its (necessary) day and is now being pensioned off.

Saunders is correct in broad historical terms. But his thesis has a degree of *post facto* historical inevitability to it, and it does not explain why the fundamental policy shift has occurred from 1979 onwards.

6.2 The objectives of Conservative housing policy during the 1980s.

Have the Conservatives simply been the agents of a long-term process, and if so why has it been so marked since 1979? The question of why the Conservatives have sought to reduce the role of council housing and replace it with owner occupation or other forms of social housing remains. Indeed the objective of Conservative policy itself remains problematic. Has it primarily been to expand owner occupation, or to reduce the role of the council sector, or to introduce a greater degree of market coordination into housing provision (see Section 5.2), or some mixture of all three? Alternatively, has the major objective been the financial one of reducing the cost of housing subsidies and transferring the cost to the individuals concerned?

I would ague that the policy has involved elements of all three objectives, but can be summarized by George Orwell's *Animal Farm* dictum 'Four Legs Good, Two Legs Bad', where the four legs equals private and two legs equals public provision. The encouragement of home ownership, private landlords and housing associations and the reduction of the council sector are all consistent with this interpretation. But as I argue below, they are not all consistent with an attempt to reduce the cost of housing to the Exchequer. The explanations for Conservative housing policy can be divided into *three* main categories; economic and financial, political and ideological, and I will examine each of them in turn.

The *economic* explanation has been advanced by Harloe and Paris (1984) among others. They argue that the major economic crisis of the 1970s led to considerable pressure for the reduction of state welfare expenditure in most Western countries, and that 'most of what has occurred in Britain is the result of the international economic crisis' (p.73). They accept that the attack on council housing has been pushed further and faster by the Conservatives than it was under the 1974–79 Labour government, but they argue that the first major recent cuts in housing spending took place under Labour in 1976 following the sterling crisis. They suggest from this that the principal motive for the cuts was financial and that capital expenditure on housing offered a relatively easy target that (unlike health or education) affected only a minority of the electorate. They conclude that cuts in housing expenditure have not solely been products of the New Right government, but have been a crucial element in the monetarist policies followed by both Labour and Conservatives since 1976 and they reject the idea that a sharp political break took place in 1979.

While Harloe and Paris are correct to point to the fact that the cuts in housing expenditure started under Labour, the principal objection to their argument is that the cuts have been carried much further and faster under the Conservatives than under Labour. In seeking to highlight the similarities in the economic situation faced by both parties, they underemphasize the quantitatively and qualitatively different nature of the policies pursued by the two parties. Whereas Labour undertook the cuts with reluctance as an essentially short-term response to a financial crisis, it can be argued that the Conservatives undertook the cuts with enthusiasm as part of their wider goal of rolling back the state in favour of the market and home ownership. Given Harloe and Paris's view that what has happened in Britain is part of a common response to a general economic crisis in the 1970s, they accord little weight to political and economic considerations. Labour party policy is seen as just a weaker version of Conservative policy.

It is also possible to explain council house sales policy from a *financial* perspective. Put simply, council housing has proved a greater source of revenue to the Conservatives than all the other privatizations combined. The sale of council housing raised £9.5 billion over the period from 1979 to 1986 compared to the £7.7 billion raised from other privatizations (Forrest and Murie, 1988, p.93). The revenue has not only indirectly funded and offset other housing spending, in that local authorities may retain 20 per cent of receipts, it has also enabled government to keep the budget deficit and PSBR lower than would otherwise have been possible without raising tax. There is no doubt that the sale of council housing has become an important element of the government's financial strategy. The key question, however, is not whether the sales policy is financially beneficial to central government in the short term (it clearly is) but whether financial benefits from sales constituted the central rationale for the policy. It is argued that they did not.

Second, the housing expenditure cuts have been highly selective. Forrest and Murie argue there has been major *re-orientation* of state expenditure away from direct subsidies to council housing and toward increased subsidies for owner occupation and means-tested housing benefit. Thus they argue that: 'It would be misleading to attribute changes in housing policy as logical and necessary outcomes of fiscal restraint'. On the contrary, the changes are the direct result of a series of explicit Conservative decisions to support owner occupation at the expense of council renting.

But, if this has indeed been the thrust of Conservative housing policy, it raises the question of why? The *political explanation* is that the Conservatives have seen the prospect of electoral gains from the disposal of council housing and its replacement by owner occupation. There is some support for this idea. There is a long history (Forrest, 1983; Swenerton, 1981), to the idea that home ownership makes for political conservativism and in 1979, Margaret Thatcher declared that: 'Thousands of people in council houses and new towns came out to support us for the first time because they wanted a chance to buy their own homes.'

There is some evidence from studies of voting patterns that tenants who have bought their homes are much more likely to vote Conservative than council tenants who have not, but this is not necessarily a result of tenants buying their home. It could result from more affluent tenants disposed to the Conservatives being more likely to buy than those tenants disposed to Labour. It would be necessary to examine voting patterns before and after purchase to check whether the right to buy converts voters from Labour to Conservative. Viewed overall there are a number of problems with a narrowly political explanation of Conservative housing policy.

The *third* potential explanation is an ideological one. It is that Conservative policy towards the council sector has been primarily motivated not for financial or party-political reasons, but for reasons of ideology. This ideology is a double, or even a triple, edged one. One part of it consists of a strong and deeply rooted suspicion of state housing provision and management which is seen to be inherently bureaucratic and inefficient. In addition, there is the nineteenth century view that state assistance encourages fecklessness and indolence. As William Waldegrave, then Minister of Housing, put it in 1987 it is important: 'to get people of the most deadly of all social drugs — the drug of dependence — on the state, or bureaucracy or whoever' (quoted in Malpass, 1990, p.166). This view of the inherent dangers of state provision were clearly put in the 1988 White Paper *Housing: The Government's Proposals*.

The reverse side of the coin is, of course, a strong belief in the inherent efficiency and efficacy of the market as the most appropriate and satisfactory form of provision. It encourages self reliance and promotes choice, and individuals benefit from or pay the costs of their own actions. This type of market orientated individualism has long been a part of Conservative thinking, but it can be argued that as a result of the influence of Hayek and others, that since the 1970s it has had a much greater influence.

In addition, home ownership has long played an important part in Conservative political ideology. Mrs Thatcher's reference in her 1979 speech to 'Anthony Eden's dream of a property owning democracy' is indicative of this and the late Ian Gow, commented to the Building Societies' Association in 1985: 'We should set no limit to the opportunity for owner occupation in Britain ... In those societies where property is widely owned freedom flourishes. But where the ownership of property is concentrated in the hands of the State freedom is in peril'.

It can therefore be argued that the basis of the attack on council housing is a belief in the inherent superiority of home ownership over council renting. But, as we have seen, Conservative policy shifted from 1986 onwards. Whatever the nuances of Conservative ideology (and ideologies or belief systems are, in their very nature, very slippery, difficult creatures to pin down), it can be argued that it is an ideology about the organization of housing which has shaped Conservative housing policy rather than financial or political calculations. And at the core of that ideology is the idea that the market is a far superior means of coordination than the state. As you will realize from some other chapters in this book particularly those on hospitals and local government, this belief is not confined to housing policy. It conforms to Conservative policy across the board.

7 Conclusions

In this chapter we have ranged across the changing structure and organization of the British housing system, and its transformation from a system dominated by private renting to one dominated by home ownership. We have also examined the history of government housing policy from the late nineteenth century onwards, paying particular attention to the radical changes in policy introduced during the 1980s. Returning to the initial question of models of coordination, it can be argued that the British housing system has gradually been transformed from a system largely dominated by the market in the nineteenth century, to one with a strong degree of hierarchical coordination and direction from 1919 to 1979 and a return to the market in the 1980s.

It can be further argued that the 1980s have seen the growing power of central government in this hierarchy. The freedom and power of local government to determine its building programme, rent levels and the like has been progressively curtailed and eroded. Yet, paradoxically, this concentration of central government power has been conducted with the goal of creating a freer market with more consumer choice. Whether this will ever be achieved or whether we will see a permanent move to greater centralization is a question for debate.

Thus, from the mid-1980s onwards we have seen central government increasingly being blamed for the record levels of homelessness, the decaying fabric of council housing and, most recently, the crisis in the home ownership market. Local councils argue that the problems have nothing to do with them, they are a result of central government policy. If this analysis is correct, the growing degree of hierarchical dominance in housing policy during the 1980s could rebound on the government's head as they (and not local authorities) are blamed for any policy failures. Arguably, this is already happening in the early 1990s.

One thing which is clear is that, despite (or perhaps because of) the major restructuring of housing finance in the 1980s there has been a sharp reduction in the number of new dwellings built from an average of 277,000 per year in the 1950s — through highs of 352,000 per year in the 1960s and 304,000 per year in the 1970s — to just 202,000 per year in the 1980s (BSA, 1989). Thus, whatever else it may or may not have achieved, Conservative housing policy did not deliver more dwellings during the 1980s than before. On the contrary, the average annual number of completions was lower than at any time since the war.

References

Back, G. and Hamnett, C. (1985) 'State housing policy formation and the changing role of housing associations in Britain', *Policy and Politics*, 13, pp. 393–411.

Bank of England (1992) 'Negative equity in the housing market', *Bank of England Quarterly Bulletin*, 32, 3, pp. 266–268.

Boleat, M. (1989) *Housing in Britain*, Building Societies Association, London.

Council of Mortgage Lenders (1990) *Housing Finance*, no.7, August.

Department of the Environment (1976) *Housing Policy, Technical Volume 1*, London, HMSO.

Department of the Environment (1987) *Housing: The Government's Proposals*, Cmnd 214, London, HMSO.

Dorling, D. Gentle, C and Cornford, J. (1992) 'The crises in housing: disaster or opportunity?', *CURDS Discussion Paper No. 96*, University of Newcastle Upon Tyne.

Englander, D. (1983) *Landlord and Tenants in Urban Britain, 1838–1918*, Oxford, Clarendon Press.

Forrest, R. (1983) 'The meaning of home ownership', *Society and Space*, vol. 1, pp. 205–16.

Forrest, R. and Murie, A. (1987) 'Fiscal Reorientation, Centralization, and the Privatisation of Council Housing', in W. Van Vliet (ed) *Housing Markets and Policies under Fiscal Austerity*, Westport, Conn., Greenwood Press.

Forrest, R. and Murie, A. (1988) *Selling the Welfare State: The Privatisation of Public Housing*, London, Routledge.

Harloe, M. and Paris, C. (1984) 'The decollectivization of consumption', in *Cities in Recession* (eds) Szelenyi, I, London, Sage, pp. 70–98.

Kemp, P. (1990) 'Shifting the balance between state and market: the reprivatisation of rental housing provision in Britain', *Environment and Planning. A.* 22, pp.793–810.

Malpass, P. (1990) *Reshaping Housing Policy: Subsidies, Rents and Residualisation*, London, Routledge.

Merrett, S. (1979) *State Housing in Britain*. London, Routledge.

Saunders, P. (1984) 'Beyond housing classes: The sociological significance of private property rights in the means of consumption' *International Journal of Urban and Regional Research*, 8.2, pp. 202–27.

Swenerton, M. (1981) *Homes fit for Heroes*, London, Heinemann.

Usher, D. (1988) 'Housing privatization: the sale of council estates', *Working Paper No. 67*, Bristol, School of Urband Studies, University of Bristol.

Waldegrave, W. (1987) 'Some Reflections on Housing Policy', London, Conservative News Service.

Woodward, R. (1991) 'Mobilizing opposition: the campaign against Housing Action Trusts in Tower Hamlets', *Housing Studies*, 6, 1, pp.44–56.

Wriglesworth, J. (1992) 'Housing market: the debt trap, *UBS Phillips and Drew Economic Briefing*, no. 262, June.

CHAPTER 8:
THE COORDINATION OF THE SCHOOL SYSTEM

Rosalind Levačić

1 Applying the models of coordination

In this chapter I shall be setting out to analyse the management of the school system in the United Kingdom in terms of three models of coordination — markets, hierarchies and networks — and to show how the relative importance of the models changes over time. My principal focus is the profound changes in the schooling system initiated by the 1988 Education Reform Act which introduced market coordination within the state school sector at the expense of local education authority (LEA) power, and heralded an intensification of hierarchical coordination by the Department For Education (DFE)[*]. In contrast, the system of coordination which evolved under the 1944 Education Act, and provided the framework for school organization until 1988, was widely characterized as a policy network consisting of three key partners: central government, local education authorities and the teaching profession.

My use of the models of coordination in this chapter is selective. In general the models of hierarchy, market and network, may be applied either to coordination *within an organization* or to coordination *between different organizations or individuals*. In this chapter, as in Chapter 9 on hospitals, the market as a means of coordination *within* an organization — the internal market — is the chief focus of interest and not the market as an external coordination device. For the other two models, hierarchy and network, I concentrate on their function in coordinating *between* the three layers of a pyramid consisting of the central government department for education, the local education authorities and the schools. I do not examine the internal workings of these organizations, though they are to a greater or lesser degree internally coordinated by hierarchy. I am also selective in my treatment of networks, focusing only on one particular type of network — the *policy network* — which coordinates the different organizations and interests concerned with a common area of policy.

In order to illustrate how the models of coordination may be used analytically, I have applied them to selected historical developments to show how the emphasis on the different models has changed over time.

2 1833-1944: the development of state hiearchical coordination

Initially, the provision of education was left to a combination of market and network coordination operated by parents, guardians and charities, mainly of a religious nature. However the increasing recognition of the importance of education both as a private and a public good led in the nineteenth century to a slow growth of state involvement.

2.1 Reasons for state involvement

Education is an important private good because it has such a significant influence on individuals' future roles in society, their income and lifestyle. The type of education a child receives also has external effects and so is a public good. Education in the widest sense determines individuals' attitudes, values and culture and is therefore of crucial importance to families as well as to promotional groups, and to the state since a civilized society in which democratic political institutions can flourish requires educated and socialized citizens. There is a further collective interest in the development of a well-educated and trained workforce in order to promote national economic prosperity.

The private good characteristics of education lead many parents to attach great importance to the kind of education their children receive and therefore to provide and pay for it themselves. State intervention to provide education for children whose parents cannot or do not wish to pay for it and also to determine the type of education all children receive is justified in mainstream opinion by market failure in the field of education (see Chapter 2). A further reason given for supporting government involvement in education is in order to promote social justice so as to give all children an equal opportunity to achieve their potential, both in order to gain qualifications and in order to appreciate learning for its own sake. In this sense education is also a merit — good.

2.2 1833–1944: state funding and organization of schooling

The state first provided grants to elementary schools run by voluntary bodies, predominantly the churches, in 1833. A central government department and Her Majesty's Inspectorate (HMI) were then set up to monitor the use of the grants. The 1870 Elementary Schools Act (1872 in Scotland) required School Boards to be set up in areas where voluntary provision was inadequate. Thus began the dual system of state and state-aided denominational schools we retain to this day. Attendance at school from the ages of five to ten years was made compulsory in 1880 in England and ten years later free elementary education was available for all who wanted it, though fee paying in state and state-aided schools continued.

The next major extension of state hierarchical coordination was the 1902 Education Act which abolished School Boards and gave responsibility for education in England to local government, creating some 300 local education authorities, the forbears of the present 107 local education authorities. In Wales the new local government units were given responsibility for education from their inception. The 1902 Act represented a victory for church interests in that their schools' running costs were now to be paid out of local government rates, though administered by the LEAs.

In Scotland, School Boards were not abolished until 1918 when they were replaced by larger, single-purpose education authorities. Education remained centrally administered from London until 1939 when the Scottish Office, created in 1885, moved to Edinburgh.

In the period up to 1944 much was done to expand secondary education in terms of the numbers going to secondary schools which remained fee paying and mostly selective. Pupils not transferring to secondary school remained in elementary school until statutory leaving age which, in England, was raised to 14 in 1918. The Hadow Report (1926) recommended that all pupils should progress from a primary phase of education ending at 11 to a distinct secondary phase in a secondary school. Academically able children should be selected for grammar schools to the age of at least 16 while the majority should go to technical or secondary modern schools which were to have 'parity of esteem'. Reorganization on these lines was recommended to LEAs by the Board of Education in 1928; by 1938 over half of pupils aged above 11 were in secondary schools.

2.3 Control of the curriculum

State prescription and testing of the curriculum is clearly a form of hierarchical regulation. Central government first prescribed the curriculum in the Revised Code of 1862, a strict set of regulations for elementary schools and teacher training colleges. The Code served to monitor the use of government grants as elementary schools were paid according to the attendance and attainments of their pupils. The Code continued until 1889, though in a gradually more flexible form, and was replaced by grants paid for attendance and for a satisfactory general inspection.

Between 1904 and 1926 the Board of Education continued to control the elementary curriculum through regulations. Central control was removed in 1926 and replaced by a *Handbook of Suggestions*. Progressive ideas on the primary curriculum and teaching methods developed within the education profession began to take root in the inter-war period. The secondary curriculum continued to be much more tightly controlled in the inter-war period through Board of Education regulations and the School Certificate leaving examination.

3 1944–1975: the golden age of the partnership

The 1944 Education Act was a response to the desire to promote equality of educational opportunity and to strengthen the role of the Board of Education which had diminished in the inter-war years.

3.1 The provisions of the 1944 Act

The Board of Education was replaced by the Ministry of Education, and the Minister charged with the responsibility to:

> promote the education of the people of England and Wales and the progressive development of institutions devoted to that purpose and to secure the effective execution by local authorities under his control and direction.

Equality of educational opportunity was promoted by ensuring that all children received a free secondary education up to the age of fifteen, with provision for raising the leaving age to sixteen at some future date. The Act did not specify that secondary education was to be selective but this was an accepted expectation. LEAs were therefore required to undertake a huge building programme to provide separate secondary education for all pupils. The Act also rationalized the number of LEAs and extended LEA control of church schools.

The Ministry of Education possessed a vital instrument — the control of finance. In order to encourage the post-war expansion of education, each LEA received a central grant earmarked for education which was a fixed percentage of its education expenditure. Categorical or specific grants for particular activities were also paid by the Ministry which scrutinized LEA expenditure to ensure that it was spent as intended. Ministry of Education control diminished after 1958 when central grants for specific services were replaced by a block grant for all services for each local authority to determine how to spend.

The 1944 Act intended a diffusion of power between the three partners — Ministry, LEAs and schools — in which each could balance and check the others. The rough division of responsibilities was that the Ministry directed overall education policy and the supply of resources, the LEAs built, maintained and staffed schools, and enforced attendance, while head teachers were largely responsible for what was taught and how the school ran on a day-to-day basis. However, the 1944 Act left considerable ambiguity regarding the specific powers of each of the partners, so enabling the relative influence of each one to alter over time within the same legislative framework.

3.2 The role of LEAs in relation to the centre

Despite the 1944 Act's intention that the centre should have power to direct national education policy and its implementation, the LEAs over time increased their influence at the expense of the centre (Ranson, 1980). In the first twenty years, the Ministry was able to promote the development of secondary education with the backing of the LEAs in the context of a general acceptance of selective secondary education. However, the Labour government elected in 1964 was committed to ending selection. It did not legislate for comprehensive reorganization but issued a famous circular, 10/65, requesting LEAs to submit plans for reorganization. Under the 1944 Act the DES could not insist on changing an LEA's school system; it could turn down or approve proposals for reorganization coming from the LEA. The only other instrument used by the centre was its control of local authority capital spending. Circular 10/66 announced that building project funds would only be released for schemes compatible with comprehensive reorganization. However, a number of mainly Conservative LEAs did not want to abolish their grammar schools and were able to delay matters until a Conservative government was elected in 1970. When Labour returned to power in 1974 they were unable, under existing legislation, to force a number of LEAs to comply with circular 10/65. This episode showed that 'The centre, bereft of funds and the necessary statutory instruments, had become manifestly unable to secure policy implementation through persuasion alone' (Ranson, 1980, p. 110). Thus the DES lacked the necessary hierarchical instruments of command over rules and resources.

3.3 The role of LEAs in relation to their schools

The 1944 Act envisaged a significant role for governing bodies in the management of schools which did not materialize. In response to a growing movement for greater parental involvement, the Taylor Committee (1975–6) on governing bodies was set up. It reported in 1977 that:

> A feature of many areas, especially county boroughs, was the close control by the LEA, and within it by the dominant political party, of the composition of managing and governing bodies ... In those areas where there is some freedom of resource allocation at the school level, it is the head rather than the governors who makes the effective decisions.
>
> *(Taylor Committee, 1977, p. 11)*

LEAs thus controlled the organizational structure of their educational institutions, subject to DES approval of any proposals for change. Prior to 1989 LEAs controlled the admission of pupils to schools and, subject to parental appeal, allocated pupils to schools. LEAs managed their teaching force, and could appoint or redeploy teachers to particular schools. Members and officers were the main influence in appointing head teachers and deputy heads. LEAs determined the level of spending on education and the allocation of resources to individual schools.

3.4 Control of the curriculum

Writing in the late 1970s Lawton (1980) observed that:

> The DES now has little formal control over the curriculum. The control of the curriculum ,has, however, not yet been a subject which has caused conflict between the DES and LEAs. LEAs, although technically responsible for the curriculum of schools, have traditionally (that is since 1945) left the control of the curriculum to governors who have normally left it to the head teachers who may or may not leave it to their assistants.
>
> *(Lawton, 1980, pp. 8–10)*

David Eccles, Conservative Minister for Education, in 1960 coined the memorable phrase 'the secret garden of the curriculum' to describe its embrace by the teaching profession to the exclusion of government and lay influence. His attempts to 'make the Ministry's voice heard more often and positively' by setting up a Curriculum Study Group and then in its place the Schools Council failed to make any inroads into professional control of the curriculum.

From the late 1960s increasing criticism of curricular practice in schools was voiced by 'traditional' educationists, lay people, DES civil servants and politicians. The abolition of the 11-plus in most areas, the diffusion of child-centred teaching methods in primary schools and the problems faced by the newly created comprehensives in educating children through the entire ability range were the main factors giving rise to unease outside the mainstream of the teaching profession. Then, starting in the mid-1970s the DES began to raise its profile in the matter of the curriculum and press its case for some departmental influence in order to discharge its 1944 Act responsibilities for promoting the education of the nation.

3.5 Policy networks in education

The much proclaimed 'partnership' between central government, local education authorities and teachers in running education is a good example of a *policy network*. defined by Rhodes (1991, p. 120) as:

> ...characterized by stability of relationships, continuity of a highly restricted membership, vertical interdependence based on shared service delivery responsibilities and insulation from other networks and invariably from the general public (including Parliament).

The key participants in the English and Welsh network, in the middle post-war period were the DES/Welsh Office, the LEAs and the So-

ciety of Education Officers, the Schools Council and, particularly at local level, the teacher associations. This concept of a policy network is
part of a theory of governmental agencies known as resource dependency
or exchange theory. The key idea is that the different participants are
interdependent but also have at their command different kinds of resources such as rules, organizational structure, finance, ideology and the
allocation of tasks, which are bargained, negotiated and exchanged.
While central government has the power to legislate this does not
translate directly into control over teachers' professional ideology or
classroom practice. Also LEAs, by virtue of the fact that they administered the schools, could dilute central government control and influence.
As in the case of the 1944 Act, legislation which sets down the rules
governing the hierarchical arrangements connecting central and local
government is only part of the picture. Much depends on how the rules
are interpreted and the expectations which the parties in the network
have built up on the basis of custom and accepted values. Thus the legislative framework of the 1944 Act and the practices that became accepted under that framework established a policy network in the mid-
post-war period in which the DES was relatively impotent and much
of the delivery of education was left to LEAs and teachers.

Over time the relative power of the key participants in the policy
network can change. The 1988 Education Reform Act considerably enhanced the power of central government, which subsequently increased
it through further legislation. This was possible because in the UK local government powers are not protected by the constitution but depend
upon what legislation passed through Parliament permits them to do,
requires them to do and prevents them from doing.

4   1976 onwards: the breakdown of the partnership

In 1976 the then Labour Prime Minister, James Callaghan, made a
speech at Ruskin College critical of educational standards and serving
notice on the teaching profession that they must share control with lay
people. More extreme voices from libertarian and radical right-wing
groups (such as the Hillgate Group, 1986) decried the lamentable standards in state schools and lack of parental choice. These ideas were
part of a wider breakdown in consensus over the welfare state in the
1980s, started in the 1960s by 'radical right' thinkers advocating a
much diminished role for the state. To counterbalance the concept of
market failure, libertarian economists developed the idea of
'government failure' — reasons why government intervention also
caused inefficient and inequitable resource allocation (see Levačić,
1991).

For the first ten years after the Ruskin speech, the DES slowly asserted central power at the expense of the other partners and in particu-

lar challenged the hegemony of the teaching profession. The DES
sought to influence the school curriculum through a series of documents
and circulars. By 1981 the DES was asking LEAs to draw up curricular
policies and two years later to inform them on progress. The 1985
White Paper, *Better Schools*, firmly stated and elaborated the government's principles for the curriculum for all pupils: it should be broad,
balanced, relevant and differentiated.

> The objectives set out ... make it necessary to alter practices in
> many schools. The Government shares the view ... that more
> emphasis needs to be given to science and technology; to practi-
> cal application of knowledge and to practical skills throughout
> the curriculum.
>
> *(Cmnd 9469, 1985,* Better Schools, *para. 76)*

The Department of Employment also got in on the act by promoting
with money the technical and vocational education initiative (TVEI)
for 14–19 year olds. Professional control of the curriculum was attenu-
ated: in 1984 the Schools Council was wound up and the Council for the
Accreditation of Teacher Education set up to vet all initial teacher
training courses.

The 1980 Education Act stipulated that the LEA and school governors
must comply with parental choice of school unless the child's admission was incompatible with the school's selection criteria or 'would
prejudice the provision of efficient education or the efficient use of resources'. LEAs could therefore still protect schools with declining pupil
rolls by restricting the numbers of pupils admitted to popular schools.
The 1980 Act improved parent's access to information by requiring
schools to publish their public examination results in brochures. The
Education Act of 1981 in Scotland went considerably further in providing for parental choice of school and not permitting the twelve education authorities to operate artificial admission limits. The 1980 Act
also provided grants for able children of low income parents to attend
independent schools.

Following the recommendations of The Taylor Committee, the 1980
Education Act laid down that elected parents and teachers must serve
on the governing body. The 1986 Education Act increased the number of
parent governors depending on the size of school and, by providing for
coopted governors, ensured that the LEA could not pack a governing
body with councillors. LEAs were also required to give the governors a
sum of money for the school to spend on books, materials and equipment.

Thus the 1988 Education Reform Act was not a sudden break with the
past but a decisive step in the direction already being taken by central
government. It had slowly gathered to itself more resources in the form
of legislation and financial control and developed a consensus towards a
national curricular framework. The concept of the partnership was
wearing thin by now. Central and local government relations had dete-
riorated with the centre's determination to control local government

spending and the 'secret garden' had been invaded. However, the government still felt frustrated by its lack of impact on the processes and outcomes of schooling.

5　Education reformed

In formulating and enacting the 1988 Education Act the government felt confident enough to ignore the wrath of the old partners. The legislation encompassed further and higher education as well, but I will consider only the measures affecting schools, the major ones being the imposition of a national curriculum, greatly enhanced management powers for head teachers and governing bodies, and the creation of a quasi-market for state schooling.

5.1 Local management of schools

Presenting the case for the Bill on its second reading in the House of Commons, the Secretary of State for Education, Kenneth Baker, proclaimed:

> If we are to implement the principle of the 1944 Act that children should 'be educated in accordance with the wishes of their parents' we must give consumers of education a central part in decision making.

> The purpose of the bill is to secure delegation and widen choice ... When governing bodies and heads control their own budgets, decisions will be taken at a local level.

> (Hansard, 1 December 1987)

The set of measures by which the LEA control of schools was dismantled is known as *local management of schools* or LMS, under which LEAs must delegate to schools a budget to cover almost all their running expenses. The governing body decides how to spend the budget as it thinks fit for the purposes of the school and is responsible for determining the staffing establishment and for appointing, disciplining and dismissing all staff, although the LEA remains the employer in LEA schools.

Strict guidelines determine the budgets the LEA allocates to its schools and drastically limit what the LEA can retain centrally. The LEA must allocate school budgets by a formula which should reflect 'the objective needs' of each school. At least 75 per cent (rising to 80 per cent in 1993) of the money delegated to schools (the Aggregated Schools Budget) has to be allocated according to the number and ages of the schools' pupils. The DES used prescription, backed by legislation and some categorical funding for LEAs, to insist that even the most reluctant LEA delegated power to its schools. To ensure that LEAs decentralize decision making to school level; the DES has become markedly more centralized *vis-à-vis* LEAs (Thomas and Levačić, 1991).

5.2 A quasi-market for schools

The decentralization of managerial decision making to school level and the enhanced role of the governing body had widespread support, including that of all the main political parties. Head teachers are, on the whole, in favour of the delegation of management to school level, provided the size of the school budget is adequate.

The same cannot be said for the elements of increased competition introduced by the 1988 Act. 'More open enrolment' ensured that the LEA could no longer refuse to admit pupils to a school which had fewer pupils in its intake year than the 'standard number' — an upper limit derived from measuring the school's accommodation capacity. However parents can only obtain a place at their chosen school if it has surplus capacity or if they gain a place on appeal. More open enrolment meant that LEAs could no longer protect schools with falling rolls by holding down the intakes of more popular schools. Thus a direct link was forged between consumer preferences and the size of the school budget. Pupil driven formula funding, together with more open enrolment, act very much like a voucher system. With vouchers parents would be given a credit for £x to spend at a school of their choice at which their child obtained a place.

Further competition was provided by the creation of grant maintained schools (GMSs). After a majority vote by parents to opt out of the LEA system and, if approved by the Secretary of State, a school becomes grant maintained by the DFE and the value of its budget is subtracted from the LEA's Revenue Support Grant. GMSs have also received more generous capital funding from the DFE than LEA schools.

By late 1992, 315 out of 25,000 schools had become grant maintained with a further 160 in the pipeline (Dean, 1992). Some of these schools were motivated by the desire to avoid LEA reorganization. Threats to opt-out became an effective means by which opponents scuppered or delayed reorganization plans and thus made it more difficult for LEAs to rationalize surplus school places and so reduce costs. In 1991 it was announced that grant maintained schools would be able to change their admissions criteria so enabling comprehensive GMSs to become more selective.

The creation of city technology colleges (CTCs), run by trusts and funded partly by the DFE, has also added to competition for pupils in inner city areas. The city technology colleges are more generously funded and hence better equipped than their maintained rivals. Hence, there is considerable resentment in the maintained sector that CTCs and GMSs are not competing on even terms.

The argument in favour of more competition as a means to raising educational standards is twofold. The first element of the process is that of self-improvement and diffusion of best practice. The head teachers, the governors and school staff will endeavour to raise educational standards in their school in order to attract pupils and funding. The second element of the process is that of Darwinian selection. Schools with poor standards will lose pupils, become financially unviable and close. The exit of the worst schools raises average standards. However, the process of exit for schools remains slow and complex, with LEAs required to engage in lengthy, expensive consultation procedures, after which their proposals may get rejected by the Secretary of State.

The argument that competition will improve educational standards has met with much criticism. For example the Campaign for the Advancement of State Education argued that:

> The change in the admissions procedures to open enrolment is designed both to give the appearance of extending parental choice by increasing the number of children admitted to 'popular schools' and to concentrate resources in larger, more 'economic' units. The corollary is that other perfectly good schools will be allowed to deteriorate due to loss of revenue and resources in an increasingly under-financed situation ... This will result in ever widening differences between the quality of education.
>
> *(Quoted by Haviland, 1988, pp. 5–6)*

5.3 The national curriculum and testing

> The national curriculum ... is the bedrock of our reform proposals ... We are proposing a curriculum which:
>
> (a) promotes the spiritual, moral, cultural, mental and physical development of pupils at the school and of society; and
>
> (b) prepares such pupils for the opportunities, responsibilities and experiences of adult life...
>
> After religious education come the three core subjects of English, maths and science, and the seven other foundation subjects — history, geography, technology in all its aspects, a foreign language in secondary schools, music, art and physical education. In Wales, Welsh will have a firm place in the curriculum.
>
> ...We seek a balanced package of assessment arrangements including national tests ... Published results will be on a class or school basis.
>
> *(Kenneth Baker, Secretary of State for Education,* Hansard, *1 December 1987)*

The 1988 Act set up two bodies whose members are appointed by the Secretary of State: the National Curriculum Council (NCC) to advise on devising the national curriculum; and the School Examination and Assessment Council to advise on assessing and testing the national curriculum as well as on the existing examinations system. These were combined into a single Schools Curriculum and Assessment Authority under the Education Act 1993. National curriculum tests, known as Standard Assessment Tasks (SATs), are being introduced for all pupils at the ages of 7, 11, 14 and 16. GCSE and A level as well as SATs results of all schools are to be published in the press.

The reaction of the teaching profession to the final takeover of the 'secret garden' has been mixed. There are some aspects of the national curriculum which appeal to egalitarian values — in particular the national curriculum as an entitlement for all. In this sense it carries forward the 1944 Act's fundamental principle of universal secondary education which, even with comprehensivization, was not achieved because many less able pupils received a restricted curriculum, being allowed to drop subjects, in particular foreign languages and science. However, initial professional reaction to the national curriculum was largely hostile because outside prescription on what should be taught denigrated the status of teachers as professionals. There is considerable objection to the tests, especially to the publication of results which, because they are unadjusted for differences in pupils' ability, are misleading indicators of educational value added and yet are being used by lay people to judge between schools.

The 1988 Act only established the framework; the crucial features of the national curriculum and its assessment are being determined as it is being implemented from 1992 to 1997. Initially the NCC developed the national curriculum through subject working parties of educationalists, but with changes in DFE ministers, the government became even more interventionist (Graham, 1992) in using its powers to approve statutory curriculum orders. As a result the national curriculum orders and test arrangements, many aspects of which were being accepted by teachers, have undergone revisions and are (in 1993) meeting with increased resistance.

5.4 Educational reform in Northern Ireland

Responsibility for schooling is exercised by the Northern Ireland Department and by non-elected Education and Library Boards. Similar measures to those in England and Wales were introduced a year later. The proposed national curriculum specifies six areas of study (English, maths, science and technology, environment and society, creative and expressive arts, and languages for secondary schools, and includes the Irish language for those schools teaching it). Assessment is due to occur at ages 8, 11, 14 and 16.

Parents were given a statutory right to express a preference for a school and artificial limits on intake numbers are not permitted. Financial delegation was introduced with formula funding and similar provisions for delegated management of staffing and other resources to governing bodies. Additional funding is provided to schools which are or become integrated (i.e. take both Protestants and Catholics) in order to encourage this. A major difference is that there are no provisions for opting out.

5.5 Educational reform in Scotland

Scotland has always prided itself on the quality of its education system. It has a collectively more united teaching profession and the policy network has continued to prevail, with the Scottish Office Education Department (SOED) promoting a national curriculum and testing through consultation. Scotland has had open enrolment since 1981. The Self-Governing Schools (Scotland) Act 1989 enabled schools to opt out of education authority control, though hardly any have. The School Boards (Scotland) Act 1988 established School Boards with a majority of elected parents as members. These Boards have considerably less power than governing bodies in England. A much less prescriptive form of local management of schools is being proposed for 1994, in which powers would be devolved to head teachers not school councils.

The partnership model is more in evidence in Scotland than elsewhere and the Scottish Office felt less need than the DFE to extend hierarchical control because it has always exerted greater influence within its policy network.

6 Educational reform: hierarchy and markets

The 1988 Act and subsequent developments have markedly strengthened hierarchical control by the centre, particularly by the DFE, and at the same time replaced LEAs' hierarchical control of schools by quasi-market relationships. The centre has asserted itself as the dominant player in the policy network and in effect abandoned notions of partnership.

As I indicated at the beginning, this chapter focuses on hierarchy and markets as modes of coordination *between* different organizations which are arranged in a superordinate and subordinate set of relationships. In the case of education the hierarchy extends from its apex at the DFE (Welsh Office, Scottish Office or Northern Ireland Education Department) either through (local) education authorities and thence to their schools or through the Schools Funding Agency offices (being set up under the Education Act 1993) and grant maintained schools.

6.1 Defining the internal market

An internal market mimics the market form of coordination. Within the organization there are sub-units which act as buyers and sellers, exchanging goods and services with each other. Competition is promoted by ensuring that the buying and selling units have alternative parties with whom they can exchange, and so trade with external agents is usually encouraged. The internal market is an organizational form which originally developed within large multiproduct companies and is now being experimented with in public sector organizations, such as the health service and community care, as well as education.

A decentralized organizational structure is a prerequisite for setting up an internal market since there must be sub-units within the organization which can trade with each other. The changes brought about in the structure of local education authorities by local management of schools parallel those which occur when a private sector firm moves from a centralized to a decentralized structure. A centralized structure for a firm is known as a U-form structure, whereas a decentralized, multidivisional structure is called M-form. McGuinness (1991) offers the following definitions:

> The U-form is a hierarchy organized on functional lines in which the chief executive office has responsibility for both long-run ('strategic') planning of the organization as a whole and day-to-day ('operational') coordination of the functional departments (production, marketing, purchasing, personnel, finance). Each functional department is hierarchically organized, and is in the charge of a middle manager responsible for coordinating activities within his or her department...

> In the M-form, below the top level of management, the hierarchy is organized on an operating rather than on a functional basis. Each division controls the operations of a fairly self-contained part of the organization's activities (for example, a particular product line, or a geographical area) ... The head of each division is responsible for its operating performance which is judged by indicators of overall success in its markets (for example, by operating profits, sales growth, or market share). Divisional heads therefore have incentives that, compared to the U-form, are aligned more closely with corporate (global) goals and which discourage over-pursuit of functional (sub-global) goals. Each division is itself organized on U-form lines.

(McGuinness in Thompson et al., 1991, pp. 75, 77)

The key feature of a decentralized organization is that top level management (the chief executive office), having foregone U-form detailed control, needs to replace it by an alternative form of regulation.

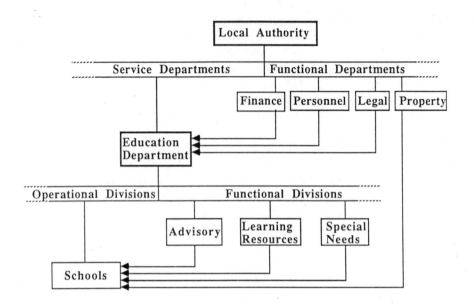

Figure 8.1   *Pre-LMS: the LEA as a U-form organization*
Source: Levačić, 1993

This requires setting measurable objectives for the sub-units and their managers, monitoring the achievement of these objectives and rewarding or penalizing accordingly. The internal market, therefore, is an alternative mode of internal coordination to hierarchy — the coordination mechanism inherent to a U-form organization. Networks will operate to some extent in both U-form and M-form organizations but are likely to be more important in a decentralized organization.

6.2 The internal market applied to the school system

The next section discusses how the concept of the internal market applies to the school system. A more detailed discussion is provided by Levačić (1993).

In applying the concept of the internal market to the organizational structuring of schools, we need to know where it is appropriate to draw the organizational boundaries of 'State Education plc'. With respect to the new structures being set up there seem to be three possible models, depending on how policy evolves.

Model 1

The first possibility is that the organizational boundary is drawn round the LEA and the schools it maintains. LMS replaces LEA hierarchical control of schools with an internal market.

Model 2

The second possibility is that we draw the boundary around the entire state school sector. The DFE (not the LEA as in model 1) is the 'top level management' with an internal market regulating all types of state school — maintained (LEA) schools, grant maintained schools and city technology colleges.

Model 3

In the third model, favoured by the radical right, all schools become autonomous institutions chosing their own curriculum, with a very weak 'top level management' function for the DFE and LEAs ceasing to exist. Schools are funded by means of vouchers provided by central government to parents who are free to cash them in at any school which will admit their child. Under the most radical type of voucher scheme, schools could top up vouchers with fees and there would be no clear boundary between state and independent schools. In this model market coordination is dominant and is more akin to external market coordination than to an internal market.

MODEL 1: THE LEA AS AN INTERNAL MARKET

Prior to local management of schools, local authorities were U-form organizations with separate functional departments for finance, property, personnel and so forth, as illustrated in Figure 8.1. Each of these functional departments provided services direct to schools, largely on terms decided at central office.

In contrast, LMS has created an M-form type LEA, as illustrated in Figure 8.2. Schools have become semi-autonomous operating units and the functional departments have had many of their functions transferred to schools, which are now treated as cost centres in the accounts. Many of the central functional departments have become sellers of their services to schools in competition with external suppliers.

In terms of the M-form structure in Figure 8.2, the schools have, under local management, become divisions with considerable managerial discretion. This M-form structure has set up two kinds of internal market relationships depending on whether the schools or the local authority and its central departments are buyers or sellers.

Formula funding establishes the LEA as a buyer of education services from its schools. Through the formula it determines the price it offers schools for educating a particular type of pupil and also the terms on

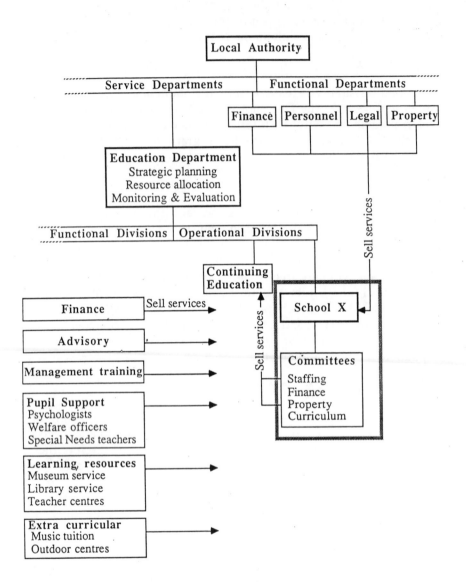

Figure 8.2   *LMS: the LEA as an M-form organization*
Source: Levačić, 1993

which it will discriminate between schools on criteria of size, condition of the buildings and so on. Within the ceiling set by government the LEA decides which expenditures it will retain itself and not delegate. The LEA regulates the internal market by determining, in conjunction with central government, the number and types of schools and their admissions criteria.

In the second set of internal market relationships the LEA acts as seller to the schools. In terms of Figure 8.2 direct trading between the operating divisions (schools) and the functional departments replaces the hierarchical allocation of these services to schools by the LEA. LEA personnel instead of providing such services through a bureaucratic hierarchical linkage have to earn income by selling their services to schools, who will be free to buy alternative services from outside the LEA. The services now purchased by schools include buildings and ground maintenance, advisory and music instrument teachers, library and museum services, financial administration and legal advice.

The key process that drives the internal market is competition. As sellers of education services schools compete with others within the same LEA, as well as with any schools within their local market that are maintained by another LEA, by the DFE or CTC trust as well as with independent schools. As purchasers schools have a greater choice of supplier of services. However, one of the major features of a competitive market, competing by price, is not available to state schools.

MODEL 2: THE DES AS TOP-LEVEL MANAGER OF THE INTERNAL MARKET

The initial framework set up by the 1988 Reform Act implied that Model 1 was likely to be the dominant one. Subsequently, however, the Education (Schools) Act 1992 and the Education Act 1993, have further diminished the powers of the LEA. The former Act removed from LEAs the power and money to run their own inspectorates and so delivered a body blow to their monitoring function. Each school must now tender for an inspection every four years from a private inspectorate registered by the newly created Office for Educational Standards. Schools deemed at 'risk' after such an inspection will, if they fail to improve after a year, be put in the hands of an Educational Association which will either recommend the school for closure or oversee its improvement. Schools are still being given financial inducements to become grant maintained and such schools are to be funded by a new Schools Funding Agency. When between 10 and 75 per cent of an area's schools are grant maintained both the LEA and the Schools Funding Agency will have joint responsibility for planning educational provision and agreeing admissions arrangements. The legislation now provides for a potentially very high degree of central control of schools by the DFE and by the Treasury and the Department of the Environment through tight control of local authority finances. It would appear that a system is evolving of a high degree of central government control of the curriculum and of funding to reinforce it, in which schools compete for pupils (to the extent that surplus places remain) and are free to make their own financial and resourcing decisions. This model is aptly described as a franchise.

6.3 The rationale for internal markets as a control mechanism

The justification of public sector internal market arrangements on efficiency grounds is the claim that they incur lower transactions costs than hierarchical coordination but can be regulated to ensure that consumer access is maintained regardless of income. The advantages of the internal market depend on the extent to which it copes better with the bounded rationality, opportunism and asset specificity features of organizations highlighted in Williamson's (1975) markets and hierarchies approach (explained in Chapter 2). The fundamental issue for efficient organizational design is where the knowledge required for making particular decisions is best located within the organization. Centralization is an inefficient means of coordination when the knowledge required for effective decision making is not possessed by headquarters management due to bounded rationality and because opportunistic subordinates have insufficient incentives to generate and communicate the required knowledge up the hierarchical chain. One of the main arguments in favour of local management of schools is that the head, teachers, governors and parents are better placed to know what mix of resources is best suited to the educational needs of the school's pupils.

It is widely argued (see for example McGuinness, 1991) that organizations abandon the U-form in favour of the M-form as they become larger and operate in more complex and uncertain environments because the M-form structure copes better with problems of bounded rationality and opportunism. It does this by separating operational from strategic decision making. The former become the responsibility of the divisions leaving top level management to concentrate on strategic decision making. They can now do this more effectively because they are not subject to information overload and poor communication channels which impede hierarchical managerial control in the U-form organization. The opportunistic tendencies of middle managers are channelled to the fulfilment of organizational goals by setting them targets, monitoring outcomes and rewarding good performance. The internal market ensures that the divisions produce the kinds of goods and services which customers want and do so cost effectively.

The predominant advantage of centralization is that only headquarters can plan for the organization as a whole, given that it can obtain and process the required information. Top management can be motivated to pursue the organization's goals and allocate resources accordingly, whereas in a decentralized system the divisional managers will pursue the interests of their divisions — and then only if motivated to do so. For decentralization to be effective in realizing the organization's goals the objectives of the divisions have to be carefully specified and coordinated by top management.

Competition between schools is criticized on the grounds that it will be less effective than the previous system in fulfilling the goal of equality of provision (see for example Miliband, 1991). A further criticism is that LMS will be a less cost-effective way of making educational provision in a locality because it hampers the central planning function of the LEA (Tomlinson, 1988). This point is in essence one about asset specificity. Schools, both as buildings but even more so as viable communities, are highly specific to their purpose. It takes time to build up the staff and pupils for a new school and closing a school is costly in terms of the disruption to staff, pupils and parents. In order to function, a market has to be dynamic — some producers flourish and grow while others decline or cease to trade. As Williamson's analytical framework suggests, market coordination is more costly when there is asset specificity.

A further concern is that the monitoring and control function which headquarters management undertakes by measuring divisional managers' performance against quantitative targets cannot be effectively performed for decentralized public sector organizations. In the restructured school system the national curriculum and testing are an essential element of the monitoring and control function, but there is widespread disagreement on whether this can or should be done. For instance, Mintzberg (1979) considers the M-form unsuited to public service agencies like education authorities because of their inability to measure the achievement of their social goals and because the divisions (schools) are seldom divested (that is it is difficult to close schools). He concludes, therefore, that public service agencies which have adopted M-form have to remain uncontrolled, or exert control through regulation of work process or by setting up 'artificial' targets. The national curriculum is criticized by some on similar grounds, that it will lead to teaching to the 'test' rather than to a broad and relevant curriculum.

6.4 Regulation and the internal market

It is clear from models of the centralized organization and from discussion of empirical examples of such decentralization that the key to using decentralization as an effective way of improving organizational performance is to ensure that the middle managers, to whom decision-making responsibility is delegated, are motivated so as to act in ways which are consistent with the goals set for the organization by top management. At the heart of this problem is the opportunism of em-

ployees and the bounded rationality of the superordinates. The standard solution to the problems arising from opportunism in the context of
firms is for headquarters management to set middle management clear
and measurable targets, monitor these targets and evaluate and reward
middle managers accordingly. In a commercial setting these targets are
readily quantified in terms of profits, cost reduction, sales growth,
market share and so on.

But what in the education setting can replicate such a control system?
This problem has not been created by LMS: there was considerable concern under the previous system that educators were not sufficiently accountable for their work. The government is now putting in place two
quite different but related systems of accountability. One is hierarchical regulation in the form of the national curriculum, inspection to judge
the quality of its delivery in schools and quantitative measures derived from national testing. The other mode of accountability is the
market itself, relying on parental judgement to confirm through school
choice which are good schools and which are poor schools. As resources
follow the pupils, so good schools will flourish and poor schools either
improve or leave the market place. The role of the national curriculum
and published test results in the market model of accountability is to
inform consumer choice.

The third model of accountability is professionalism. This relies
upon the ethic of the professional acting in the best interests of his or
her clients. In the ideology of the teaching profession, this means always acting in the best interests of the child as determined by the
teachers. If the ultimate clients of the education system — those using
it and paying for it — can rely upon the professionalism of teachers to
deliver the kind of education they want, then professionalism removes
the problem of opportunism. It is clear that the government does not
trust in regulation by professional values. On one hand, the quality of
education is ultimately in the hands of teachers. The danger is that excessive reliance on hierarchical control reflecting values antithetical
to teachers may worsen teacher performance rather than improve it.
On the other hand, in a situation where professionals' values and practices are not approved by service users and tax payers, then the internal
market may well induce the providers either to pursue consumers' goals
or to persuade consumers to value the professionals' goals.

7   Summing up

As the discussion in the last paragraph shows, assessing the efficacy of
the internal market as a coordination mechanism is not just a technical
matter of judging the extent to which bounded rationality, opportunism
and asset specificity apply to a particular organizational setting. It
involves value judgements about the relative importance of different
organizational goals. If one thinks that the school system should be

more responsive to the whole range of individual demands for different kinds of provision within schools then one is much more inclined to favour the internal market for schools than if one considers that uniformity of provision is essential to promote social integration and social equality.

NOTE

* The Department of Education and Science (DES) became the Department for Education (DFE) in 1992. DES is used only in reference to the past.

References

Dean, C. (1992) 'Opting-out revolution proceeds at snail's pace', *Times Educational Supplement*, 6 November.

Great Britain (1985) *Better Schools*, Cmnd 9469, London, HMSO.

Graham, D. (1992) *A Lesson For Us All*, London, Routledge.

Haviland, J. (1988) *Take Care Mr Baker!*, London, Fourth Estate Ltd.

Hillgate Group (1986) *Whose Schools? A Radical Manifesto*, London, Hillgate Group.

Lawton, D. (1980) *The Politics of the School Curriculum*, London, Routledge & Kegan Paul.

Levačić, R. (1991) 'Markets and government: an overview', in Thompson et al. (eds) (1991).

Levačić, R. (1993) 'Local management of scbools as an organizational form: theory and application', forthcoming in *Journal of Education Policy*.

McGuinness, T. (1991) 'Markets and managerial hierarchies' in Thompson et al. (1991).

Miliband, D. (1991) *Markets, Politics and Education*, London, Institute for Public Policy Research.

Mintzberg, H. (1979) *The Structuring of Organizations: a Synthesis of the Research*, Englewood Cliffs, NJ, Prentice-Hall.

Ranson, S. (1980) 'Changing relations between centre and locality in education', *Local Government Studies*, vol.6, no.6, pp. 3–23.

Rhodes, R. (1991) 'Policy networks and sub-central government' in Thompson et al. (1991).

Taylor Committee (1977) *A New Partnership for Our Schools*, Department of Education and Science and Welsh Office.

Thomas, G. and Levačić, R. (1991) 'Centralizing in order to decentralize? DES scrutiny and approval of LMS schemes', *Journal of Education Policy*, vol. 6, no. 4. pp 401–16.

Thompson, G., Frances, J., Levačić, R. and Mitchell, J. (eds.) (1991) *Markets, Hierarchies and Networks: the Coordination of Social Life*, London, Sage.

Tomlinson, J. (1988) 'Curriculum and market: are they compatible?' in Haviland, J. (1988).

Williamson, O.E. (1975) *Markets and Hierarchies: Analysis and Antitrust Implications*, New York, Free Press.

CHAPTER 9:
RUNNING HOSPITALS

Christopher Pollitt

1 Introduction

Most people born since 1960 were born in a hospital. Unless current trends change substantially, most of us will die in a hospital. This enormous concentration of births and deaths in hospitals is new — in a relatively short space of historical time the hospital has become one of the most prominent institutions in our lives. 'In 1800 there were only 3,000 patients in hospital. Medical knowledge consisted of nurses' gossip, and sick men's fancies and the crude compilation of a blundering empiricism' (Abel-Smith, 1964). By 1987 there were more than seven million annual deaths and discharges from hospitals in England and Wales (Central Statistical Office, 1990, p.64).

The hospital is also one of the most costly of our public institutions, one of the most technologically advanced and one of the most complex in terms of the range of skills and occupational groups which are to be found working within it. Given their complexity, cost and salience it is not surprising that hospitals have frequently attracted the attention of politicians and policy makers. In the UK in the late 1980s and early 1990s political interventions have been particularly intense.

2 Scope

'Running hospitals' could have a number of different meanings, so it is worth spelling out here what will be covered and what will not. First, we shall be examining what goes on *inside individual hospitals* — how the different groups of staff are organized, who controls the money, who has the authority to decide particular issues, and so on.

In addition, however, we shall be looking at hospitals *collectively*, as a *connected* system. Does this system grow haphazardly, or according to market forces of some kind, or in accordance with a plan?

Although the modern hospital is a feature of all advanced industrial societies, in keeping with the overall focus of the book we shall be concentrating mainly on UK hospitals. What we say about these will not necessarily be applicable to the internal workings of hospitals in other countries, and certainly not to hospital *systems* in other countries. Indeed, the striking differences of arrangements abroad are a useful reminder of how artificial (and therefore in principle alterable) are our own organizational and political forms. For this reason some space will be devoted to a comparative analysis of hospital systems in the USA and Sweden.

3 NHS hospitals 1948–1989: hierarchies — and networks

Most of this chapter will concern the market-oriented reforms introduced by Mrs. Thatcher in her 1989 white paper, *Working for Patients* (WfP). However, to understand why that document marked such a sea-change in the environment of NHS hospitals we need to have some sense of what went before. In this section, therefore, an attempt will be made to provide a brief overview of the way in which hospitals were run from the inauguration of the NHS in 1948 through to 1989.

The 'nationalization' of the hospitals was perhaps the most radical element in the original design of the NHS. Whereas General Practitioners (GPs) were left as independent contractors both the old municipal and the 'voluntary' hospitals were absorbed into the new service as public hospitals, supervised by fourteen Regional Hospital Boards (RHBs). Hospital doctors became salaried employees of the state.

The story of 1948–1989 is, from one perspective, that of a series of modifications to this basic model, that is a collection of hospitals, great and small, each with its own management committee but supervised at a higher level by an appointed board or authority which, in turn, reported to the Ministry of Health (later the Department of Health and Social Security and then the Department of Health). Thus we can summarize the main modifications as follows (see Harrison, 1988, Chapter 2 for more detail):

1 1948–1989: Hospitals loosely supervised by the RHBs but mainly run by their own local Hospital Management Committees (HMCs). Little new hospital building. Treasury kept a fairly tight lid on NHS spending.

2 1962: The then Minister of Health announced a *Hospital plan for England and Wales*. This proposed a centrally coordinated building programme for ninety new hospitals, and a progressive standardization around the concept of a district general hospital with a full range of medical specialties. During implementation this plan turned out to take much longer than had been anticipated, and to cost much more (Owen, 1976).

3 1974: Major modification of the administrative structure of the NHS (DHSS, 1972). Henceforth there were to be, in effect, five tiers — individual hospitals, Districts, Area Health Authorities, Regional Health Authorities and the Department of Health and Social Security itself. The hope was that the various services of the NHS would henceforth be better coordinated within a framework of long-term plans (DHSS, 1976).

4 1982: One of the middle tiers (Area Health Authorities) was abol-

ished. This move represented a growing impatience with the cumbersomeness of the machinery created by the 1974 reform.

5 1983: The Conservative government announced that it was going to introduce a general manager into each unit, District and Region. Previously the mode had been one of governance by 'consensus teams' of administrators, consultants, nurses etc. (Schultz and Harrison, 1983). Now a single manager was to assume overall responsibility at each level (National Health Service Management Inquiry, 1983).

6 1983: A series of experiments with new budgeting systems was begun. These attempted to make groups of doctors and nurses more conscious of the costs of their activities and more active in seeking ways of improving the efficiency and effectiveness of expenditures. In 1986 some pilot schemes for a new system called Resource Management (RM) were begun.

Yet this progressive refinement of a set of administrative hierarchies was by no means the whole story. Throughout the various changes and schemes of 1948–1989 the medical profession retained a great deal of autonomy from administrative or managerial control. Hospital consultants were a particularly powerful and independent group. They tended to be organized not in a formal hierarchy (though they had representatives in such hierarchies) but rather as a series of local professional networks.

The evidence of much of the research of the 1970s and 1980s was that consultant networks often proved extremely resistant to the authority of managers/administrators (Harrison et al., 1992). This was an important feature of the running of the hospital system, not least because it left consultants with the power effectively to commit large proportions of hospitals' resources in ways which did not necessarily accord with the longer term plans being developed by the administrative hierarchies (Elcock and Haywood, 1980). As demands on the hospital service grew (through demographic changes and technological progress) this freedom to commit scarce resources became more and more problematic (Kings Fund Institute, 1988). The new budgeting systems referred to above (especially RM) were in part attempts to persuade consultants to adopt a more 'managerial' attitude to the resource consequences of their clinical decisions.

4 Working for patients

The publication of the Conservative government's white paper *Working for Patients* in January 1989 marked a radical change of direction for the running of NHS hospitals. Previously, hierarchically orchestrated planning had been supposed to deliver an equitably distributed, effective and efficient set of public hospitals within which consultants were left to exercise their clinical autonomy. Now competition for patients and funds was to supply a new dynamic. Local management would be encouraged to 'get on with the task of managing, while remaining accountable to the centre for its delivery of services' (Cmd. 555, 1989, p.12). The term popularly applied to describe this proposed set of arrangements was a 'provider market'.

The principal contents of the white paper affecting the running of hospitals are shown in Table 9.1.

These changes will produce a flow of funds through the NHS in the pattern shown in Figure 9.1.

Look at the left hand side of Figure 9.1. There you can see that the DoH allocates funds to the Regional Health Authorities (RHAs) and

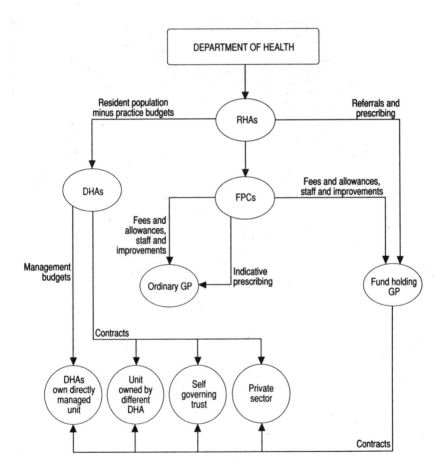

Figure 9.1   *The dynamics of British health policy*

Source: Harrison, S., Hunter, D.J. and Pollitt, C., 1990, Fig.A2., p. 173

Table 9.1 Key points for the hospital service in the 1989 white paper
Working for Patients

1	There is to be a clear organizational separation between the roles of providing hospital services (the job of the hospitals themselves) and purchasing hospital services for the population of a defined area (the job of the District Health Authority and of certain GPs — see point 4 below).
2	A DHA in its purchasing role, will contract for the services it estimates its local population will need with whichever hospital offers the most attractively priced bid, subject to also meeting quality standards. This hospital will not necessarily be located in that particular district.
3	Thus an internal provider market will be created, with hospitals competing for the revenue they will obtain through contracts with DHAs (and GPs — see point 4).
4	Some of the larger GP practices may apply for special practice budgets. With these they, too, may purchase hospital services for the patients on their list. Thus some GPs, as well as DHAs, will be looking for the best contract.
5	DHAs will be able to purchase services from private, as well as NHS hospitals. Further expansion of private provision will be encouraged by tax relief for health insurance premiums for the over 60s.
6	NHS hospitals may apply to the DoH (the DHSS was renamed Department of Health in 1989) to opt out of DHA control and become self-governing trusts. 'The government proposes to give NHS hospital trusts a range of powers and freedoms which are not, and will not, be available to health authorities generally. Greater freedom will stimulate greater enterprise and commitment...'
7	A process of medical audit will be introduced in every DHA to ensure that doctors systematically monitor the quality of their work. Also consultants will be given more precise job descriptions than has hitherto been common.
8	At the centre a new NHS Management Executive will be created, reporting to an NHS Policy Board chaired by the Secretary of State. The Board 'will determine the strategy, objectives and finances of the NHS in the light of government policy'. The Executive 'will deal with all operational matters within the strategy and objectives set by the Policy Board' (Cmnd. 555, 1989, p.13).
9	RHAs and DHAs will be retained but slimmed down in numbers to make them more businesslike. Local authorities will lose their former right to appoint some DHA members.
10	The Resource Management Initiative (RMI) will be extended from its original 6 pilot sites to a total of 260 acute hospitals by 1992. This will give doctors and managers much better information about patient diagnoses, treatments and costs.

they then sub-allocate to each District Health Authority (DHA) depending on the resident population of that district (there is a subtraction of any GP practice budget money in the district which then goes direct to those GPs for their own use in respect of the hospital care needed by patients on their lists). The DHA then acts as purchaser of services for its population, choosing between the 'best deals' offered by its own hospitals, hospitals sited in other DHAs, self-governing trust hospitals (point 6 in Table 9.1 above) or private sector facilities.

Now look at the right hand side of the diagram. The 'Fund holding GPs' are those with practice budgets (point 4 in Table 9.1) — hence the long arrow down the right hand side and across the bottom to the four different types of hospital, showing that funds flow from these GPs to the hospitals. The other 'Ordinary GPs' are financed by the Family Practitioner Committees (FPCs), subsequently retitled Family Health Service Authorities (FHSAs).

At the outset WfP proved remarkably unpopular. The DoH spent millions of pounds promoting it with videos and 'roadshows' and booklets to households, but successive public opinion polls showed that large majorities of the general public disliked the 'reforms'. The British Medical Association (BMA) financed a major public campaign criticizing the proposals, including the distribution of leaflets in doctors surgeries. The then Secretary of State for Health, Kenneth Clarke, accused the BMA of inaccuracies and self-interest while many voices accused the government of having produced a scheme which would fragment the NHS and encourage greater use of the private sector providers of health care.

Acrimonious struggles, some of them public, broke out at many of the hospitals which were possible candidates for self-governing trust status. Wider policy debates were also vigorous. There is no room here to examine all of these, so we will concentrate on four issues of especial salience for our theme: consumer choice, the role of the private sector, efficiency and quality.

5 Consumer choice

'Consumers' (patients and potential patients — that is nearly all of us) had figured little in the running of NHS hospitals since 1948. With WfP, however, we encounter the language of the market. One of the big advantages of markets — at least according to politicians of the 'new right'— is that unlike bureaucratic hierarchies they offer *consumer choice*. Mrs Thatcher wrote in the foreword to WfP that 'We aim to extend patient choice, to delegate responsibility to where the services are provided and to secure the best value for money'.

One way into the issue of patient choice is to look at the information likely to be available to users of the NHS. In markets the price system can be the basis for a strong 'horizontal' exchange of information between producers and consumers. How might this work in the case of the WfP internal market? The white paper and its supporting documents leave this fairly vague, but it does not appear that most patients, most of the time, will have that much information on which to base any choices of, say, which hospitals to go to. Purchasers (that is DHAs and fund-holding GPs) will receive cost (and sometimes quality) information from providers (hospitals). It is hard to imagine that GPs would sit down with patients and go through all this information (even if they understood it all and had it at their fingertips). More likely they would say 'I think St. Lukes is the best hospital for you Mrs Jenkins.' Thus patient choice in hospital care is most unlikely to resemble the classic shopper choosing between different products of known price and quality. Instead, the patient will be represented by DHAs or GPs in a set of contract negotiations to which patients will have no direct access. As one early analysis put it: 'The proposals show no commitment to mechanisms for developing and delivering services to individuals and groups in ways which incorporate their own perceptions of their needs' (Harrison et al., 1989, p.15). The government has claimed that, in the provider market, 'the money will follow the patient'. Thus far it seems more a case of the patient following the money. Most of the early contracts (more than 90 per cent by value) were 'block' contracts by which DHAs in effect 'booked' blocks of beds in particular hospitals. Surveys indicated that purchasing authorities seldom seek lay opinion, or give it much weight in these matters.

6   The role of the private sector

Under both Labour and Conservative governments the interface between the NHS and the private sector of health care has from time to time generated controversy. WfP was no exception, with some commentators on the left suggesting that it was a thinly-disguised strategy for promoting the private sector and gradually dismembering the NHS.

Certainly the Conservative government was well disposed to private medical care and had taken a number of steps throughout the 1980s to encourage its growth. The tax concession in WfP (see Table 9.1, point 5) was merely the latest in a series of supportive measures. By 1988 about 9 per cent of the population were covered by some form of private health insurance — twice as many as a decade earlier. Around 6 per cent of acute hospital beds were in private hospitals, with an increasing tendency for these hospitals to be grouped together in commercial chains. Some of these were owned by US companies such as American Medical International (AMI) and Humana. More significantly, perhaps, the percentage of NHS consultant income which derived from private practice rose from 13 per cent in 1975 to 31 per cent in 1990 (Norwich Union Healthcare, 1992).

It is important to remember that the private sector is, and always had been, composed of a wide variety of types of organization. There are nursing homes, hospices and chiropodists as well as acute hospitals. There is a mixture of non-profit and commercial for-profit institutions, some large, some small, some local, some international. During the 1980s two types in particular expanded — nursing homes and for-profit acute hospitals. It is the latter which are the focus for the strongest political disputes. Critics claim that they undermine the equitable methods of the NHS (similar cases to be treated similarly) by providing a privileged minority with a way of queue-dodging and enjoying a higher class of amenities than are available in many NHS hospitals. Against this it is argued that these hospitals actually relieve pressure on an overburdened NHS, and that they draw additional (private) finance into health care which the government would not otherwise provide. It is also pointed out that, increasingly, the NHS is itself purchasing treatment for its patients from private facilities and that local partnership and contractual deals between health providers were proliferating before WfP. The critics, however, are unimpressed. They argue that many of these deals would be unnecessary if the NHS were properly funded in the first place. They also point to the way in which aggressively commercial hospitals in the major population centres push up salary rates and attract away scarce NHS staff who have been trained at the taxpayer's expense.

We cannot hope to resolve this (strongly ideological) debate here. There are, however, two general observations which may be worth making. First, the internal market foreseen by WfP will involve NHS providers competing for NHS contracts with private providers, including private profit-oriented providers. This *may* result in NHS hospitals trying, for better or for worse, to copy the practices of commercial hospitals. Second, in the past the NHS has been *so* dominant in the provision of acute hospital care that it was possible to describe the UK system with hardly a mention of the private sector, this is now beginning to change. It would seem that more people are at least partly 'exiting' the NHS than before ('partly' because many of them will still be using the NHS for part of their health care — especially primary care). The question is raised, therefore, of how much further that process can go before either the NHS is forced to change its ways or it becomes a 'second class service' dealing mainly with 'unprofitable' conditions and with those who cannot afford private insurance — not the 'universal' service envisaged by its creators?

7 Efficiency

Efficiency is a third issue around which argument has raged. The supporters of WfP insist that an internal market will promote productive efficiency. The white paper itself pointed to evidence that efficiency varied enormously from one hospital to another. 'In 1986–7 the average cost of treating acute hospital in-patients varied by as much as 50 per cent between different health authorities, even after allowing for the complexity and mix of cases treated' (Cmnd. 555, 1989, p.3). Under the new system, it is suggested, the costlier hospitals will have to reform themselves or they will not be able to compete for contracts.

This is a powerful argument but only if one accepts at least three assumptions which lie unspoken behind it. These are:

1   Higher average costs are a good indicator of inefficiency, not of some other factor, for example a higher quality service or unavoidably higher local costs.

2   That the cost data on which judgements like this are made is accurate and reliable.

3   That the internal market will result in relatively easy 'exit' of patients from high cost, inefficient hospitals to low cost, efficient ones. If such transfers cannot for some reason take place then the pressure on high cost institutions to reform will disappear.

The critics of WfP attack each of these assumptions.

With respect to the first one, they point out that the NHS has never produced reliable information about the relative quality of the clinical services being provided in one place compared with another. Most of the judgements that 'this is a good hospital' are impressionistic and many of them are based on the *amenity* aspects of hospitals (for example furnishings and decoration, food) or on *status* (the presence of a famous surgeon) rather than on the actual effectiveness of the medical care. Therefore in most cases no one knows whether or not higher costs actually reflect superior effectiveness or higher *medical* quality. Therefore forcing costs down (especially in a health service which is already pretty cheap overall by international standards) may have negative, but hidden consequences for effectiveness and quality. Such changes would not become visible to the public unless and until two things happened: first, the medical profession became much more open than it has ever been about the quality of its own practice and, second, that reliable and intelligible ways of measuring quality were developed and installed in all hospitals. WfP gives little sign that either of these developments sit high on the government's agenda.

The second assumption is also said to be unrealistic. The NHS has long been notorious for the poor quality of its management information, including financial information. This has been somewhat remedied by the managerial reforms of the 1980s but the slow progress with Management Budgeting and resource management schemes indicates that there is still a long way to go (Pollitt et al. 1988; Packwood et al. 1991).

The third assumption — about efficiency — has probably attracted the most criticism. Both doctors and Community Health Councils (CHCs) have voiced distaste for the idea that patients would be obliged to move around the country to find the cheapest hospital for a particular service. Such moves would make it difficult and expensive for friends and relatives to visit and could therefore cut the patient off from their local support networks. Of course, these extra costs would, by and large, fall on the individuals concerned. They would not appear as costs to the purchasing DHA or fund holding GP — to them they would be 'externalities'.

It is too early to be sure what actual gains in efficiency may be resulting from the WfP provider market. After the first year of contracts there seemed no evidence of any widespread general improvement (Ovretveit, 1992, p.10) but this was also a period in which ministers were insisting on a cautious, 'steady state' approach.

8 Quality

If efficiency is already a fiercely contested issue quality seems well on its way to becoming another. The basic problem is that until now there have been no reliable measures of the comparative quality or effectiveness of most of the medical services offered by NHS hospitals (Harrison et al., 1990, Chapter 5). This is an area which has remained shrouded in professional mystery. This is an unsatisfactory situation anyway, but it becomes doubly so when price competition is unleashed.

The government's response to this problem was to decree that all health authorities should set up arrangements for medical audit (Table 9.1, point 7) and that quality assurances should be written into purchaser/provider contracts. This would certainly represent an improvement on the depth of quality and effectiveness information which characterized the first forty years of the NHS. However, it is not yet clear how reliable and comparable much of this information will be, or how much of it will actually reach consumers. Medical audit has been set up largely as an intra-professional activity in which doctors will discuss each other's activities protected by elaborate confidentiality (Pollitt, 1993). There is no guarantee that similar methods will be used in different locations, so the resulting data is frequently not comparable from one provider to another. Managers may get just a brief doctor-written summary of the proceedings, and final consumers, CHCs etc. may get little or no information. References to quality in contracts may be no more than a general requirement that the provider shall maintain a medical audit system. These are delicate matters for both the profession and for government. It is too early to say exactly how medical audit will develop, and what information it may yield for the wider public.

Medical audit is, however, far from being the only quality initiative underway in the post-WfP NHS. Indeed, most of the rhetoric around 'quality' actually refers to non-medical aspects of services — to the pleasantness of receptionists, the flexibility of visiting hours, the availability of information leaflets, the efficiency of appointments systems, the attractiveness of hospital food, the use of 'patient satisfaction' questionnaires and so on. Since WfP there has been a huge amount of such activity, some of it apparently rather successful and some fairly poorly thought-through and superficial (Centre for the Evaluation of Public Policy and Practice, 1991; Dalley and Carr-Hill, 1991). It is noticeable that many of these non-medical quality initiatives are manager-driven and that doctor participation is frequently muted. In other words here is another example of the ability of doctors

to keep themselves separate and largely to avoid or deflect the growing power of managers in a way that nurses and the other professions
allied to medicine cannot.

9   Comparisons: hospital care in the USA

The American hospital system hardly deserves the term 'system'.
Rather it is a huge hodge-podge of institutions of widely different
types. It is hard for those of us brought up within an NHS-dominated
health care sector to understand the almost total lack of any central
planning authority, the absence of any formal hierarchy (even locally)
and the prevalent ideological assumption that health care is an essentially private matter for the individual to arrange, not a right of citizenship or a publicly-provided service. The USA — uniquely among
advanced western economies — has never developed either a national
health service or even (as many Europeans countries have) a system for
national health insurance.

Yet despite these huge differences with the UK system there are
some interesting points of comparison. For our purposes in this chapter
we will concentrate on two of them: first, how the dynamics of competition work in the market place for hospital services and, second, the relationships between the medical profession, managers and consumers.

American hospitals are, as has already been said, of a number of different types. There are some *local government-run* and *municipal* hospitals. There are many so-called 'non-profit' hospitals, in some ways not
unlike the old voluntary hospitals in Britain. These have charitable
status which means that when they make financial surpluses (as they
frequently do) these are supposed to be channelled back into the hospital, not siphoned off to shareholders as profits. Finally there are *'for-
profits'* hospitals run as businesses with the aim of yielding a level of
profit that will satisfy investors. After Saltman and von Otter (1992)
we may term this a *mixed market*, since it contains both publicly — and
privately — capitalized institutions competing one with another

During the 1970s and 1980s two major trends have been apparent, both
representing responses by providers to the dynamics of an increasingly
competitive market. First, they clustered together in chains and groups
of institutions to give themselves more market leverage and control.
Thus an organization which controlled, say, thirty hospitals instead of
one could make economies in its costs by bulk purchasing of medical supplies and equipment and other services. Such a chain could also operate
sophisticated central accounting and management control systems and
could more easily move investment to those parts of the country (or segments of the market) where demand was expanding. Most of the largest
chains were for-profit but non-profits also began to cluster together for
strength. In 1987 Hospital Corporation of America (for-profit) ran the
largest chain, with 471 hospitals.

This kind of market grouping is termed 'horizontal integration' — putting together a set of basically similar institutions. Health care organizations also practised 'vertical integration' — merging with or taking over institutions operating at other points in the spectrum of health-care services. Thus a hospital group might take over some nursing homes and some pharmaceutical laboratories. Then the hospital could control the costs of its laboratory services and would also have 'tied' nursing homes into which patients could be discharged when they were no longer sick enough to warrant occupancy of an expensive hospital bed.

The second major trend was 'institutional isomorphism'. This means that non-profit hospitals 'conformed, homogenized, and adjusted their roles to the model of for-profit hospitals, because of the specific organizational and financial advantages these hospitals appeared to offer'. In other words, the non-profits behaved more and more like profit-oriented businesses. It sounds strange to the ears of NHS users to hear that the President of Sisters of Charity Health Care Systems, Sister Celestial Koebel, should be describing 1986 as a year to 'negotiate for expansion and position for growth' (Stevens, 1989, pp. 335–6).

This may be an important indicator for the long-term future of the post-WfP hospital system in the UK. The lesson appears to be that in a market where non-profit hospitals have to compete directly with for-profit hospitals the former may be obliged more and more to copy the behaviour of the latter. Of course the starting position is very different in the UK. The private, for-profit hospitals represent a much smaller share of the total hospital service than in the USA. The NHS is still dominant. Yet, as noted above, the 1980s did witness a growth in the private sector, together with a government-backed increase in the number of NHS/private 'joint ventures'. These trends could accelerate once the provider market gets underway and purchasers are more easily able to turn to private as well as NHS hospitals for services.

Returning to the USA, some further features of the last fifteen or so years are worth mentioning. Within hospitals (of all kinds) two functions showed particular development — financial management and marketing. An increase in competition makes both these aspects of the organization especially important. Financial managers keep tight control of costs and revenues. Marketing experts plan the ways in which the hospital can show its most appealing image to potential purchasers of hospital care. The marketing managers look for some feature which distinguishes their hospital from competitor hospitals, and then concentrate on that. It could be low cost, or accessibility, or high quality, or some special piece of new equipment, or a new service no one else provides yet, or some combination of these things. For example, some hospitals offered VIP suites, one of which 'reportedly included a mauve carpet and two-cushion couch, which can be made into a bed for a guest; luxurious towels; two private-line telephones; a small refrigerator

stocked with soft drinks; fruit juices and beer and wine (if the doctor
approves); and a VCR' (Stevens, 1989, p. 336).

Although national ownership, planning and control of the system has
never been attempted it would be a mistake to conclude that in the USA
the state has had little to do with the market for hospital services.
On the contrary it has played an active and, since the mid-1960s, increasingly expensive role. For it has fallen to the state to address the
problem of those millions of citizens who cannot afford decent care. Unsurprisingly, the elderly and the poor figure prominently in this category, and a high proportion of the poor are single women and/or come
from the ethnic minority groups.

Despite occasional Presidential support the many national health
insurance bills which have been introduced into Congress have all come
to grief. Government has therefore tackled the access problem by developing special programmes for those groups who are most conspicu-
ously in need. The two biggest are Medicare, for the elderly, and Medicaid, for the poor. Following their introduction by President Johnston's
democratic administration in the mid-1960s the cost and complexity of
these programmes soared. By the end of the 1980s Medicare, a feder-
ally-financed insurance-based programme, was providing health-care
coverage for more than 32 million people at a cost of $58 billion for hos-
pital services and $37 billion for physician and outpatient services.
The Medicaid programme was differently financed: here the federal
government made grants to the States and the States were obliged to
provide matching grants themselves. The programme covered about 24
million low income persons and cost the federal authorities $35 billion.
Despite these huge expenditures, neither programme offers full coverage of all health-care services that may be medically prescribed, and
neither covers the whole of the target population. Medicaid is particularly inadequate in this respect — complex eligibility rules mean that
roughly half the people below the official poverty line do not qualify
for Medicaid.

Since the early 1970s, successive administrations have tried to control
the burgeoning costs of these two programmes, but with only limited
success. A major watershed was crossed in 1983 when the government
changed the basis of its Medicare payments to hospitals. Previously
the hospital billed the programme for its customary charges, and the
Medicare paying organizations paid. From 1983, however, Medicare
would only pay the national or regional *average* of what a particular
procedure (for example a coronary artery by-pass, an appendectomy)
costs, not what the hospital said it actually cost. This meant that hospitals which charged higher than average prices could lose money and
that those with lower than average prices could make profits. One effect of this new system (something similar to which is also being used
by many private purchasers of care such as big corporations buying
health care for their staff) is to accentuate the importance of financial

management within hospitals. Hospitals now need complex data systems to tell them how the precise balance between costs and revenues is changing for each of hundreds of different conditions and procedures. They also need to police doctors very closely, because doctors who take longer than average to deal with their patients, or who use more drugs or laboratory tests, may be losing money for the hospital.

What part do patients play in the running of hospitals? A few, as we have seen, can choose luxurious VIP suites. Others (about 12–15 per cent of the population on most estimates) have no insurance at all, and either pay for care out of their own pockets or go without it. The 'competitive strategy has ... failed to stem the tide of rising health expenditures, and its effect on the availability of medical care for the uninsured and underinsured can only be described as disastrous' (Marmor et al., 1990, p. 177). Many Americans certainly have 'choice', in the sense that they can choose (amid a barrage of marketing by mail, television and publications) an insurance policy. Many (not all of these policies) will then allow them to choose a doctor and a hospital. Like their British counterparts, however, they will usually have little or no reliable quality information on which to base these choices. But as for the larger *policy* choices:

> In a decade devoted to competition and free enterprise, the consumer of health services, the patient, has been almost invisible in the policy-making process. The average patient has no direct, controlling stake in the economic and political process that determines health policy in the United States...
>
> Meanwhile, the overriding importance of financial incentives in hospitals has centralized and concentrated power over money in agencies extrinsic to both hospitals and patients. These include major employers, insurers, and specialists in 'managed care', whose role it is to identify potentially high-cost patients, such as a patient with AIDS, and organize a program designed for efficient utilization of resources. Individuals are being told, in effect, that doctors, as entrepreneurs, and hospitals, as businesses, are no longer to be trusted as agents and advocates for the consumer; but that the large payers are to be trusted, even though their goals are overtly the goals of management efficiency.
>
> (Stevens, 1989, pp. 348–9)

Where do doctors stand in all this? One major casualty of the market has been clinical autonomy. This is not to say that doctors have entirely lost their monopoly over diagnosis and prescription of treatment. Nor that they have ceased to be powerful figures in the hospital world. And it is certainly not to suggest that they are poorly paid: on the contrary, US doctors on average earn a much higher multiple of the national average wage than do British doctors, and many in high status posts draw lavish salaries and benefits packages.

Yet despite high incomes (one of the rewards of the market, at least for the successful) and continuing dominance over some kinds of decisions, the scope and degree of clinical autonomy for the majority of US doctors practising in hospitals are less than for their NHS counterparts. (Schneller and Kirkman-Liff, 1988, pp. 600–2; Harrison and Schultz, 1989). More of their decisions are checked or subject to 'second opinions', even if these second opinions are from other doctors. The following are some of the ways in which US doctor behaviour has been increasingly controlled over the last decade or more:

- Programmes are run under which nurses or other doctors screen and approve admissions to hospital. If an admission seems 'inappropriate' according to that hospital's guidelines the admitting doctor will be asked to reconsider.

- The patient's length of stay is monitored. If a patient is in hospital for longer than is statistically usual for his or her condition the doctor may be asked why and pressed to consider an early discharge.

- Retrospective peer review (that is consideration by other doctors) of medical charts for selected patients. This is similar to medical audit. It is done to check the quality of the doctor's clinical decisions — have all the appropriate tests been run, the correct drugs selected etc.? Peer review can be 'internal' (carried out by known colleagues within the same hospital) or 'external'. The Medicare programme has set up an elaborate system of external peer review organizations which monitor samples of cases from all hospitals serving Medicare patients. (By contrast post-WfP medical audit will be overwhelmingly 'internal'.) These 'Professional Review Organizations' (PROs) can deny the hospital payment where inappropriate care has been rendered, or even apply to Washington to have a particular doctor or hospital disbarred from taking Medicare patients in future. PROs used to be primarily concerned with identifying wasteful, high cost medicine, but since the late 1980s they have come to focus more and more on actual medical quality of the service provided (Pollitt, 1993).

- Mandatory second opinions are obtained from other doctors when certain kinds of surgery are recommended by the patient's first doctor.

The crucial point is that the endless rise in costs has finally obliged organized purchasers (big employers; the federal and state governments in the case of Medicare and Medicaid) to tackle medical autonomy head on. It is the cost consequences of medical autonomy which, in an open-ended market, have forced it onto the agenda. One could argue that this collision has come sooner in the US than in the NHS because, unlike the British Treasury in the case of the NHS, the US government lacks the power to control the total size of the medical markets. The post-WfP 'provider market' will still be 'capped' in the sense that the total NHS budget will be fixed annually by central government. Whereas the total spent on health care runs at around 6 per cent of the GNP in the UK it has risen to over 11 per cent in the USA. Because there is no overall cash limit or cash plan, government has to attack costs in detail and at a more local level. Furthermore, once purchasers begin to put real pressure on the price of hospital services, the providers, anxious to maintain their profit margins, begin to increase their own internal controls over what doctors can and cannot do. Hospitals no longer want to hire the cost-careless doctor: nowadays it is becoming difficult to pass on these higher costs in the form of higher prices to purchasers. This may be a general indicator for the post-WfP NHS: in the long run it may lead to closer control of medical activities, and to the release — to managers at least — of much more information on efficiency and, eventually, effectiveness.

10 Comparisons: hospital care in Sweden

Sweden has for long had a publicly operated and financed national health service. Although broad policy is made at the national level detailed policy is made, and most hospitals are actually run, by county councils (*landsting*). Since the early 1970s various policies have been introduced to emphasize primary care — and somewhat de-emphasize hospital care — within the health care system as a whole. Nevertheless hospitals continued to expand, draw in more staff and consume more resources. Over 60 per cent of health-care expenditures are financed by a direct personal taxation, raised by the county councils. This tax represented 4.5 per cent of personal income in 1960 but this proportion had grown to 13.5 per cent in 1985 (Saltman, 1988).

During the late 1980s Sweden began to experiment with a number of market-like mechanisms in what had previously been an elaborately, consensually-planned hierarchical system (Saltman and von Otter, 1992). We will confine our attention to just one of these, a hew set of arrangements for maternity services at Stockholm County. Since 1987 expectant mothers have been able to choose which maternity clinic to deliver their babies in. The clinics which attract more mothers then receive additional funding from the county (approximately equal to the marginal cost of a normal delivery) for each woman who chooses them. Apparently this has led to a noticeable redistribution of funds between the clinics and to 'losing' clinics modifying their procedures and practices in order to try and make themselves more attractive to expectant mothers.

Saltman and von Otter term this kind of arrangement *public competition* because only publicly capitalized units, not commercial ones, compete. It stands in contrast to both the US and the WfP model, which are *mixed markets* (Saltman and von Otter, 1989; 1992). They say that the Swedish public competition model has the following distinguishing characteristics:

- The market is limited to publicly-owned and capitalized institutions (at least, this was true of the maternity experiment, though not of some of the other Swedish experiments).

- The patient chooses the physician and the hospital. In the WfP system the patient chooses his or her GP, but thereafter most of the choosing is done by the doctor. Thus the Swedish market is *consumer led*, whereas the WfP market is *agent-led*.

- Institutional budgets, instead of being fixed for a year at a time, are continuously flexed in proportion to the volume of patients attracted and the quality of care delivered. Saltman and von Otter concede that a 'quality adjustment' is not yet a working component of the Stockholm scheme, and that quality measurement problems remain. Nevertheless, in the case of the maternity clinics it would not be that difficult to supply expectant mothers with certain data such as maternal and perinatal mortality rates, infection rates and various other indicators of effectiveness.

Of these three features the first two offer the greatest contrast with the WfP model. The second — direct choice of hospital by patients (albeit usually guided by their primary care doctors) is not currently part of the UK government's plans. It could conceivably be added to a WfP-type system at a later date. However, the first feature — the limiting of the market to public institutions — may be equally significant. This is designed to produce a different market *structure* from a 'mixed market'. In particular it is intended to preclude the kind of 'drift' we saw in the American example where public and non-profit hospitals felt themselves obliged, during the 1980s, increasingly to ape the aggressive marketing and service specialization strategies pursued by the for-profit private institutions. Whether the WfP arrangements will ever develop in this same direction is open to debate. In the UK, unlike the US, the public hospitals are dominant. Also, to date, ministers have tried to regulate the market quite closely, and to dampen some of the more divisive features of competition. It is impossible to forecast how long this policy stance will be maintained.

11   The medical profession and market reforms

It is not surprising that the BMA decided to campaign against the WfP reforms. Not only did these proposals, in their view, 'destroy the comprehensive nature of the service' they also threatened the roots of medical autonomy. At the time of writing, it appears that the BMA has lost the battle at national level, but that the test of the defensive power of local medical networks is still continuing. What follows is therefore speculative, though closely based on the analysis of medical power introduced earlier in the chapter.

Why do we say that the battle at national level has been lost? Because the government has forged ahead with its plans without making any major concessions. Contracts have been drawn up, medical audit committees set up, several waves of NHS trust proposals have come forward and been approved, and a new contract of employment has been imposed on GPs.

But the profession's greatest defensive strength lies in its local networks, webs of autonomy that may reshape or stall a policy even if at national level the BMA or the royal colleges have decided that further resistance to government is fruitless.

Why did WfP threaten the roots of medical autonomy? First, unlike the introduction of general management in 1983 or the restructuring of 1974 WfP actually confers on managers new instruments for influencing or even controlling doctors' behaviour. To begin with the whole internal market revolves around contracts. Contracts must specify, at minimum, the type, quantity and cost of the medical work that is being purchased/provided. This is new: it has made the quantity and cost of the services provided by doctors progressively more *visible* (at least to managers) than before. It will set bench marks of what is expected and thus open up possibilities for controlling work levels in ways that were the exception rather than the rule in the pre-WfP NHS. This contracting process will be largely in the hands of managers (though they will obviously be wise to listen to medical advice).

Second, the government had made it clear that management needs to have some access to the information on quality which is coming out of the medical audit process, even if this is only in highly aggregate form. Again, this gives managers a window, which over time they may be able to enlarge, onto an area (the effectiveness and quality of medical work) which was previously usually concealed from them.

Third (Table 9.1, point 7), consultants have been given more precise job descriptions than ever before. Again, this is part of the process by which managers will now be able more explicitly to define what individual doctors are expected to do — and to monitor their compliance.

This is not to argue that medical autonomy will be reduced to nothing. We are describing a change of degree, a change by which a profession which has enjoyed very great work autonomy may now lose some of that autonomy, though remaining highly influential and privileged. Managers will still be in no position to second guess or interfere with a doctor's decisions to admit individual patients, diagnose this or that condition or select a course of therapy. They would not wish to take on such a responsibility, for which they are not in any way trained. What shrewd managers may be able to do, however, is to monitor the general pattern of a doctor's decisions, and to raise issues with the doctor when that pattern looks likely to lead to a job description or a contract not being fulfilled. And if the internal market is working the manager will be able to point out to the medical staff, both individually and collectively, that failure to meet expectations may now, through the contract system, lead directly to a loss in revenue for the hospital. The kind of information generated by Resource Management schemes (Table 9.1, point 10) will be central to this kind of monitoring. This will put most managers in a stronger position, both in terms of information and sanctions, than they have been in the past.

1 2   Markets and networks

In this final section we will attempt to summarize and tabulate the main arguments and counter arguments we have encountered concerning the use of market mechanisms to determine the provision of health care services. Table 9.2 (see pages 207–10) sets out these arguments, itemizing the main alleged advantages in the left-hand column and then listing the objections and counter objections in the remaining three columns.

In conclusion it may be said that after two years of operation it is still far from clear what the behavioural characteristics of the new WfP provider market will eventually turn out to be. Thus far it has been heavily regulated, and presumably this has muted some of the more troubling features of markets (for example, the segmentation of different classes of consumer). Even here, however, there have been occasional signs of competitive divisiveness, such as fund-holding GPs purchasing quicker service for their patients than is routinely available through the local DHA (see for example Andersen, 1992). In future it may be that current policies continue, that ministers and their agents head off glaring new inequities, restrain monopolistic and oligopolistic providers from exploiting their market strength and find ways of cushioning against the sudden collapse of provider institutions which are badly managed or which occupy disadvantageous market 'niches'. But if the market is to have all its teeth drawn in this way, will it still be able to act as the great engine of efficiency which its advocates envisage?

Alternatively, ministers may be persuaded that, with the 1992 general election won, it will be safe to 'take the brakes off' and see what changes less fettered competition will bring. At the time of writing (early 1993) this seems the less likely option, but so long as the basic market mechanism is in place it will remain a possibility in a way that it was not prior to the fundamental changes of 1989.

Table 9.2 Public service markets: some potential advantages and disadvantages

Advantages	Qualification/ objections	Response	Counter response
(1) Increases incentive to be *efficient*, because lowest-cost producers can increase their market shares (of patients,students, etc).	(1a) Efficiency gains will be at their maximum only if the market is highly competitive. Oligopolistic or monopolistic situations may yield no efficiency gains.	The government can regulate markets so as to detect and eliminate monopoly and oligopoly.	Can government actually do this? How, without wasteful duplication, can it avoid many local monopolies? And won't the *weight* of regulation needed cancel out the efficiency gains?
	(1b) If providers/ suppliers are privately capitalized and for profit they will seek to extract *profits*, unlike publicly capitalized or voluntary/non-profit providers. Thus the price of the service could be unnecessarily high, especially if competition is weak.	Whether profit-making *will* out-weigh efficiency gains is an empirical question, not a foregone conclusion. In some cases the efficiency gains seem to have been very substantial (e.g. some contracting out). Also, services can be regulated to prevent excess profit taking.	Yes, it is an empirical question, so it can go either way! As for monitoring for excess profits, how successful have governments been in trying to do this in the private sector? And how complex/expensive will such regulation have to become? So why not stick to public competition only, and avoid mixed markets?
	(1c) If market competition is intense there are likely to be frequent 'winners' and 'losers' among providers. If the latter 'go to the wall' continuity and security of supply will be lost. This is especially damaging in services where individual contact over time is important, e.g. education, residential care, community services.	The government can create a 'safety net' to prevent the total collapse of any particular provider. Provider units which are doing badly can be restructured and restaffed. Security and continuity can thus be assured.	How much will such a safety net cost? How far will the knowledge that it exists sap the drive for efficiency? Won't creating the ability to predict the failure of individual units (so as to bring the safety net into play) also mean a large exercise in central data-gathering and control?

Advantages	Qualifications/ objections	Response	Counter response
	(1d) In the public services efficiency and effectiveness are not the same. Market incentives to pursue low-cost efficiency may divert energy and attention from the search for effectiveness and quality.	Historically most public services have been monopolies, with few efficiency incentives and limited cost-consciousness. It is sensible, therefore, to give increased emphasis to efficiency. Also, in many cases, there is no contradiction between effectiveness/quality and efficiency.	The specific motivations and cultures of many public servants are intimately bound up with particular and distinctive 'missions' of 'their' services. To give priority to efficiency is to undermine the very 'publicness' of these activities.
(2) Increases consumer choice and thereby send clear signals to providers about what service consumers actually want.	(2a) In some cases (e.g. health care, education) the professional providers may usually know best. The service may be too complex for the individual purchaser to understand what is available and what the full range of consequences may be	The professionals have always claimed to know best, but that is what one would expect — it is in their interests to take this line. Yet there have been many cases where, once 'liberated' consumer views have been shown to diverge from professional opinion.	To give greater weight than in the past to purchaser/consumer views is one thing. To reduce the professional to an automatic respondent to consumer demands is, however, very short-sighted
	(2b) Markets are inegalitarian in so far as they exclude some consumers altogether — those who cannot afford to pay for the service. These consumers (e.g. those 15% of Americans who do not have health insurance) have no choice..	No consumers need be excluded. Markets can be designed so that *either* services remain free at the point of access *or* poor consumers receive income supplements or vouchers or state-provided insurance	In practice (e.g. benefit systems in the UK or Medicaid/Medicare in the US) such consumer-subsidies by government are often less than comprehensive. In mixed markets especially they also tend to create 'second class consumers'.

Advantages	Qualifications/ objections	Response	Counter response
	(2c) Anyway, markets only increase consumer choice where monopoly and oligopoly can be avoided. In some public services in some localities this will prove very difficult to achieve.	With creative management the number of local monopolies can be minimized, and such as remain can be subjected to close external monitoring and scrutiny. Anyway, many of the purchasing authorities will be powerful too.	There is a lot of learning to do here, so one cannot be confident that tight regulation will be effective. Also what sanctions could be used against a monopoly hospital or school without hurting the public they serve?
	(2d) Even if markets are reasonably competitive they do not necessarily increase real consumer choice very much. In some internal market designs it is a public purchasing authority rather than individual consumers which can choose.	Even WfP-type markets improve the service because they increase its efficiency. And well-managed public purchasing authorities will be very responsive to consumer wishes.	Public purchasing authorities are more likely to be driven by considerations of economy and efficiency than other considerations (such as effectiveness, access, etc.) so one is entitled to be sceptical about their 'responsiveness'.
(3) Markets reduce the scope for 'political' or 'ideological' interference in basic services.	(3a) What is wrong with 'political interference' anyway? Politics isn't a bad thing, to be minimized — rather it is a legitimate attempt to find consensus and express communal values.	This is a romantic/idealistic view of politics. In practice political intervention tends to create inconsistencies and inefficiencies and to emasculate management. The market is impersonal.	The market is actually unfeeling. The automatic application of efficiency tests that are usually founded on quasi-commercial values is not to be preferred to public debate, policy making and the articulation of collective solutions.

Advantages	Qualifications/ objections	Response	Counter response
	(3b) Anyway, political influences are not necessarily diminished. 'Designing' and re-designing the market (regulation) is often a highly political process.	Market 'design' is an appropriate role for politicians because it is strategic. But the *tactics* of how to operate in those markets can be assigned to managers and consumers.	The response is idealistic. In practice politicians are very likely to intervene in tactical as well as strategic issues.
(4) Mixed markets will generate more funds for popular public services because once given the choice many individuals will be willing to pay more for 'extras'.	(4a) The empirical evidence on this point seems highly ambiguous. Funds may shrink rather than grow, or the growth in funds may not 'trickle down' to the less well-off.	The empirical evidence is ambiguous because different types of market operate in different ways. With the right design additional funding from consumers can be stimulated.	But where will that extra funding go? Into fripperies like cosmetic surgery or potted plants in the reception area? In the US a much higher percentage of GNP is spent on health care than in the UK, but it doesn't seem to result in a healthier population.
	(4b) In any case this again assumes (see 2b above) that consumers *can* pay. Many cannot.	But many can, so why should they be deprived of the opportunity of doing so?	Because this tends to create a two class service, with stigmatization of the 'cheap' version (again, see 2b above).
	(4c) Administrative costs may be much higher (as a percentage of total costs) in a regulated, imperfectly competitive market than in a properly planned public service.	Yes, they *may* be. But only if you assume an *imperfect* market versus a *perfect* planning system. That is a biased assumption.	Not *that* biased! After all, UK governments have minimal experience in designing competitive markets. The proposed changes in health care, community care and education are leaps in the dark.

References

Abel-Smith, B. (1964) *The Hospitals, 1800–1948*, London, Heinemann.

Andersen, P. (1992) 'Health chiefs aim to put patients on GP fast track' *Health Service Journal*, 9th August p.5.

Central Statistical Office (1990) *Annual Abstract of Statistics*, no. 126, London, HMSO.

Centre for the Evaluation of Public Policy and Practice (1991) *Evaluation of Total Quality Management Projects in the National Health Service: First Interim Report to the Department of Health*, London, CEPPP, Brunel University.

Cmnd. 555 (1989) *Working for Patients*, London, HMSO.

Dalley, G. and Carr-Hill, R. (1991) *Pathways to Quality: A Study of Quality Management Initiatives in the NHS: A Guide for Managers*, University of York, Centre for Health Economics.

DHSS (1972) *Management Arrangements for the Reorganized National Health Service*, London, HMSO.

DHSS (1976) *The NHS planning system*, London, HMSO.

Elcock, H. and Haywood, S. (1980) *The Buck Stops Where? Accountability and Control in the National Health Service*, Institute of Health Service Studies, University of Hull.

Harrison, S., Hunter, D.J., Johnston, I. and Wistow, G. (1989) *Competing for Health: A Commentary on the NHS Review*, Leeds, Nuffield Institute Report.

Harrison, S., Hunter, D.J., and Pollitt, C. (1990) *The Dynamics of British Health Policy*, London, Unwin Hyman.

Harrison, S., Hunter, D.J., Marnoch, G., and Pollitt, C. (1992) *Just Managing: Power and Culture in the NHS*, Basingstoke, Macmillan.

Harrison, S., and Schultz, R.I. (1989) 'Clinical autonomy in the United Kingdom and the United States: contrasts and convergence' in G. Freddi and J.W. Bjokman (eds) *Controlling Medical Professionals*, London, Sage, pp. 198–209.

Harrison, S. (1988) *Managing the National Health Service: Shifting the Frontier?* London, Chapman and Hall.

King's Fund Institute (1988) *Health finance: assessing the options*, London, King's Fund.

Marmor, T.R., Mashaw, J.L. and Harvey, P.L. (1990) *America's Misunderstood Welfare State: Persistent Myths, Enduring Realities*, New York, Basic Books.

National Health Service Management Inquiry (1983) *Report* (The 'Griffiths Report'), London, DHSS.

Norwich Union Healthcare (1992) *UK Private Specialists' Fees: is the Price Right?* Eastleigh, Hampshire, Norwich Union.

Ovretveit, J. (1992) *Purchasing for Health Gain* (paper prepared for the annual conference of the European Healthcare Management Association, Karlstad, Sweden), Uxbridge, Brunel University.

Packwood, T., Keen, J. and Buxton, M. (1991) *Hospitals in Transition: the Resource Management Experiment*, Buckingham, Open University Press.

Pollitt, C., Harrison, S., Hunter, D.J. and Marnoch, G. (1988) 'The reluctant managers: clinicians and budgets in the NHS', *Financial Accountability and Management*. vol. 4, no. 3, Autumn, pp. 213–37.

Pollitt, C. (1993) 'The politics of medical quality: auditing doctors in the UK and the USA' *Health Services Management Research*, (forthcoming).

Saltman, R. B. (1988) 'Sweden' in Saltman, R.B. (ed.) *The International Handbook of Healthcare Systems*, Westport, CT., Greenwood Press, pp.285–93.

Saltman, R. B. and von Otter, C. (1989) 'Public competition versus mixed markets: an analytic comparison', *Health Policy*, 11, pp. 43–55.

Saltman, R. B. and von Otter, C. (1992) *Planned Markets and Public Competition: Strategic Reform in Northern European Health Systems*, Buckingham, Open University Press.

Schneller, E. S. and Kirkman-Liff, B. L. (1988) 'Health services management change in the United States and the British National Health Service', *The Journal of Health Administration Education*, vol. 6, no. 3, Summer, pp. 593–609.

Schultz, R.I., and Harrison, S. (1983) *Teams and Top Managers in the NHS: A Survey and Strategy*, London, King's Fund Project Paper No. 41.

Stevens, R. (1989) *In Sickness and in Wealth: American Hospitals in the Twentieth Century*, New York, Basic Books.

CHAPTER 10:
LOCAL GOVERNMENT

ALLAN COCHRANE

1 Introduction

Until the mid-1970s, local government was seen as a relatively unprob-
lematic part of the British political system, despite attempts to
'modernize' it in the 1960s and early 1970s. Its task was to deliver a
fairly clearly defined set of services (including primary and secondary
education, council housing and social services) at local level, reasonably efficiently and with a degree of (local) democratic control. It was
not a subject of high political (or academic) controversy. Indeed, despite steadily increasing levels of spending and employment through
the 1960s and into the 1970s, it was widely perceived as a political
backwater where nothing of importance was ever really decided. It
was a worthy world of aldermen and town clerks, only rarely enlivened
by the whiff of scandal arising from corruption over planning applications or the issuing of building contracts.

The principles underlying the division of labour between central and
local government were never clearly stated, but this merely seemed to
confirm the lack of controversy surrounding them. There was no real interest in answering the question of who ran local government. The convenient fiction was maintained that councils were responsible for the
allocation of resources at local level, as long as in practice they did not
seek to challenge the position of central government and the priorities
of central government departments. Bulpitt confirms that, 'Like children,' local authorities 'were expected to be "good", respectable indoors
and outdoors, and respectful to the centre. Misbehaviour was frowned
upon, but its consequences were conveniently left unclear' (Bulpitt 1989,
p.66).

There were effectively three systems of local government within the
UK at this time. In England and Wales the 1972 Local Government Act
created the system (of county councils, metropolitan counties, districts
and metropolitan districts alongside the Greater London Council (GLC)
and London boroughs which had already been created in the 1960s)
which was introduced in 1974 and survived with little change until the
mid-1980s. Similar reforms took place in Scotland a year later to produce that country's system of regional and district councils. In Northern
Ireland local government was a matter of greater controversy, because it
was more clearly associated with the distribution of resources
(including jobs) based on political and sectarian patronage.

Table 10.1 Principal functions of local authorities in Great Britain at the end of the 1980s.

	Metropolitan		England and Wales Non-Metropolitan		Greater London	Scotland		
	Joint Authority	District Councils	County Councils	District Councils	Borough Councils	Regional Councils	District Councils	Island Councils
Social Services		•	•		•	•		•
Education		•	•		.1	•	•	•
Libraries		•	.9		•		.2	.2
Museums and Art Galleries		•	•	•	•	•	•	•
Housing		•		•	•		•	•
Planning Strategic		.4	•			•		
Planning Local		•	•	•	•		.2	.2
Highways		•	•	•	•		•	•
Traffic Management		•	•		•	•		•
Passenger Transport[6]	•		•			•		•
Playing Fields and Swimming Pools		•	•	•	•		•	•
Parks and Open Spaces		•	•	•	•	•	•	•
Refuse Collection		•		•	•		•	•
Refuse Disposal	.5	.5	.8		.10		•	•
Consumer Protection		•	•		•	•		•
Environmental Health[7]		•		•	•		•	•
Police[3]	•		•			•		•
Fire[3]	•		•			•		•

NOTES

1 Outer London — London Boroughs. Inner London — Inner London Education Authority (joint Board) until 31 March 1990, thereafter — Inner London Boroughs.

2 Except in Highlands, Dumfries and Galloway and Border regions, where the function was regional.

3 There are joint police forces and joint fire brigades in some areas. In London the police authority is the Home Secretary and the Fire and Civil Defence Authority controls the fire brigades.

4 Strategic planning in metropolitan districts is coordinated by a joint committee of the districts. A joint planning committee also handles strategic planning for London.

5 In metropolitan areas, refuse disposal may be either a joint authority or a district council function.

6 Passenger transport in London was carried out by a separate body, London Regional Transport.

7 Regional and island councils in Scotland controlled water and sewerage, in addition to the usual environmental health duties.

8 In Wales, the waste disposal authorities and waste collection authorities were district councils.

9 In Wales some districts operated a library service.

10 Shared in groups of London boroughs.

Source: CIPFA, 1989, p. 3.

While reforms in the rest of the UK in the early 1970s created larger and, arguably, more powerful forms of local government, in Northern Ireland at the same time councils were effectively marginalized, left with few mainstream responsibilities, while housing and social services were transferred to regional agencies and joint boards. Throughout the UK, however, the fact that the discussion of local government tended to focus on organizational questions, boundaries and the sharing out of service responsibilities rather than disagreements over political programmes, merely confirmed its position as a political backwater.

But after the mid-1970s local government became the focus of major debate throughout the UK and had an increasingly high profile not only at local level, but in the national newspapers, radio and television. There was a remarkable transformation, in which 'excessive' council spending was blamed for the country's economic problems, councillors were heavily criticized for financial irresponsibility and local government officers attacked for inefficiency and constructing 'bureaucratic empires' on the basis of self-interest. A series of controversial reform packages was introduced with the aim of substantially reshaping the ways in which local government operated. Yet, despite all the changes at the time of writing (in 1993) it still does not look as if matters have been resolved (see Table 10.1 for principal functions of LAs).

Local government finance remains a subject of national controversy and local government 'reform' looks set to be a matter of continuing debate, into the twenty-first century. As a result it is dangerous to make long-term predictions. So it is important to stress that this chapter is principally intended to show how the models of coordination may be used in analysing the ways in which local government is managed from the centre. It is not just — or even mainly — an attempt to spell out the current state of local government but is organized around one key question, namely: How do the models of coordination developed earlier in the book help us to understand the operation of the UK's local government system? Each model is considered in turn and its usefulness is assessed by looking at the history of relations between central and local government between the mid-1970s and the early 1990s.

2 Hierarchy in central–local relations

The dominant — common sense — interpretation of local government within the post-war UK state system is an explicitly hierarchical one. We tend to take for granted the idea that central government makes decisions which are then implemented by local government. Perhaps, on reflection, we might reformulate this concluding that the rules within which councils operated were laid down from above, both in terms of what was permitted and what was required. But, however we qualify it, in this model councils are held to be responsible for the local delivery of services whose provision has been nationally determined. The scope for local determination is limited to ensuring that account is taken of differing local needs and that services are efficiently delivered. In positive terms the model can be expressed as follows: 'Westminster and Whitehall provide the legal framework and exercise a general oversight, but it is local people who make the rules work' (Hill, 1970, p.22). We tend to take it for granted that, in some sense at least, the centre is also 'running' local government.

Underlying this interpretation of the local government system seems to be a belief in a structure based on rational planning expressed through bureaucratic hierarchies. In this case, the logic is modified by a disjunction between central and local levels. It is accepted — implicitly at least — that a completely centralized system will not work, because local variations mean flexibility is required. But the degree of variation is limited by central rules (on levels of finance and how it may be expended), unspoken agreements about what is acceptable (and unacceptable) and the existence of professional groups responsible for the implementation of policy at local level.

In some ways, this interpretation seems to fit the UK system quite well. There is no constitutional guarantee of local autonomy here as there is in some European countries, in part, of course, because we have no written constitution. Here the legal position — the closest we get to a constitution — is that all the powers of local councils derive from legislation passed in Westminster and are expressed in various specific and more general local government acts. The powers and responsibilities of councils are to be found in a series of local government acts, education acts, housing acts, planning acts, children acts, and mental health acts among others. Local authorities in the UK have no general competence or power to act for the benefit of the people resident within their boundaries. In principle, each power they have is the consequence of some responsibility that they have been given. It is in this sense that the UK is often described as a 'unitary state', that is one in which 'the power to delegate or revoke delegated power remains in the hands of the central authority' (Rose, 1982, p. 50). If councils seek to undertake activities for which they have no specific power, they are said to be acting 'ultra vires' (outside their powers) and can be held liable in a court of law.

The growth of local government in the years after 1945 as part of the post-war welfare state can be seen to have reinforced its subordinate position within a hierarchy. One consequence of the initial post-war nationalizations was that previous local government powers — for the running of hospitals, electricity and gas supply — were removed. Water and sewage responsibilities were lost in the early 1970s. They were replaced with expanded responsibilities in the fields of education, housing, the personal social services and town planning, explicitly handed down from above as demands from the centre. In some areas — such as education and social services — there are clearly identified central inspectorates which help to reinforce the subordinate position of local government. And in town planning, the possibility of appeal to the relevant minister makes the formal position equally clear.

Named officers and committees are delegated specific responsibilities within legislation. This has in the past probably been clearest in the field of education (traditionally the biggest spender within local government), since the relevant councils were labelled education authorities, the membership of education committees was statutorily defined to include a range of cooptees and directors of education were given responsibilities which made them responsible to the centre as well as to the council of which they were officers. Similar responsibilities exist within the social services, particularly in the field of child protection. Finance officers, too, are given the responsibility of ensuring that the spending programmes of a council can be met by the income which the council can reasonably (and legally) expect to receive in the course of the year. In some circumstances (if councillors were ignoring this fiduciary responsibility) finance officers would be expected to take over the running of the council.

District auditors — who are independent of the councils and employed by a separate agency (the Audit Commission in England and Wales and the Audit Service in Scotland) — also have the role of ensuring that councils behave with propriety in their financial dealings. In particular, they have the power to penalize councillors and officers for 'wilful misconduct'. In the mid-1980s Lambeth and Liverpool councils were prosecuted for 'wilful misconduct' over the way in which they conducted the setting of their local taxation in 1985. It was argued that they 'wilfully' delayed setting the rate in such a way that significant income was lost to the council and councillors were individually and collectively surcharged to repay the sums of money allegedly lost as well as the costs of the court cases — amounting to about £250,000 in the case of Lambeth and over £500,000 in the case of Liverpool.

The financial position of local government also suggests a subordinate role in other ways. Until the late 1980s councils in England, Scotland and Wales did, of course, have access to significant locally generated taxation whose levels they could set (albeit within increasingly tight limitations). But even then, most local authority spending (over 60 per cent) was funded by central government grant. Since the changes of the late 1980s this has been emphasized because (at least in England and Wales) the collection and distribution of business taxes (the uniform business rate) is now a national responsibility too, so that only around 15 per cent of local authority income is now locally determined. Legislation in the mid-1980s enabled the Secretary of State for the Environment (the department responsible for local government in England and Wales) and the Secretary of State for Scotland (where new legislation was first introduced) to fix the levels of spending by named local authorities, which went outside certain centrally determined guidelines. This effectively meant that levels of local taxation were also determined centrally (hence the process was labelled ratecapping in England and Wales, while in Scotland concern was expressed about the ways in which a 'hit-list' of local authorities was chosen for attention by the Scottish Office). Despite the move to new forms of local taxation (the community charge or poll tax) in the late 1980s which were intended to *increase* local accountability and reduce the need for direct central intervention, these powers have been retained.

The programme of the third Thatcher government — elected in 1987 — had grand ambitions to reshape Britain's local government system having already abolished a tier of local government in 1986 (the GLC and the metropolitan counties). No area of local government escaped scrutiny. In education, proposals included the introduction of a national curriculum, encouragement to schools to opt out of local control making them more directly responsible to the Department of Education, support for city technology colleges also outside the local authority system, and a move towards the local management of schools within tight financial guidelines. In housing, limitations on council house building were reinforced, while existing council estates were encouraged to leave local authority control and move into the housing association sector, or be taken directly into central control in housing action trusts. And the existing rules requiring some local government services and maintenance activities to be provided on the basis of competitive tendering between independent bidders was extended to cover more areas.

So, it looks as if the legal framework within which local government has to operate is quite restrictive and hierarchical. The various grant regimes and methods of calculating GREAs (Grant Related Expenditure Assessments), needs assessments and SSAs (Standard Spending Assessments), coupled with powers to cap first rates and more recently community charge and council tax levels, suggest a significant increase in central political power, and the bureaucratic power of the Department of the Environment, the Welsh Office and the Scottish Office. Power is delegated from above, and the centre retains the ability to limit spending and to police what is being done (see also Chapters 7 and 8).

But it is hard to explain some of the difficulties the centre has had in implementing its policies simply in terms of the hierarchical model. If central–local government relations are understood as hierarchical, then it becomes difficult to explain why all the changes of the 1970s and 1980s were necessary, since they were introduced precisely because local authorities did not automatically accept the authority of the centre. In effect as long as there were no disagreements between central and local government, it looked as if the hierarchical model worked, but as soon as disagreements developed (in practice as soon as attempts were made to work through hierarchical authority) then it looked increasingly unconvincing.

If matters were as simple as a hierarchical model would suggest, then it would be difficult to explain the high levels of conflict which have characterized central/local government relations since 1975, when Tony Crosland (then Secretary of State for the Environment in a Labour government) first announced that 'the party was over' for local government. If the centre were able to run the local welfare state at one remove through local councils, then one would expect matters to have been settled relatively quickly through a series of central decisions, more or less speedily filtering down to local level. In practice, however, local government has been remarkably resistant to pressure from above.

In the early years of the 1980s, matters seemed relatively clearcut. The overwhelming academic consensus was that local government and local democracy were under attack from the centre. It was identified as a period of centralization, and one in which the changing rules of finance were fundamentally, probably fatally, undermining the scope for local autonomy. According to Stewart, 'in place of local choice will be the decision of the Secretary of State who is seeking ... remarkably unrestrained power' (Stewart, 1984, p.9). It was claimed by some that the provisions of the Local Government Planning and Land Act marked 'the beginnings of the wholly centralized state' (Burgess and Travers, 1980, p.188). In Scotland, complaints were made about the arbitrary nature of the Scottish Secretary's 'hit list' of local authorities whose spending he defined as 'excessive and unreasonable' (Keating et al., 1983). It was almost universally agreed that councils were losing their scope for independent action.

By the middle of the 1980s, however, it seemed that many of the more direct financial assaults had not been very successful in their own terms — it was, for example, increasingly clear that neither levels of spending nor employment (particularly white collar employment) had decreased significantly. Despite a decline in capital expenditure (that is spending on equipment, buildings and infrastructure financed by long term loans), current expenditure (that is spending on services, mainly financed by tax and grant income and short-term loans) actually rose in real terms up to the end of the 1980s and numbers employed also rose, although there was a decline in the employment of manual workers and a growth in part-time working (Fleming, 1989). More positively, there was continued evidence of new initiatives developing at local level (including, for example, the expansion of local economic development, the spread of decentralization policies and devolved management structures, a growing concern for equal opportunities, and more recently for green issues). None of this suggested an area whose significance was withering.

The process of local government reform in the 1980s can be explained in part by a belief in the effectiveness of the hierarchical model of co-ordination at central level. The evidence suggests that some senior civil servants and leading national politicians believed that they could determine what happened at local level by legislating for it. White papers tended to talk in terms of the UK as a 'unitary state' and the frequency of legislative reform suggests that there was a belief that eventually it would be possible to construct the appropriate 'rational' structures of government. Unfortunately, the evidence of the 1970s and 1980s also suggests that such a view is difficult to sustain in practice. Every change from above seems to have been met by adjustments elsewhere in the system first to take account of and then to evade the intended consequences of the central legislation. As we have already noted, even the attempts to reduce local government spending were much less successful than the political rhetoric on both sides would have suggested. If the relationship between central and local government is a hierarchical one, it is certainly far more complex than any simple model of hierarchy would suggest. It looks rather more like a constant process of negotiation in which the negotiators are not always clear of the ground rules — and the centre always has the possibility of changing them, but can rarely predict the consequences of such changes with any accuracy.

3   The market critique

The market model has been used to construct a powerful critique of existing structures of local government and it influenced some of the most important reforms of the 1980s. The main elements of the critique were not specific to local government in the UK, but were developed more broadly in looking at public provision within welfare states. The arguments of those seeking to introduce market mechanisms are clear enough. They have two main elements. The first is the view that learning from markets will encourage an increase in efficiency (with a stress on 'value for money'), and the second that it will increase direct accountability to 'consumers'. This approach implies a shift away from a view of local government as responsible to citizens (through political pressures and elections) towards one in which it is responsible to consumers (through forms of market pressure).

The argument goes further to suggest that public service provision in local government (as in the rest of the welfare state) has historically operated in the interests of the groups which run it — particularly the professionals who gain directly from it in terms of income, employment and status — whilst private sector provision is more genuinely controlled by the public because it is forced to respond to their demands as purchasers and consumers.

It is argued that bureaucratic pressures will encourage budget holders to try to maximize their budgets or staff instead of concentrating on efficient service provision. This is said to be an inevitable consequence of bureaucratic organization and the result of a series of rational choices made by the bureaucrats themselves (see for example, Niskanen, 1973). Writers in this tradition stress that they are not concerned to make moral judgements or to apportion blame, but to show that, given the rules within which they have to operate, rational individuals will choose to behave in the ways predicted (that is for their own benefit) rather than in the ways hoped for by the architects of the welfare state, who necessarily believed in the altruism of welfare professionals — in acting for others and not themselves. Instead, it is suggested that controlling the largest possible budget, or the largest possible number of staff, is the bureaucratic equivalent to profit maximization in a competitive environment. This is likely to lead to levels of spending and forms of spending which have more to do with the priorities of bureaucrats than the needs of those they are intended to serve or, indeed, the ambitions of the governments which fund them.

Some of the implications of this critique for the operation of individual councils will be quite clear and can be expected to include privatization of services, contracting out and the search for market surrogates such as vouchers. Most importantly, it suggests that a straightforward hierarchical model simply will not work, particularly when it requires coordination *between* rather than *within* organizations. There are three main reasons why supporters of the market model would argue that a hierarchical approach to central–local relations will not work.

The first picks up on criticisms of central planning which suggest that the centre is unable to gather all the information required to make detailed decisions on resource allocation, and — still more damning — even if civil servants could gather the necessary information it would be so extensive that they would be unable to process it in a way which made such decisions possible. At the start of the 1980s, some supporters of market approaches suggested that the UK's system of central–local relations actually encouraged the feeding of inadequate and misleading information from local to central government, since councils were dependent on the centre for most of their funding and local treasurers spent a great deal of their time trying to maximize the available grant from the centre (by what was called 'creative accounting'). One commentator concluded that there were 'huge economic incentives for local authorities to overspend' within the grant system which existed at the start of the 1980s (Jackman, 1981, p. 777).

This issue points to a second problem identified within the system of central–local relations: namely the — necessary — inefficiency of a system in which one set of 'bureaucrats' (at the centre) is expected to police another set (at local level) with the help of a complex set of instructions and guidelines. Not only does the operation of these soon turn into an almost incomprehensibly Byzantine process of detailed bargaining which few can understand, but also it fails to take into account the effects of bureaucratic self-interest in different organizations at various levels of the hierarchy. If it is the case that bureaucratic success is measured in terms of budgets or staff, then the incentive of civil servants to reduce the budgets of those lower down the hierarchy at local level will be limited since their own budgets are likely to be determined — in part at least — by those of the organizations over which they have nominal authority.

A third — related — weakness of the hierarchical model identified by the market critique is that the people making the decisions are not those having to pay for them. And the lines of accountability are also highly confused by the appearance of hierarchy, which suggests that it is officials in the Department of the Environment, the various Departments of State to which local authorities are accountable, rather than the national and local tax payers who provide the funds. Local electors have a distorted view of the decisions they are being asked to make, since it looks as if services provided at local level are paid for by local taxes which only cover a relatively small proportion of actual expenditure. Until the late 1980s this distortion was (according to these arguments) reinforced because many of those benefiting from spending were not paying *any* local taxation because they were not householders and therefore not ratepayers, but were, nevertheless, able· to vote for higher levels of expenditure. However much the rules of grant allocation from the centre were manipulated and adjusted, it was argued that they could not deal adequately with this problem. A new set of arrangements was required. It was argued that since local electors would 'have no incentive to be efficient unless they are substantially responsible for financing the services ... an efficient tax must fall on electors' (Foster et al., 1980, p. 235).

The implications of these arguments for central–local relations might, in principle, look fairly straightforward. Indeed they suggest that central–local relations should cease to be an issue, because — as far as possible — responsibility both for raising and spending money on local services should be located at local level (this was, incidentally, also one of the options presented by the Royal Commission on Local Government Finance — chaired by Sir Frank Layfield — which reported in 1975). In practice, as we shall see in the next section, matters were rather more complicated than that despite the support for the market model expressed by senior politicians in the 1980s.

4 The experience of the 1980s: mixed success for markets.

This section will focus on two aspects of change in the 1980s, both of which were of significance for central–local relations and both of which were influenced by ideas drawn from supporters of market approaches. The first is the piecemeal introduction of forms of market mechanism into local government as part of the welfare state (some of which look similar to those introduced in the National Health Service at the same time and discussed in Chapter 9), and the second is the extensive programme aimed at restructuring the system of local government finance.

Julian Le Grand uses the term quasi-market to describe some of the changes which were introduced in many areas of welfare state in the 1980s. The term is helpful because it highlights the extent to which the new methods sought to imitate the operation of markets, without yet having all the features we normally associate with them (for example, in terms of extensive competition, the identification of individual consumer choice, and the measuring of profits). In developing quasi-markets 'the intention is for the state to stop being the funder *and* the provider of services. Instead it is to become primarily a funder, with services being provided by a variety of private, voluntary and public suppliers, all operating in competition with one another' (Le Grand, 1990, p. 2). These quasi-markets differ from more 'conventional markets in one or more of three ways: not-for-profit organizations competing for public contracts, sometimes in competition with for-profit organizations; consumer purchasing power in the form of vouchers rather than cash; and, in some cases, the consumers represented in the market by agents instead of operating by themselves' (Le Grand, 1990, p. 5).

Moves in this direction are likely to have major affects on service delivery but here we are only concerned about their implications for central–local relations. One might expect the extension of quasi-markets to reduce potential areas of conflict between central and local government, and to undermine existing hierarchical assumptions, as competition develops between agencies, and new ways of allocating resources become the norm. In practice, however, the experience of the 1980s allows rather less definite conclusions to be drawn. The new arrangements have often been experienced at local level as increased restrictions and tighter control

Perhaps the most obvious way in which market methods were imposed by central on local government was in legislation requiring the privatization of specified aspects of their work and the awarding of contracts for those services to other agencies through a process of compulsory competitive tendering (CCT). The main emphasis of CCT was in areas such as refuse disposal, housing maintenance or street cleaning or in ancillary work (such as catering, vehicle maintenance or the cleaning of council property). Central government set down strict rules about how CCT was to take place (for example, excluding 'good employer' clauses, and forbidding most forms of positive discrimination or affirmative action). Local authorities have had to comply with these and have often had to reorganize their departments so that they can bid for contracts against other private sector organizations. There is evidence that CCT has reduced costs in some areas, but like much central legislation, it has also encouraged the search for loopholes at local level, to the extent that, according to a report from one monitoring body, most work put out to tender is still carried out by 'in-house' direct service organizations (LACSAB, 1990).

The experience of increased central control is particularly clear in the field of housing and has already been extensively discussed in Chapter 7 where Chris Hamnett catalogues a lengthy series of legislative changes, each of which seems to have reduced the power of councils.

Hamnett comments that the powers of central government increased through the 1980s as a paradoxical consequence of attempts to create a freer market with more consumer choice. In practice the development of quasi-markets in local government in the 1980s did not resolve or bypass many of the problems of central–local relations identified at the start of the decade. On the contrary it seems to have reproduced them in a different form. In part this may be because central government continues to have legitimate interests in controlling or influencing not only aspects of funding, but also aspects of provision. It also becomes involved in policing the 'rules of the game' and plugging loopholes in its regulations. Market mechanisms have in practice largely been used as part of the battle to impose central authority. This was, perhaps, particularly clear in attempts to reform the financing of local government.

Numerous attempts were made in the 1980s to change the ways in which local government was financed. Indeed one complaint frequently made by local authority treasurers was that the rules changed so frequently that it was no longer possible to make rational decisions about spending from year to year. Nevertheless, there were two main principles underlying the changes which were being introduced from above. The first was the perceived need to control levels of spending at local level, and the second was to increase the accountability of those under-taking that spending. In the early 1980s both of these principles found expression in moves to increased central control. More and more precise and apparently rigorous formulae were developed to determine appro-priate levels of spending and various financial mechanisms were used to encourage (or force) councils to stick to central guidelines. It was the departments of central government which were to decide when spending was 'excessive and unreasonable' and to cut (or 'clawback') grant when that was felt to be the case. By the mid-1980s departments of central government not only had the power to cut the levels of grant which they gave to councils, but they were also able in particular cases to de-termine how much they could raise in local taxation (at that time still the rates).

In large part, moves to increased central (hierarchical) control were justified with the help of arguments drawn from market approaches, because it was argued that excessive state spending (including that of local government) was undermining the profitability of the private sec-tor in the UK. The accountability implied in this set of arguments was to the funder, that is central government, representing national taxpay-ers, and this justified the increasingly complex structures of financial monitoring and control which were set up.

But, as we have seen, moves to tighter control were not as successful in restricting spending as might have been expected. Imposing rules from above and attempting to manipulate grant levels brought increased complexity (and more work for bureaucrats) without delivering what was wanted. Mixing market and hierarchical models of coordination simply seemed to result in increased confusion.

In the second half of the 1980s, the implications of market ap-proaches were taken a step further in attempts to develop a different model of accountability not to the centre, but to local residents and local taxpayers. One underlying assumption was that there would be a shared interest between a centre seeking to reduce levels of state spend-ing and local taxpayers seeking to reduce the levels of tax which they had to pay. The introduction of the community charge (or poll tax) in the late 1980s can be understood as part of the continuing campaign to gain control over local decision makers, implying a fiscal alliance be-tween the centre and local voters against professionals and wasteful lo-cal politicians. But the argument went further than this, following those such as Foster et al. (1980) who argued that making local voters responsible for paying for the services they received would also ensure that they elected councils which would provide the services they wanted at costs which reflected 'value for money' and increased effi-ciency.

The tax was introduced to replace domestic rates in Scotland in 1989 and in England and Wales in 1990. Each resident over the age of 18 was to pay a charge set by his or her local authority to cover the costs of lo-

cal services over and above those met by grant from central government
(in the case of England and Wales including centrally collected income
from business rates), income from charges for particular services (such as
leisure facilities, planning applications etc.) and (in Scotland) non-do-
mestic (that is still locally collected business) rates. Concessionary
levels were available for some categories of resident (such as students
and those dependent on social security) but in principle everybody was
expected to make *some* payment (at least 20 per cent of the charge
levied).

The official name of the tax — the community charge — was intended
to highlight the notion that residents were paying for a package of
services supplied by or organized through the local council. Consumers
were expected to judge whether the cost of the package they received
was reasonable and to express their judgement by electing the council
likely to manage the delivery of an appropriate package most efficiently.

Supporters argued that:

> Every voter, now faced with paying their share of council ex-
> penditure will have a powerful incentive to consider the possi-
> ble costs of their candidate's policies before they cast their
> vote... Accountability and responsibility will reappear in many
> communities where, in recent years, both have been lamentably
> lacking ... and this will create significant, and probably sub-
> stantial, electoral and demographic pressure on authorities to
> reduce their expenditure.

(Adam Smith Institute, 1989; quoted in Midwinter, 1989, p. 12)

There seems to have been a strong belief that providing the right sort
of comparative information at local level would encourage vot-
ers/consumers to draw conclusions in line with those of central government. Pressures from above would be reinforced by electoral pressures
from below. Party political broadcasts in the late 1980s, therefore,
stressed differences between 'poll tax' levels in Conservative controlled
authorities (such as Wandsworth) and Labour controlled authorities
(such as neighbouring Lambeth). It was hoped, too, that the reports of
the Audit Commission (a quango set up in the early 1980s to monitor local government and the health service in England and Wales) were
used to draw attention to differences in the 'economy, efficiency and effectiveness' with which different authorities delivered that service.
More recent proposals for the Audit Commission to assess the extent to
which councils have met certain standards in the delivery of specific
services suggest that this belief remains a strong one.

With hindsight it is all too easy to see some of the flaws in the vision which underlay the poll tax, particularly as a means of running local government from above.

It is difficult to identify the precise packages provided in different
places, and distinguish between what is provided by various agencies

at local level. Most people find it difficult to distinguish between what is provided by different levels of government, not only district and county or regional levels, but also between local and central government. In addition, it is frequently difficult to make any clear judgement about services provided by voluntary agencies, receiving support from a wider range of statutory and non-statutory (even private sector) bodies.

The arguments for the tax also underestimates the welfare element of local government. Since not everybody benefits from all of the services provided through local government, it is not clear what each taxpayer/elector is paying for. Certainly taxpayers are not *only* paying for services from which they benefit directly. It is difficult to know quite how a childless person should assess the contribution he or she should make to the education system, or how young people should judge the share of the charge used to support the old. Some of those receiving services — for example the children in child protection cases — have no electoral voice and pay no tax. This does not mean, of course, that voters are unprepared to pay for these services, but it calls into question the principle that they are making choices as consumers between packages of services received by them. Those paying taxes are also paying for the 'consumption' of services by others.

In any case the charge itself only raised a small element of the overall costs of local government — the legislation which introduced the poll tax in England and Wales also effectively left central government responsible for a significantly *increased* proportion of local government finance because it was accompanied by the introduction of the uniform business rate, as well as the 'residual' power to cap spending and thus charge levels. It is difficult to see how local decisions could significantly influence local levels of tax when those were effectively determined at national level, both in overall terms and, still, through the various grant regimes, in practice for individual local authorities.

Paradoxically, although the *proportion* of local government spending financed from central sources increased in the late 1980s and into the early 1990s, this masked a reduction in the level of grants paid from the centre. In England and Wales the share rose only because central government took control of the business rates and in Scotland, where business rates remained locally determined, the share fell. So, the introduction of the community charge (an unpopular tax) was made more difficult because money raised from local residents (and voters) was expected to cover a higher proportion of council costs.

As a result, levels of local taxation rose without a corresponding improvement in services. The local election results of 1989–1990 suggest that it was the central government, rather than local government, which was blamed for this. The political unpopularity of the tax led to changes (in the 1991 Budget) which reduced still further the proportion of local spending funded locally (to not much more than 10 per cent in England and Wales), as VAT was raised to reduce community charge levels. The attempt to fund a higher proportion of local spending from the taxation of local residents was over.

The political retreat from the poll tax at the start of the 1990s, following Margaret Thatcher's replacement as Prime Minister by John Major, seems to have brought an end to this particular experiment in market approaches. After all the attempts to shift the costs of spending on to those who use services, we are left with a policy which seems to have the opposite effect. The 'council tax', intended to replace the community charge involves a move away from a flat rate 'charge' for services back to a property based system, albeit a less complicated one than the old rates. It also heralds a move away from the notion that everyone should pay, since those on state benefit will not be expected to do so and the tax will once more be levied on households. Although reforms of the 1990s (including proposals to restructure local government by getting rid of the two tier system) may still be influenced by market models, they are no longer justified with quite the same enthusiastic reference to those models.

5 Policy networks and local government

Looking at the hierarchical and market models raises important questions about the operation of the UK state system. But both also leave a lot of questions which still need answering. Neither takes enough account of the ways in which organizations relate to and negotiate with each other in practice, nor of the processes of internal bargaining which take place. In one, it is assumed that a unitary state can hand down policies from above: in the other it is assumed that markets can be constructed to cover almost all areas which are currently the responsibility of states. The experience of the post-war period suggests that both assumptions are, at least, highly questionable. And it looks as if combining the two in an attempt to control local government more effectively through the introduction of market methods (which seems to have been the dominant approach of the 1980s) is particularly inappropriate. Central–local relations look more like a complex maze than an expression of hierarchical or market models.

In this context the network model is particularly helpful. It has been developed extensively by analysts of central–local relations in the UK, most fully in a book by Rhodes, entitled *Beyond Westminster and Whitehall: Sub-central Governments of Britain*. He starts by arguing that the influence of the centre 'lies in its ability to cajole, bully and persuade (but not command), and even this ability may not call forth the desired degree of compliance' before going on to suggest that there is no single centre (Rhodes 1988, p. 1). There are rather 'multiple centres or policy networks', each of which is centralized but between which there is little coordination (Rhodes, 1988, p. 3). In other words, for

Rhodes, it is, strictly, inappropriate to talk of 'central–local' relations as if there were a centre which could control local agencies. The system is more complex and fragmented than such a phrase suggests. For him, the system of 'central–local' relations is a product of many such networks, linking centre and locality often apparently independently of each other, but also influencing each other in ways which are rarely clearly understood by those involved.

Rhodes argues that there is a tension at the heart of the UK state system between the tradition which assumes that the centre knows best and the reality of the centre's dependence on local and other forms of sub-central government for the delivery of services. And for him that tension can best be understood in terms of policy networks, which link the centre and localities, rather than in terms which stress the importance of local (or indeed, national) party politics. These policy networks can be defined as the systems of (vertical) linkages between professionals (and associated councillors) and civil servants responsible for policy within departments of central government. In other words there are separate networks in the fields of education, housing and social services which do not always interact with each other.

The experience of the 1980s shows the value of Rhodes' approach particularly clearly, if only because it highlights the dangers of ignoring policy networks. The politics of UK central government at that time were characterized by the belief that it was possible to transform the structures of economy, society and politics by taking a lead from the top, in what Rhodes describes as a 'command operating code at variance with the differentiated polity' with which it had to deal. It was assumed that change could be achieved through the issuing of 'commands' from above and from a relatively unified centre (whether represented by Prime Minister, Cabinet or political party). 'The command code', says Rhodes, 'represents a failure to comprehend that British government is a multi-form maze of interdependence. To operate a code at variance with this reality is to build a failure into the initial policy design' (Rhodes 1985, p. 55). As a result there was a substantial gap between what was promised in political rhetoric and what could be delivered in practice.

The driving force of Thatcherite politics was to be found in their economic policies and in the case of local government that meant that one might expect substantial cuts in spending on the local welfare state. But the nature of the UK's political system made that difficult to achieve in practice because policy networks were centralized, while the centre was fragmented. The policy networks of the welfare state ensured that central government itself was more divided than the 'command' model expected: spending departments (including education and social services) were represented at the centre, although expenditure was carried out on a decentralized basis through local government. While it might be possible to sustain an overall attitude which stressed the need for limits to local government spending, the Treasury had to negotiate with other departments of state as well as through them with local governments and other sub-central governments. Meanwhile those parts of the centre with interests in service provision were likely to continue to encourage expansion at local level, even if the overall policy of central government favoured retrenchment. In practice the centre found it difficult to speak with one voice.

So, for example, the government might be arguing strongly for reductions in spending as part of an overall economic programme, while at the same time, civil servants within the Department of Education and Science, or the Department of Health were arguing with their counterparts at local level for increased spending on particular schemes. The Department of the Environment is in a particularly uncertain position. In arguments with the Treasury, it is likely to support more spending in the areas for which it is responsible through local government, yet in its relations with local government it acts as the policer of budgets — indeed it effectively plays the Treasury role. And matters are made still more complex because, even in this context of departmental pressure for retrenchment, some parts of the Department — those responsible for housing, planning and other spending areas — might also be encouraging increased spending. These internal conflicts of interest are reflected through policy networks.

At the same time substantial pressures for resistance developed at local level. One crucial aspect of change in the early 1980s was an increased politicization at national level, following the election of the first Thatcher government. Rhodes suggests that this introduced 'grit in the well oiled machinery of the policy networks' (Rhodes, 1985, p.53). It did so partly by encouraging a substantial politicization throughout the system, so that local politicians (of both major parties) increasingly sought to influence decision making through their contact with senior party politicians, making it difficult to achieve effective 'command' from above. It also did so by encouraging more conscious and deliberate resistance from below by councils, particularly but not only those controlled by the Labour Party. Increased politicization at local level was also encouraged by the pressures of rising unemployment, which brought demands for more welfare services from below, at the same time as responses to economic decline brought pressures for retrenchment from above (see Rhodes 1988, pp. 210-14).

In his discussion of policy networks, Rhodes concentrates on linkages within the state system. He tends to underplay the significance of what happens outside that system. In general, Rhodes plays down the independent value of local politics, instead suggesting that a growth in local or territorial politics tends to be a consequence of shifts elsewhere in the system. His explanation for the growth of local challenges to the centre in the 1980s is essentially that the centre did not understand how to manage the system properly. Within his analysis, therefore, local politics is a product of the central–local government system, rather than an independent element within it. Yet, this means his explanation of change in the 1980s loses some of its force, because local politics does have a life of its own, to the extent that changes at local level may have forced responses from the centre as much as central initiatives encouraged rebellion at local level. The initiatives associated with the new urban left (sometimes labelled the 'loony left' in the tabloid press) at the start of the decade, for example, had little to do with traditional policy networks. The policies of the authorities such as the Greater London Council, London Boroughs such as Islington, Camden and Lambeth and others such as Sheffield and Manchester which aroused most wrath from the centre were the least traditional, whether in the fields of local economic policy, equal opportunities, race relations or sexual politics. As one leading Conservative politician (Norman Tebbitt) put it in 1984: 'The GLC is typical of this new, modern divisive form of socialism. It must be defeated. So we shall abolish the GLC' (quoted in Lansley et al., 1989, p. 47). Statements of this sort reflect a conflict which goes beyond any which could easily be explained in terms of policy networks.

As we saw earlier, too, political changes at national level may also be important to the operation of central–local relations. Of course, Rhodes acknowledges this in principle, but his theoretical approach makes it difficult to incorporate this form of politics in practice. He would tend to explain it as an external shock to the system, rather than an integral part of its operation. This is problematic because elections and the governments it produces are perhaps the most obvious expressions of the operation of politics in the UK. Rhodes' insights into political processes which are usually hidden within forms of bureaucratic hierarchy seem to have the weakness of making it more difficult to explain or understand the significance of more open forms of political decision making. Despite their obvious value in the analysis of central–local relations, network models like that of Rhodes have the potential disadvantage that it is difficult to introduce factors which are not initially represented as having key roles within the model, however important they later turn out to be. They are in danger of being closed systems.

In Chapter 3 Grahame Thompson raises some other problems associated with network forms of coordination, some of which are worth thinking about again in this context. The first he raises is a concern about democracy and democratic control. Networks may effectively insulate decision makers from accountability to electors or (as market models would suggest) consumers. There is a danger that using network models may obscure instead of clarifying relations of power in the UK state system, thus effectively reinforcing the power of elites. It makes it difficult to identify those who have power, because it assumes that it is spread more widely through a 'differentiated polity'. But it is not clear quite how 'differentiated' it really is. There are already tight controls over those who are admitted to the networks, partly because they are professionalized (that is, to be a player in the game one has to have a professional label), with different professions having access to different networks. And they are also hierarchical. Each level of the same networks is only accessible to some grades of staff and levels of political leadership. Some networks are only open to senior managers and politicians who are defined or define themselves as political elites. As in many other areas of social and political life, this tends to mean that the main decision makers are male, white university graduates.

Secondly, Thompson points to the possibility of corruption within informal networks, which depend on discretion. It would be misleading to accuse any of the participants in central/local relations of corruption, in the sense of abusing their positions to make personal gain, and no such claim is made here. Indeed, perhaps corruption is too strong a term, but it is not too difficult to see how moving away from strict notions of rule-driven bureaucratic hierarchy may mean that discretion will be used to benefit one group (or even individual) rather than another. An informal system of rewards (and punishments) may be required to oil the wheels of the system. The main political parties have not been afraid to accuse each other of 'corrupt' dealings in the allocation of central grants. In the late 1970s the Conservative controlled shire counties claimed that they were being deliberately disadvantaged not by the grant system itself, but by the way it was being manipulated by the civil servants to the advantage of large Labour controlled urban authorities. Similarly in the early 1990s it was claimed by some Labour authorities that the grant system was manipulated to benefit a small number of Conservative controlled councils which were then — as a result — able to set very low levels of community charge.

6 Conclusion: beyond the models

Each of the three models we have considered has something to offer in the analysis of the local government system within the UK. Each has a contribution to make in helping us to understand the ways in which local government is run. But each is also only able to give us partial answers to the questions which concern us.

The hierarchical model is helpful because it highlights the extent to which councils are ultimately under the control of central government and the departments of central government are reliant on those of local government to implement their policies at local level. But it exaggerates the extent to which the centre is able to control local government, as well as the extent to which it is possible to identify a coherent set of policies to be implemented through the central–local system.

The market model is helpful because of the attention it draws to the behaviour of bureaucrats, challenging the notion that it is possible to have a hierarchy dominated by an ideology of rational benevolence. It forces us to think about the logic of human behaviour, instead of believing in the stated intentions of organizational pyramids. In the end, it is less convincing in providing a model of change, because some of its supporters fail to acknowledge that welfare markets are likely to be bureaucratically managed, and, once that is acknowledged, then the issue may become one of how best to organize bureaucracies rather than how best to introduce markets. (See Dunleavy 1991 for an approach which builds on public choice theory to produce a more developed analysis of the politics of bureaucracy.)

The network model is helpful because it directs our attention to the complexity of the central–local government system. It highlights the paradox between the apparent centralization of the UK political system and its actual fragmentation, particularly in terms of delivery systems (through sub-central governments) but also within central government. But there are also problems with the network model particularly because it tends to minimize the significance of open party politics at local and national levels. Both of the other models have rather more to say about politics in the sense of a conflict between different interests for scarce resources.

If each of three models has its problems, it should also be clear that bringing them together is quite a helpful way of looking back and assessing the experience of the 1970s and 1980s. Each model is just that — an attempt to develop a simplified expression of how decisions are made and organizations behave. Such models are essential if we are to be able to understand the most important processes at work. As a result, however, each is also bound to be partial, if only because no model of social life can ever incorporate its full complexity. But at least in this case it is possible to use the models so that their individual weaknesses are compensated for by their collective strengths, as each is used to question the other and draw our attention to different aspects of change.

Despite their combined strength, however, all of the models have a shared weakness which is apparent in their analysis of central–local relations. None of them is very convincing in placing those relations in their wider social and economic context. The major events and constraints which shape what is possible tend to be introduced from the outside into systems which respond to them. The danger of this is that it makes it difficult to acknowledge significant shifts which are taking place and easy to concentrate instead on the incremental adjustments within hierarchies, markets and networks. Yet, it is increasingly clear that local government is being reshaped as part of wider processes of social and economic change (see for example Cochrane, 1991; Stoker, 1990). The crisis of the local government system which started in the 1970s and was not yet fully resolved at the start of the 1990s, was part of the wider political crisis through which the UK passed at the same time, as the old certainties of Keynesian welfarism were called into question (see for example Cochrane, 1993). Local government was one of the key battlegrounds over which the important political battles of the late twentieth century were fought. Sometimes it is easy to miss that in the more measured discussion of models of coordination.

REFERENCES

Adam Smith Institute (1989) *Wiser Councils, The Reform of Local Government*, London, Adam Smith Institute.

Bulpitt, J. (1989) 'Walking back to happiness? Conservative party government and elected local authorities in the 1980s' in Crouch, C. and Marquand, D. (eds.) (1989) *The New Centralism: Britain Out of Step in Europe*, Oxford, Basil Blackwell.

Burgess, T. and Travers, T. (1980) *Ten Billion Pounds. Whitehall's Takeover of the Town Halls*, London, Grant McIntyre.

CIPFA (1989) *Local Government Trends 1989*, London, Chartered Institute of Public Finance and Accountancy.

Cochrane, A. (1991) 'The changing state of local government restructuring for the 1990s', *Public Administration*, vol 69, no. 3, pp. 281–302

Cochrane, A. (1993) *Whatever Happened to Local Government?* Buckingham, The Open University Press.

Dunleavy, P. (1991) *Democracy, Bureaucracy and Public Choice. Economic Explanations in Political Science*, London, Harvester Wheatsheaf.

Fleming, A. (1989) 'Employment in public and private sectors', *Economic Trends*, no. 434, pp. 91–3.

Foster, C.D., Jackman, R. A., Perlman, M. with the assistance of Lynch, B. (1980) *Local Government Finance in a Unitary State*, London, Allen and Unwin.

Hill, D. (1970) *Participating in Local Affairs*, Harmondsworth, Penguin.

Jackman, R. (1981) 'How to control local government spending', *Journal of Economic Affairs*, vol 1, no. 3, pp. 177–8.

Keating, M., Midwinter, A. and Taylor, P. (1983) 'Excessive and unreasonable: the politics of the Scottish hit list', *Political Studies*, vol. 31, no. 3, pp. 394–417.

LACSAB (1990) *CCT Information Service Survey Report No. 1*, London, Local Authorities' Conditions of Service Advisory Board/Local Government Training Board.

Lansley, S., Goss, S. and Wolmar, C. (1989) *Councils in Conflict. The Rise and Fall of the Municipal Left*, London, Macmillan.

Le Grand, J. (1990) *Quasi-markets and Social Policy. Studies in Decentralisation and Quasi-markets*, Bristol, School for Advanced Urban Studies, University of Bristol.

Midwinter, A. (1989) 'Economic theory, the poll tax and local spending', *Politics*, vol. 9, no. 2, pp. 9–15.

Niskanen, W.A. (1973) *Bureaucracy: Servant or Master? Lessons from America*, London, Institute for Economic Affairs.

O'Dowd, L. (1989) 'Devolution without consensus. The case of Northern Ireland' in Anderson, J. and Cochrane, A. (eds.), *A State of Crisis*, London, Hodder and Stoughton.

Rhodes, R. (1985) 'A squalid and politically corrupt process? Intergovernmental relations in the post-war period', *Local Government Studies*, vol. 11, no. 6, pp. 35–57.

Rhodes, R. (1988) *Beyond Westminster and Whitehall: Sub-Central Governments of Britain*, London, Unwin Hyman.

Rose, R. (1982) *Understanding the United Kingdom,* London, Longman.

Stewart, J. (1984) 'Storming the town halls: rate capping revolution'. *Marxism Today,* no. 28, p. 4.

Stoker, G. (1988) *New Management Trends,* Luton, LGTB.

Stoker, G. (1990) 'Regulation theory, local government and the transition from Fordism' in King, D. and Pierre, J. (eds.) *Challenges to Local Government,* London, Sage.

CHAPTER 11:
MANAGING THE CIVIL SERVICE

Keith Dowding

1   Introduction

The 1980s brought the biggest managerial changes in the civil service
for a century. The reforms started with a concerted effort by a Conservative government to reduce the numbers of civil servants and the costs
of administering the state. It increased the contracting out of services,
privatized sections of the civil service, created a small team under
Derek Rayner to look at the efficiency of selected parts of the government machine, introduced new management systems, and finally under a
reform known as *The Next Steps* — following the subtitle of a report
produced under the tutelage of Rayner's successor Robin Ibbs — it has
started the process of creating semi-autonomous agencies for service delivery divorced from the policy-making machinery of Whitehall.
This chapter will explain these changes, their rationale and their
likely consequences. It is concerned with management of the civil service. Only in the final section will some of the political consequences of
these managerial changes be briefly discussed.

2   Civil service reforms

The modern reforms have come about following a period of criticism of
the efficiency and effectiveness of the public sector as a whole. However, many of these criticisms are not new and should be placed in context. Indeed, each decade in the twentieth century has seen a report
critical of the civil service, reports from Parliament, ones commissioned
by Government or ones issued by the Royal Institute for Public Administration. Few have been effective however. The most famous report
which was largely responsible for transforming the civil service in the
latter half of the nineteenth century was the Northcote-Trevelyan Report of 1854. It is worth recalling some of its recommendations to compare with more recent views of administrative efficiency. The report
suggested six main reforms which created the civil service as it existed
throughout most of the twentieth century.

1   The civil service should be divided between superior and inferior
    posts corresponding to intellectual and mechanical tasks.
2   Entry into the civil service should be for young men who are then
    trained 'on the job'.

Table 11.1 The Fulton Report and civil service change since 1968

Findings	Recommendations	Implementation
Generalist philosophy	'Preference for relevance' degrees	Rejected
Generalist philosophy	Administrators should specialize	'Open structure' , littleeffect
Little management training	Civil Service College and management training	Implemented but most training in departments
Staff management inadequate, career planning inadequate, promotion too dependent on seniority, Treasury should not combine financial and management functions	Civil Service Department headed by Prime Minister to absorb the Civil Service Commission	Established 1968; abolished 1981; Financial Management Iniative and new training 1985; Treasury regains financial and management functions 1988
Departmentalism and proliferation of grades	Unified grading and job evaluation	'Open structure' ,little effect. *Next Steps* changes direction
Too inward	Two way transfers with private sector	Pension rules modified with little effect. Mrs Thatcher brings in private sector advisers
Too much secrecy	Inquiry into Official Secrets Act	Franks Report 1972 on Section 2 Official Secrets Act 1989
Oxbridge dominated	Inquiry into recruitment. Larger graduate entry	Davies Report 1969, Administration Trainee grade. Enlarged entry but reduced 1981

Source: Drewry and Butcher, 1988, *The Civil Service Today* up-dated and modified by the author

3   Recruitment should be on merit based upon competitive examinations overseen by an independent central board.

4   The examinations should be based upon the arts (rather than the sciences) and for the superior positions be on a par with the university education.

5   All promotion should be on merit.

6   The civil service should become less fragmented and allow individuals to move from department to department and be given a more uniform pay structure.

It is worth while pausing to consider the reasons behind some of the reforms mooted in the Northcote-Trevelyan Report. First, the civil service, dependent as it was upon a patronage system, was notoriously inefficient and filled with the indolent who secured promotion not on merit but on personal favour. Northcote-Trevelyan wanted to overcome this problem by an entry requirement based upon merit and they looked to the dominant intellectual tradition of the time in the schools and universities. Hence the arts bias in the examination system which remains to this day. They also wanted young men trained 'on the job' in order to stop 'the dregs of all other professions' entering the civil service as a secure haven having failed in their original choice of employment. It took a long time for many of the reforms to be implemented but Northcote-Trevelyan is still referred to today as a benchmark when discussing the desirability of any changes in the civil service structure.

The Fulton Report (1968) was likewise commissioned following doubts as to the efficiency of the civil service, particularly its ability to deal with modern technological society. Its main conclusions are contained in Table 11.1. Clearly Fulton wanted greater specialization, greater mobility between the civil service and the private sector, less secrecy, and some privatization, plus the setting up of a Civil Service Department and College to reduce the influence of the Treasury. Table 11.1 also describes how far Fulton was implemented. Modern reforms which, as we shall see, derive more from the recent initiatives under Mrs Thatcher's premiership to take the civil service closer to some of Fulton's recommendations than the immediate responses of the government and civil service. Most critics argue that Fulton failed in its objective since the civil service itself was given the task of implementing Fulton and its general conservatism and self-interest ensured that most of the changes were abandoned (Kellner and Crowther-Hunt, 1980, Chapters 4 and 5). Mrs Thatcher demonstrated a greater determination to force change and brought in civil servants who fitted her description of 'one of us' to ensure that radical changes were brought about.

3   Introducing market incentives

3.1 Reforms started under Mrs Thatcher

The first assault on the civil service was in many ways simply a number reducing exercise. Table 11.2 shows the numbers of civil servants from 1797 to 1991. We can see a fairly steady peacetime growth with more rapid spurts at the time of the First and Second World Wars. Numbers did reduce during the 1950s and early 1960s, though they picked up again during the later 1960s and 1970s. From 1979 the numbers of civil servants fell rapidly. However, many of these losses were losses from the public sector rather than losses in jobs (at least at first). Privatization of the naval shipyards and other blue-collar workers reduced the numbers by something like 100,000. Privatization of productive work and the contracting of many services, such as cleaning, both fit into the ideology of the Conservative administration that the market is a more efficient producer of services than the public sector.

Table 11.2   Civil servant numbers 1797–1991

Year	Number of civil servants	Year	Number of civil servants
1797	16,267	1914	280,900
1815	24,598	1922	317,721
1821	27,000	1939	347,000
1832	21,305	1944	1,164,000
1841	16,750	1950	746,000
1851	39,147	1960	643,000
1861	31,947	1970	701,000
1871	53,874	1979	732,000
1881	50,859	1986	594,000
1891	79,241	1989	569,000
1901	116,413	1991	554,000
1911	172,352		

Sources: G. Drewry and T. Butcher *The Civil Service Today*, 1988, p. 48; *Civil Service Statistics 1988–89; 1990-91*.

The classic defence of straightforward hierarchical organization within a public bureaucracy involves the idea that civil servants are implementors who methodically apply rules to particular cases 'read off' from their rule book. They have clearly demarcated spheres of competence and can act as impersonal cyphers for their politician masters' policies. Recently, however, the straightforward hierarchical mode of efficiency has been challenged. Dominant wisdom suggests that market methods of organization are more efficient in all spheres of life. Thus recent attempts at reform up to and including *The Next Steps*, have looked to the private sector and market methods to see if they can improve upon the strict hierarchy of the civil service. What were the roots of dissatisfaction with the hierarchical mode of public provision? One was the widely perceived inefficiency of bureaucracy which found its best expression in the popular books of Leslie Chapman

(1978, 1982). Indeed Chapman was brought in by Thatcher to advise her on civil service waste. Another root of dissatisfaction was contained in the 'rational choice' models of bureaucracy developed by American economists such as William Niskanen. This is discussed later.

A main advantage of market organization is the incentives it produces for those in productive roles. Such incentives come in two forms. The first is simply 'pay packet' rewards. For example, if a company produces a product which consumers want and profits soar, then this may be reflected in the pay packets of its employees. The harder they work, the greater the production and hence the greater the rewards possible. This sort of incentive to produce more efficiently can be modelled by non-market processes if a measure of the output of individual employees can be devised. This is not always easy to do, although in fact it is often no easier to measure the output of individual workers in the private sector than it is in the public sector. Only a relatively few industrial workers work piece rate; whilst measuring the output of white collar workers in the private sector does not differ greatly from measuring the output of white collar workers in the public sector.

However, the market produces a second incentive for increased production and innovation which it is much harder for non-market processes to mimic. This is the entrepreneurial function. Entrepreneurs are innovators who take risks, usually with other people's money, but risks none the less. If they fail, then they end up worse off than if they had not tried. Even though the chances of failure are high the rewards of success are so great that the risks are worth taking for risk-taking individuals. However, bureaucrats tend to be risk averse, and for very good reasons. If a civil servant suggests innovations which patently fail then his promotion prospects dim immediately even if he hangs on to his job whilst if he succeeds the rewards of risk taking are not great. Certainly he may receive accelerated promotion but materially this does not compare with the rewards which entrepreneurs may expect in market situations. A better life-plan for the civil servant is not to take risks and secure himself a smooth path to promotion. It is hard to see how this incentive problem could be overcome. Typically, come boom or recession, only about one in ten entrepreneurs succeeds (though fewer entrepreneurs operate in times of recession, for banks are less willing to lend money); could we really operate a system of bureaucracy which allowed such a high failure rate? Could we give each civil servant the chance to fail nine times in order to see if he can succeed in some innovation once? Moreover it is harder to measure success and failure without the ready made process of market demand.

The possibility of introducing market processes within the civil service is limited, though some initiatives were attempted in the 1980s. Raynerism, the Financial Management Initiative (FMI), and the latest changes contained in *The Next Steps* are all initiatives which attempt to change the incentive structures of civil servants to make them more efficient and 'managerial'.

On becoming Prime Minister, Mrs Thatcher appointed Sir Derek (now Lord) Rayner, then head of Marks and Spencer, as an adviser on administrative efficiency. He was given a small 'unit' composed of both civil servants and outsiders. Rayner's (1982) objectives were to:

1   examine a specific policy or activity, questioning all aspects of work normally taken for granted;

2   propose solutions to problems and to make recommendations to achieve savings and increase efficiency and effectiveness;

3   implement agreed solutions, or to begin their implementation within twelve months of the start of a scrutiny.

There followed a number of scrutinies which involved these stages:

1   A strategy was created. All departments were expected to suggest areas for scrutiny.

2   The investigation which followed was usually carried out by department staff, who submitted a report to the minister within ninety working days.

3   An action plan was then created which summarized ideas for implementing savings. This had to be approved within three months of receipt of the initial report.

4   The saving had then to be implemented. This was the responsibility of the permanent secretary of each department.

5   Two years after the initial scrutiny an implementation report was drawn up to see what savings had in fact been achieved.

Rayner had no right of entry into departments and could only investigate where he was invited, however pressure was put upon senior civil servants to allow him access. In the first six years a total of 266 reviews were completed which identified annual savings of £600 million with a further £67 million of one-off savings. There are many small examples. For instance, it was discovered that government research departments spent £30 producing their own rats for experiments when they could be bought for £2 each on the open market; and it cost £90 to administer each £100 of woodland grant. But more importantly large scale possibilities for savings were identified.

By 1986, £950 million of savings had been identified against scrutiny costs of only £5 million. However, critics have argued that many of the identified savings did not occur in practice. Some have suggested that the savings made are miniscule in relation to the overall budget. Richard Rose (1987) argued that the savings in 1982–3 were only 0.4 per cent of total government expenditure. A better measure is the cost of the savings compared to the costs of running central government — about 6 per cent. Furthermore, since we are talking about vast sums of money the savings are not insignificant.

3.2 The Financial Management Initiative

The Financial Management Initiative (FMI) was designed to produce a general and coordinated drive to improve financial management in departments. The aim of FMI was to promote in each department an organization and system in which managers at all levels have:

1   a clear view of their objectives, and means to assess and, wherever possible, measure outputs or performance in relation to those objectives;

2   well-defined responsibility for making the best use of their resources, including a critical scrutiny of output and value for money; and

3   the information (particularly about costs), the training and access to expert advice that they need to exercise their responsibilities effectively.

Underlying FMI was the idea that in order to make use of resources one has to be clear about the objectives of expenditure and it was expected that all departments would develop their objectives under specific priorities. All have done so although their objectives often seem rather vague. It is also clear that departments find it much easier to establish objectives for administrative costs, which make up 13 per cent of total costs, than for the bulk of their programme costs.

The Financial Management Unit (FMU) — which later became the Joint Management Unit (JMU) — was set up jointly by the Management and Personnel Office (MPO) and the Treasury in 1982 to help thirty-one departments to examine all aspects of their work and to develop programmes to improve their financial management. Progress was monitored by two White Papers published in 1983 and 1984. Each department has taken on board a management information system like MINIS (Management Information System) — the prototype set up by Michael Heseltine with Rayner's help at the Department of the Environment — or developed systems of their own.

Attempts at budget devolution have been made by dividing departments into appropriate units or 'cost centres' each with a manager accountable for the costs under their control. For example, the Department of Health and Social Security (DHSS) (which was split into two departments in 1988) had over 800 centres (many of them local social security offices) with a manager who was responsible for keeping expenditure within a budget. However, these so-called 'efficiency drives' require examination.

One worry about these sorts of incentives, which has been voiced by the Civil and Public Services Association, is that they make local managers care as much about saving money as they do about ensuring that their clients are provided with the resources they need. Some people believe that this is a good thing; others see it as a major problem.

In order to carry out FMI the departments have had to develop ways of measuring their performances and those of their employees. In order to measure performance one must have a yardstick with which to compare it. This is much easier for administrative tasks. These include easily quantifiable running costs such as postage, staff, travel costs, photocopying and so on which can be used comparatively to measure throughput such as the number of cases dealt with and their unit costs. These measures can then be used to identify areas of underperformance, to set targets, and to form the basis of staff appraisal. Later in the process the emphasis changed to programme measurement. This is much more difficult. Comparison is much harder and costs may be spread across various divisions or even departments. Furthermore the benefits of programmes which produce collective goods cannot be quantified in the same way and proxy measures are often used in their stead. These may be misleading or downright wrong. Christopher Pollitt has noted that these efficiency measures are also, at root, political ones (Pollitt, 1986). Performance evaluation is value-laden by the sort of criteria which are used to choose those things to be evaluated. It has led in the views of some commentators to departments concentrating more upon short-term managerial innovations and agenda management than upon long-term policy goals.

The FMI requires a new type of civil servant who is trained in personnel management. In 1985 a new course was developed for those at under secretary level to teach them how to think collectively about management problems. Also in 1985 performance-related pay was introduced for all staff in grades three to seven, whilst new productivity agreements were offered to officials at deputy secretary and under secretary level to compete for discretionary payments of up to £2,000 per annum. Again what we have here are attempts at changing the incentives of civil servants. Rather than having a secure future merely by keeping their noses clean, civil servants are being asked continually to innovate with pay and promotion as the carrot. Logically the next step is to introduce the stick in the form of removing job security. Whilst not exactly a market process, as it does not follow the laws of supply and demand, it is certainly a competitive process which is the motor of markets. Of course, hierarchies have always had the motor of competition too. Civil servants have always been in competition for promotion; what has changed are the criteria upon which they are judged and the fact that the government is trying to heat up the competition by increasing the stakes.

Is all this enough? Pollitt argues that 'a government can force its employees to go through the motions, but it cannot mandate enthusiasm and "commitment" ' (Pollitt 1986, p. 165). MINIS, FMI and *The Next Steps* are just the latest of a long line of attempts to improve the efficiency of the civil service. However, there was a change of emphasis under Mrs Thatcher's administration. This change of emphasis is captured by those who suggest that the concept of 'efficiency' has replaced that of 'effectiveness'. Effectiveness is about attaining objectives and can be measured by the extent to which objectives are achieved. Efficiency is a relationship between inputs and outputs. Logically the two ought to go together. We choose our objectives and measure effectiveness by how closely we attain them. We can still measure our efficiency at attaining our objectives at any given level of attainment by comparing costs and benefits. But concentrating upon efficiency in the sense of keeping costs down can lead to losing sight of objectives. Take a homespun example. We may have the objective of keeping warm at home and find that a given mix of clothing and central heating is the most effective way of attaining this objective. Efficiency would then be to attain these levels as cheaply as possible. Buying cheap warm clothing rather than fashionable clothing would be one way. Fixing draught excluders, double glazing and lagging in the home would be another. But note the latter measures cost money in the short-term, even if they bring long-term saving. If efficiency is the by-word and pressures to keep costs down always operate in the short-term rather than looking to the future, then these long-term measures may be ignored. Efficiency then becomes equated with cutting costs, which in the homespun example may mean turning the heating down and wearing more clothes even if this is less effective at attaining our objectives. Thus short-term cost-cutting (rather than strict efficiency) has led us to lose sight of effectiveness. In recent years efficiency has come to mean cost-cutting which is in fact a long way from what it technically means. It is also significant that *The Next Steps* nomenclature suggests that the executive agency should be effective whilst the core department should be efficient. But given the logical priority of effectiveness over efficiency (for one can be efficient at any level of service) surely we should want core department effectiveness and executive agency efficiency.

3.3 *The Next Steps*

Sir Robin Ibbs took over the Efficiency Unit in 1983. His report, *The Next Steps*, is truly revolutionary in terms of civil service organization (Efficiency Unit, 1988). It suggested that we need to 'establish a quite different way of conducting the business of government'. The focus was on continued pressure for efficiency services provided by experts. Ibbs made three main recommendations that possibly:

1   agencies should be established to carry out the executive functions of government within a policy and resources framework set by a department;

2   departments ensure that their staff are properly trained in the delivery of services within or outside central government; the staff will then be in a position to develop and interpret govern-

ment policy and manage the agencies in a way that can maximize results;

3   a full Permanent Secretary should be designated as Project Manager as soon as possible to ensure that the change takes place.

The revolutionary idea was to create agencies designed to deliver services and play no part in policy making and thereby break up the unified structure of the civil service. Anne Mueller, a senior civil servant, suggested in *Working Patterns: a Study Document by the Cabinet Office* in 1987 that a two-tier civil service would emerge with the 'core' enjoying job security and career prospects with a 'periphery' staffed on a wide range of conditions of employment (Treasury and Civil Service Committee, 1987). The idea is that this would allow for a more flexible delivery without the structural rigidities of a unified career civil service. In Geoffrey Fry's (1988b) words *Working Patterns* concludes 'the Career Civil Service with its implication of permanency tends to make for staff costs to be effectively treated as if they were fixed costs, but the philosophy of FMI is to treat them as running costs (p. 436)'. *The Next Steps* was seen as the logical conclusion of FMI, for the rigid hierarchy of the career civil service does not allow for the managerial initiative Rayner and his successors are after. It is an attempt to encourage individual initiative, the entrepreneurial function outside market conditions. Peter Kemp the Project Manager for the implementation of *The Next Steps*, told the Treasury and Civil Service Select Committee that 'we are moving from a hierarchical system to a system in which the Minister and Chief Executive are in a quasi-contractual position' (Treasury and Civil Service Committee, 1990, p. 51).

There are obvious advantages in creating a periphery of workers paid at market rates rather than a unified national pay structure. A unified pay structure makes little economic or welfare sense where there are vastly different costs of living in different parts of the country — a fact recognized, but hardly compensated for, by 'London weighting'. Furthermore, it should mean that posts in short supply can be offered higher rates of pay in order to attract quality staff, whilst lower salaries can be offered for posts where there is a ready supply of workers. However, this does not necessarily mean that overall salary levels will fall, as the Treasury recognizes, a fact which has led it to fight devolution and try to keep control over pay throughout the civil service and associated agencies.

The first agency to be created was the Vehicle Inspectorate on 1 August 1988; by April 1991 a further forty-seven diverse agencies had been established, which employ over 37 per cent of the civil service. If current plans to create agencies for all policy-implementing functions are completed on schedule then only 2 per cent of civil servants will enjoy their current status by the end of the century.

The Ibbs report defines an agency as 'any executive unit that delivers a service for government', the main difference from previous agencies being the policy and resource framework under which all executive agencies operate. The agency framework allows for a reporting and accountability network between the Chief Executive, the 'parent' department and the Treasury. For each a corporate plan establishes current and future objectives and policy; the financial arrangements such as the means of controlling costs, delegation and accounting/auditing procedures; personnel issues and basic conditions of employment; plus review procedures. Once policy objectives and budgetary arrangements are set it is intended that the Chief Executive (who is also the Agency Accounting Officer) will have overall responsibility for the day-to-day executive functions which are the *raison d'être* for the agencies. The agency 'must be left as free as possible to manage within this framework...to strengthen operational effectiveness, there must be a freedom to recruit, pay, grade and structure in the most effective way'.

The policy-making and policy-implementation functions of the civil service have thus been almost completely separated. Almost though not completely, for Chief Executives are likely to be consulted during policy formation to ensure that policies are implementable. Framework agreements are reviewed and re-written every three years at present, though individual targets may be changed as new policies are introduced within the time period of the original framework agreement. However, the idea behind these changes is to create a central core of policy makers and advisors close to government: the Whitehall machine; with a periphery of policy implementors who can operate with the rigours and efficiency associated with the private sector.

4 The intellectual roots of *The Next Steps* reforms

When Mrs Thatcher came to power she had a low opinion of the civil service. She believed that the higher civil service had been responsible for the failures of the Keynes–Beveridge consensus. Nor did she think highly of the career civil servant whom, she thought, tried to see each side of every argument. Hennessy (1990) writes: 'Though always ready to exempt those who have served her closely and personally, she nevertheless detests senior civil servants as a breed. Mrs Thatcher simply does not believe that people of flair and enterprise should sign up for a job in the public service' (pp. 632–3). Her low opinion was partly formed during her earlier experiences as a junior minister at the Ministry of Pensions where she saw official advice vary as new ministers arrived. Her low opinion of the civil service is not confined to the higher echelons but extends to the lowliest clerk who is viewed as inefficient almost by default. The intellectual roots of this belief derive from a model of bureaucracy created by the American economist

William Niskanen and discussed in reports from the influential Adam Smith Institute and the Institute for Policy Studies.

4.1 Niskanen: the budget-maximizing model

Niskanen's (1971) model of bureaucratic behaviour is based upon neo-classical economic theory. In it, he imagines that every individual is a self-interested utility maximizer. That is, each person acts to bring themselves the greatest possible rewards. Firms in competitive markets maximize their utility by maximizing their profits. Profit maximization therefore becomes the motive force of their managers.

However, as bureaucracies do not have profits to maximize what determines their behaviour? Niskanen suggests that bureaucrats will maximize their budgets, because a higher budget will:

1   provide more jobs for bureaucrats and therefore improve promotion prospects;

2   tend to strengthen the demand for services making the department easier to run;

3   improve prestige and patronage opportunities;

4   generally provide more chances to deliver funds to private interests and goals.

The constraint upon maximization is that the bureau or department must supply the output expected of it by the government or the government may ignore the department's claims on future occasions. Rational choice analysts of bureaucracy have tended to treat the supply and demand for government goods and services in much the same way that classical micro-economics treats the demand and supply of traded goods and services. Demand comes from government, and in a democracy there is some control as the government is answerable to the electorate. Most rational choice writers assume that the government will tend to produce more goods than the majority of the electorate would choose under market conditions. This is because the government likes to make promises to different parts of the electorate and these promises taken together are greater than the sum total that the electorate would pay for services itself. In Niskanen's model, which is based upon his American experiences, bureaucrats are able continually to increase their budgets for two reasons. First, they have a near monopoly of information. Second, budgets are set by committees of politicians who are subject to the fragmented pressures of many diverse interest groups. Thus politicians generally support budget increases in their area of interests even though they may support cuts in the overall budget. The interaction and the fragmented nature of the pressures upon budget spending leads to a massive over supply of government goods and services, according to Niskanen's model.

Bureaux do have incentives to seek out and to implement the most efficient combination of resources but:

1   The *strength* of these incentives are not as great as they are for a profit maximizing firm. For example, a firm that makes 5 per cent profit can cut costs by 5 per cent and make 100 per cent increase in profit, but a 5 per cent reduction in costs for bureau leads to less, perhaps considerably less, than 5 per cent in spending power.

2   The factor costs (wages, fringe benefits, fees, rents, and so on) are lower than their full value because the civil service is exempted from taxes, rates and so on. Therefore over used factors of production are underpriced.

3   Some bureaux, especially those where demand grows rapidly, have no marginal incentive for productive efficiency.

There can be little or no doubt that Niskanen's and other similar arguments have influenced recent government attempts to cut back on bureaucratic waste. Many of the attempts to try to force rigid hierarchies, to be more critical of their procedures, to bring in different sorts of incentives for civil servants to consider the costs of their activities and so on, are all part of the attempt to limit budgets. However, Niskanen's model of bureaucratic behaviour is very limited. He has little to say about the internal organization of bureaucracies which for him are straightforward line agencies directly controlled from the top. The strategy which maximizes the utility of the head of each department thus determines the strategy for the whole department. However, departments in the civil service vary in structure, aims and organization. The Niskanen model is far too simple. Patrick Dunleavy has developed a model of the British civil service which uses Niskanen's 'rational choice' or economic framework assuming individual utility maximization but which takes account of the empirical realities of the British situation. He has developed a 'bureau-shaping' model of the civil service. We will briefly consider Dunleavy's model and then see what it teaches us about what we should expect to result from FMI and *The Next Steps*.

4.2 Dunleavy: the bureau-shaping model

Patrick Dunleavy was not happy with the rational choice approach to bureaucracy believing it to be too simplistic and unrealistic (Dunleavy 1991). However, he discovered that by modifying the assumptions and providing a more realistic description of the civil service he could utilize rational choice methods to explain the changes taking place. His original problem with the rational choice models was their static, unchanging nature. Yet, in recent years, as we have seen there have been major attempts at reform in Britain. These attempts at radical reform, whilst emanating largely from politicians who exist outside the

Niskanen model, are being carried out by bureaucrats — which seems to falsify Niskanen's argument. However, it does not falsify his methods if more complex models, based upon the same assumptions, are able to help explain the changes.

Niskanen assumes that each department is run by a senior official whose job it is to decide the budget for that department. The budget thus becomes the private *good* of that senior civil servant and the utility of the department is therefore equated with the utility of that senior official. However, this does not realistically describe the organization of the departments. In fact there are many senior civil servants in each department who, despite the hierarchical structure, all have a hand in preparing budgetary claims but do not all share the same interests. At any given level in the hierarchy there will be civil servants in competition with each other for promotion and recognition. As they are in control of different aspects of the department's work they will have objectives which may be at variance with those of their colleagues. (Many departments have up to eighty staff at Assistant Secretary level or above.) Officials may pursue their own objectives ranging from the individually private to the collectively public: for example, vertical promotion in the bureau, promotion across departments, upward regrading of their particular job, workload reduction, diversion of money to pet schemes, general improvement in working conditions, general pay increases across all levels of staff, budget maximization and so on.

Dunleavy argues that whilst all officials have a common interest in having as big a budget for the department as possible, they also all have an interest in getting as much as possible of the overall budget diverted to their own divisions or sections. Civil servants are mainly indifferent to budget increases for other departments, but are likely to be opposed to them if:

1   it means that a department gains in prestige *vis-à-vis* their own; and

2   it entails their own department getting less.

There is also the added collective action problem. Individual civil servants will only press for an increased budget for their own department if they think that their own demands stand a certain probability of succeeding. They will only advocate a large budget if the cost to them — in time and trouble — of making those demands are lower than the expected benefits of the increase multiplied by the probability that their efforts will be decisive in bringing about a change. The lower down the hierarchy an official is located the lower the probability of the success of their advocating budgetry increase. This leads us to expect that the lower in the hierarchy the official is located the more conservative his or her attitude will be towards change.

Dunleavy also criticizes Niskanen's simplistic conception of a 'budget'. Dunleavy argues that in fact there are at least four different types of budget and whilst civil servants want to maximize some of them they will be indifferent to increases in others (Figure 11.1).

1   *Core budget:* spent on maintaining its own operations — staff, accommodation, day-to-day activities, personal equipment (i.e. running costs).

2   *Bureau budget:* those parts of the programme for which the department is directly responsible to the government.

3   *Programme budget:* all expenditure over which the department exercises supervision or control.

4   *Super programme budget:* consists of the department's programme budget plus any spending by other departments from their own budgets over which this particular department has some control or exercises some responsibility;

The benefits to civil servants of an increase in each element of the budget are not the same. According to Dunleavy, the benefits to each bureaucrat from a budgetary increase are mostly associated with the core budget or the bureau budget. On the other hand, the costs of increasing the budget (in time spent, level of external criticism of sponsor and public) are associated with the programme budget. For example, if education costs in local education authorities rise sharply, the burden

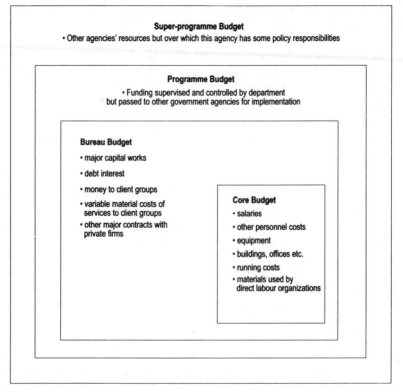

Figure 11.1   Types of Budget

of defending their record in Cabinet and Parliament falls on the Department of Education and Science, especially in the annual round of negotiations over the following year's budget. Officials in the DES had
no reason to desire a spiralling programme budget. The 1988 Education
Reform Act, as well as increasing central control in the form of a
National Curriculum and an associated system of attainment testing at
different age levels, also brought devolved budgeting and local
management into schools. This effectively by-passes Local Education
Authorities and gives the DES greater control over the programme budget (Whitty, 1990). Thus where the programme budget is not in the control of the central department, civil servants will either try to bring it
back into their control, or they will try to achieve efficiencies in that
budget in order to allow the core and bureau budgets to rise as much as
possible.

Once we have seen how the budget may be split up we can see that
four criteria are important:

1   the overall size of budget;

2   bureau budget/programme budget ratio;

3   core budget/programme budget ratio; and

4   core budget/bureau budget ratio.

These ratios can be represented in a simple diagram as is shown in
Figure 11.2. Thus we can expect civil servants to have a different attitude to the efficiency drives of the FMI. Those drives which affected
the core and bureau budget would not be as welcome as those which affected the programme budget.

As we saw, Niskanen's view of bureaux as simple line-bureaucracies
with a single set of interests is not realistic. So Dunleavy defines different types of bureaux according to how they allocate their resources
and in terms of their internal organization. He produces a list of eight
different types of bureau which have different relationships between
the different types of budget (see Dunleavy 1991, Chapter 7) and he
concludes:

> Once we recognize the distinct meanings which are attached to
> the term 'budget', the claim that bureaucracies maximize their
> budgets clearly becomes ambiguous. What particular budget
> should rationally self-interested officials seek to increase?
> The consistent answer for a public choice account would seem to
> be that officials will maximize their agency's core budget, fol-
> lowed in some cases by the bureau budget.
>
> (*Dunleavy, 1989, p. 273*)

Lower-ranked civil servants will favour increases in core budgets,
whilst higher ranked officials may favour increases in bureau budgets.
Dunleavy's own model is called the bureau-shaping model. He suggests
that rational officials adopt a bureau-shaping strategy designed to
bring their bureau progressively closer to the 'staff' rather than the

'line' agency. They maximize this objective within budget constraints but budget constraints carry with them the character and size of the agency. At each stage of this process officials seek to achieve a satisfactory level of budget, but this level is set by their previous success in getting the bureau to conform to their objectives. One of the most important consequences suggested by this model is the attempt to reduce the constraints upon the core budget over time by delinking the top officials' utilities from dependence upon an absolute level of programme or bureau budget — thus the successful bureau takes on a smaller, central, elite character over time. There are four main bureau-shaping strategies:

1   Major internal reorganizations of the bureau. Acquisitions of functions will be concentrated at a policy-making level whilst routine functions will be 'hived-off' to other agencies or private firms. Often geographical separation is a key means of achieving this result. The agency idea of *The Next Steps* is in line with this prediction.

2   Redefinition of relationships with external partners — maximize policy control whilst minimizing day-to-day accountability. Hiving-off is important, as are bringing greater control over policy to the centre. For example, the 1988 Education Reform Act fits this prediction.

3   Competition with other bureaux at the same level of government. Bureaucrats defend the scope of their activities rather than the programme budgets associated with it, so may compete to do the programme cheaper than other departments. An example of fighting over the scope of departmental activities is provided by Richard Crossman who describes Dame Evelyn Sharpe's battle to retain the 'planning' function at the Department of the Environment (quoted in Hennessy, 1990, p. 436).

4   Transformation of internal work practices to achieve more sophisticated management — that is complicate decision making in order to avoid problems of internal criticism. A glance at Hennessy's *Whitehall* (Chapter 10) allows us to see that there are now sixteen different management systems across twenty-two departments. Each department argues that its functions are unique and thus it requires a unique management system rather than having the same management system (say MINIS) as the other departments, which would allow easier external accountability.

Dunleavy argues that the empirical evidence confirms his rather than Niskanen's model. If Niskanen were right we should have expected state growth to take the form of accretion of large budgets by line agencies, expansion of already existing large agencies and a continuing centralization of state growth. None of this has occurred. Rather existing large line agencies have been broken up. New governmental growth has been concentrated outside central government in sub-national governments — local, in single-function agencies and quasi-gov-

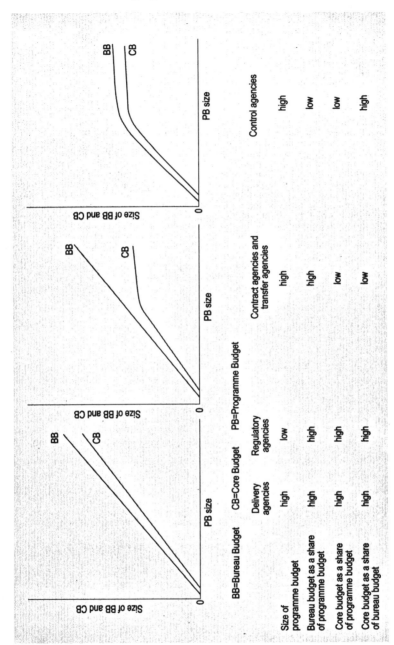

The table within the figure:

	Delivery agencies	Regulatory agencies	Contract agencies and transfer agencies	Control agencies
Size of programme budget	high	low	high	high
Bureau budget as a share of programme budget	high	high	high	low
Core budget as a share of programme budget	high	high	low	low
Core budget as a share of bureau budget	high	high	low	high

BB=Bureau Budget   CB=Core Budget   PB=Programme Budget

Figure **11.2** *Dunleavy's Budget and Rates Model*

Source: Dunleavy, 1989.

ernmental organizations. Programmes have been removed from central control through privatization, contracting out and physical removal of lower officials from the control officials. Core budgets have increased as a proportion of programme and bureau budgets and top bureaucrats have massively increased their salaries in comparison to their juniors. In 1979 top civil servants salaries were six times the basic civil service minimum; by 1987 there were 15.5 times the basic salary. How this occurred is instructive. Christopher Monckton, formerly a member of the Prime Minister's Policy Unit, writes:

> When the Review Body on Top Salaries recommended a large increase in the salaries of top civil servants in 1985, all the papers relating to the Report were given a national security classification as though the matter were a military secret which could, in the wrong hands, endanger the safety of the State. Members of the Prime Minister's Policy Unit are cleared to see papers classified up so far as Secret. We were, therefore, unaware of the existence of the Report or of any of the papers relating to it until we saw the Cabinet Minute recording that the Report had been agreed. At this point we at once protested at this scandalous abuse of the classification system and made enquiries which eventually revealed that the Prime Minister had taken our silence as acquiescence. It is no secret that the Prime Minister has realized that the wrong decision was taken.
>
> *(Cited in Fry 1988a p. 12)*

We have seen how the civil service is structured and how it has been changing in the past ten years or so and the justification behind those changes. The Niskanen model of the bureaucracy was introduced to explain the intellectual roots of the *The Next Steps* reforms, and Dunleavy's critique to demonstrate the failings of Niskanen's analysis. Dunleavy's model suggests that the reforms contained in *The Next Steps* may well be in the interests of the higher civil service allowing top administrators to concentrate upon policy formulation leaving implementation to lower levels. Whether it will lead to the greater efficiencies expected by its proponents remains to be seen.

5   Accountability in the new civil service

Many academics have claimed that *The Next Steps* process will cause problems for government accountability to parliament. This section will review those claims and argue that they are greatly overplayed, for two reasons. First, they exaggerate the extent of accountability which existed previously. Second, they exaggerate the difference that *The Next Steps* will make. There is undoubtedly a problem of government accountability in Britain but it has little to do with *The Next Steps* reforms.

Civil servants are only accountable to parliament in the sense that their ministers report to parliament on the activities of their departments. Ministers are also accountable to parliament through the questions they answer to the House. Logically accountability requires some form of independent verification of the information relayed to parliament. One of the problems for such accountability occurs when it is in the interests of both civil servants and ministers to provide the same story. This problem is exacerbated by the Osmotherly rules — drawn up following the setting up of the new Select Committees in 1980 — and Sir Robert (now Lord) Armstrong's memorandum 'On the duties and responsibilities of civil servants in relation to ministers', which make clear that civil servants should not inform parliament of anything their ministers want kept secret. The Osmotherly rules state that any civil servant appearing before the select committees 'remains subject to ministerial instructions as to how he should answer questions.' Indeed these rules allowed the government to refuse to permit certain civil servants to appear before the Defence Committee in the wake of the Westland Affair, on the grounds that as they would not be allowed to answer the questions the committee would like to ask, there was no point in their appearing before it. Armstrong's memorandum states that the 'Civil Service as such has no constitutional personality or responsibility separate from that of the elected Government of the day' (Armstrong, 1988, p.14)).

Accountability to the House rests upon a very thin foundation indeed. This foundation is nothing more than the fear of ministers (and their civil servants) of actually lying to parliament. But whilst direct lies are, at present, rare there are many means by which the House may be misled. One Assistant Secretary to the Chancellor of the Exchequer stated:

> With a minister you give a full and quick answer to what he wants. With an MP, you often know what point he is trying to make, but you answer no more than the precise questions he has asked. If he has not asked the right questions, that's his problem. Often the answer to PQs (Parliamentary Questions) are deliberately misleading.

(Quoted in Kellner and Crowther-Hunt, 1980, p.164)

What difference does the process of creating agencies mean to this accountability? One of the aims of the process is to divide policy making from policy implementation. Given that one of the problems of policy making is that it does not take into account the difficulties of implementation this may seem a strange aim, but aim it is. Accountability may be enhanced due to the existence of framework agreements which set out in black and white what the targets of the implementation phase are to be. So long as these are in the public domain they clarify, at least marginally, what was previously intra-departmental and obscure. Now Chief Executives are responsible for the activities of their agencies and in most cases will report directly to parliament themselves. (The line of accountability from agencies to parliament varies according to the framework agreements. The Patent Offices Framework

Agreement, for example, states 'DTI Ministers will answer to Parliament on the work of the Agency'; whereas the Companies House Agreement merely states that there may be cases where the 'Ministers will decide to reply'.) Reporting to parliament will occur by two means. First, Chief Executives will answer MPs questions about their areas of responsibility (ministers may refer questions they are asked to Chief Executives). These answers will be available from the Commons library and appended to *Hansard* much as ministers' answers are now. Second, Chief Executives will appear before select committees themselves. If they feel secure enough to point out implementation difficulties and, if by implication alone, criticize the policy making of government then accountability could be enhanced. However, whilst Chief Executives are encumbered by the Osmotherly rules this is unlikely. The agency process will not enhance accountability, but this is due to the Osmotherly rules, not *The Next Steps* process. Only if agencies are seen to be outside the purview of government itself; if, that is, they take on the role of private companies, as mooted by William Waldegrave during the summer of 1992, can we say that ministerial responsibility has lessened. But then if it is the Conservative government's aim to reduce the sphere of governmental influence, this policy result cannot be criticized on constitutional grounds. Not unless, that is, there are constitutional reasons why government should not reduce the responsibility of the state. There are no such constitutional grounds.

References

Armstrong, R. (1989) 'The duties and responsibilities of civil servants in relation to ministers: note by the Head of the Home Civil Service', reprinted in Marshall, G. *Ministerial Responsibility*, Oxford, Oxford University Press.

Chapman, L. (1978) *Your Disobedient Servant*, London, Chatto and Windus.

Chapman, L. (1982) *Waste Away*, London, Chatto and Windus.

Drewry, G. and Butcher, T. (1988) *The Civil Service Today*, Oxford, Basil Blackwell Ltd.

Dunleavy, P. (1989) 'The architecture of the British central state: Part I framework for analysis: Part II empirical findings', *Public Administration*, 67, pp. 249–75 and 391–417.

Dunleavy, P. (1991) *Democracy, Bureaucracy and Public Choice*, Hemel Hempstead, Harvester Wheatsheaf.

Efficiency Unit (1988) *Improving Management in Government: The Next Steps*, London, HMSO (The Ibbs Report).

Fry, G. (1988a) 'The Thatcher government, the financial management initiative, and the 'new civil service', *Public Administration*, 66, pp. 1–20.

Fry, G. (1988b) 'Outlining "The next steps"', Symposium of improving management in government, *Public Administration*, 66, pp. 429–38.

Hennessy, P. (1990) *Whitehall*, London, Fontana.

Kellner, P. and Crowther-Hunt, Lord (1980) *The Civil Servants: An Inquiry into Britain's Ruling Class*, London, MacDonald, Futura Publishers.

Niskanen, W.A. (1971) *Bureaucracy and Representative Government*, Chicago, Aldine.

Pollitt, C. (1986) 'Beyond the managerial model: the case for broadening performance assessment in government and the public services', *Financial Accountability and Management*, 12, pp. 115–70.

Rayner, Sir Derek (1982) *The Scrutiny Programme — a Note of Guidance* (revised), London, Management and Personnel Office.

Report on the Organization of the Permanent Civil Service, (1854) London, HMSO (Northcote-Trevelyan Report).

Rose, R. (1987) *Ministers and Ministries: A Functional Approach*, Oxford, Oxford University Press.

Treasury and Civil Service Committee (1987) *Working Patterns: a Study Document by the Cabinet Office*, London, HMSO (the Mueller Report).

Treasury and Civil Service Committee (1990) *Eighth report: progress in the next steps initiative*, Session 1989–90, HC 481, London, HMSO.

Whitty, G. (1990) 'The politics of the 1988 Education Reform Act' in Dunleavy, P., Gamble, A., and Peele, G. (eds.), *Developments in British Politics 3*, London, Macmillan.

CHAPTER 12:
OVERVIEW AND CONCLUSION

Tom Ling

1 Introduction

In this final chapter we have the opportunity to see how the earlier chapters fit into the wider context of the political economy and public policy of the UK and to consider the key questions which arise from the case studies. One concerns the globalization or Europeanization of the UK. Evidence of this is particularly prominent in chapters on the automobile industry and the high technology industries and in the first section of this chapter we consider the extent to which the experiences of these industries are matched by other trends in the UK.

In the second section we examine the changing public sector. Examples from housing, education, hospitals, local government and the Civil Service all suggest important recent changes. We examine the extent to which these changes amount to a systematic restructuring rather than a series of *ad hoc* responses.

The third section concerns the economy. As well as considering the apparent globalization (or, perhaps, Japanization, according to our case studies) other questions are considered. Is the economy restructuring in some fundamental (perhaps post-Fordist) way, is it becoming more efficient, has the state been 'rolled back' from the economy and what are the options facing future Governments?

Finally, we consider the social context of managing the UK. What has happened to the main social relationships such as class, gender and race? Is the UK becoming more poverty-ridden and unequal or are we seeing a new culture of freedom and opportunity? Or have things really not changed much in the society still dominated by the 'good chaps' from public schools and Oxbridge?

The models outlined in Chapters 1, 2 and 3 provide useful tools for painting this wider context. Whilst they do not dictate the analysis they do provide a useful way into further important questions. Some of these are based directly on the models. Is Britain now more shaped by markets and less by hierarchies? Are networks necessary to organizational success? They also generate other, equally important, questions such as is management becoming flatter, is the public sector more contractual in its relationships, or is the Establishment able to keep itself in a dominant position? With these questions in mind, let us consider the claim that external factors decisively shape internal developments.

2 Globalization and Europeanization

There is now considerable academic sensitivity to global, international and European factors in shaping the UK's domestic circumstances. But has the UK suddenly become more vulnerable to external influences? To begin to answer this we must untangle the different issues involved and first we should clarify our terms.

The term 'international' implies a relationship between independent nation states whilst the term 'globalization' implies both that the nation state is no longer the most significant causal unit and that most important developments within each nation state are driven by the global system. The idea of Europeanization is different again. It might imply that we are seeing a regionalization of the 'West' around three major regions; the Pacific rim, the Americas and Europe. According to this argument the characteristics of Western states are conditioned more by regional than global factors. There is an additional confusion with the word 'Europeanization' as it is sometimes linked exclusively to the European Community (EC), sometimes to what used to be called Western Europe, and sometimes to both East and West Europe. The 'relaxed' view offered here pays most attention to the EC but does not exclude the other definitions.

Whatever the terminology, the UK has always been profoundly shaped by its relationships with other states. As the key international player in the nineteenth century, the UK was able to construct a series of 'external supports', consolidated in the creation of the formal Empire. These supports allowed Britain to resist pressures to modernize and, in providing the resources necessary to win the Great War and defeat its most important European competitor, it created a heady mixture of empire, patriotism and popular culture which is still not far beneath the surface in the 1990s. This was to create both the culture and the economic resources which made modernization unnecessary and almost un-English. In Bulpitt's words, the Empire 'exerted a profoundly conservative influence on British society and politics' (1983, p. 109). Attention should be paid to this if one is to fully understand the context of the reforms of the 1980s and the impetus behind Thatcherism. Many neo-liberals believed that the UK was forced to telescope a century of reforms into a decade.

The UK today faces a rapidly changing global order. The end of the cold war, weakening US dominance over Europe, attempts to unify Europe itself, and the end of the long boom all changed the 'external support' system in profound ways. The origin of many of the UK's difficulties in managing an effective response to these changes dates back to the 1940s when the post-war British government was faced with the possibility of building alliances with a war-damaged Europe, split by the cold war; creating new ties with the nations of the old Empire (who showed every sign of enjoying their new-found autonomy); or forging a relationship with the new US superpower. This was an unenviable position and in practice, successive governments attempted all three whilst concentrating on the latter. The result was an ambivalent attitude towards Europe in general, and the institutions of the newly emerging EC in particular, without the benefits of active US support or expanding trade with the Commonwealth. Nevertheless, the post-war global settlement helped to create the most extensive economic boom in the history of the modern world and this, in turn, allowed the UK to avoid awkward questions concerning its need to modernize. Meanwhile at least its role as junior partner in the special relationship with the US and Britain's place in the Commonwealth helped to satisfy the domestic expectation that the UK should be a world player. The question of Britain's place in Europe has still to be fully answered.

As a result of these weaknesses, when the international post-war settlement began to creak in the 1970s, the UK found itself in a vulnerable position. A British government could either seek an alliance with the US in an up-dated version of the special relationship or they could opt for 'an ever closer union' with the rest of the EC. The alternative — a policy of glorious isolation — would have left the UK vulnerable to international agreements put together in negotiations lacking an effective British presence.

For Conservatives the EC option was problematic. The fact that by the end of the 1980s over half of UK exports were with the EC (having risen from just under a third in 1973) implied that the UK was inextricably bound up with the EC economically. However, the EC was dominated by a combination of Christian democracy and social democracy both of which were hostile to the ambitions of a neo-liberal government. More to the point, the Conservative Party had for long viewed itself as the Party of the flag, monarchy and national sovereignty. For some Conservatives this was the very essence of the Party and its was threatened by the growth of a 'united states of Europe'. The fact that the German Deutschmark was the key currency did nothing to abate these concerns.

If a pro-EC stance was out of the question, the preferred Atlanticist stance was also awkward. The US was in such a dominant position that it had no need to enter into alliances with the UK if these required it to compromise US interests. The outcome of this was an apparent anti-Europeanism which angered pro-EC sections of the Party, with few manifest benefits which might have been used to placate backbenchers and voters alike. It was a key factor leading up to Mrs. Thatcher's resignation as Party leader of the Conservatives and it remains a major stumbling block for the Conservative Party managers. Arguably, the Conservative Party's best hope is to promote an expanded Europe to include as wide a range of nations as possible. This would limit the capacity of the EC to take firm steps forward and would thereby delay the difficult choices facing the Conservative Party (possibly indefinitely).

The EC also has implications for the Labour Party. The strategic intent of the Party leadership is to work within the EC to strengthen the social democratic emphasis upon redistribution and welfare, and within Britain to enhance its capacity to compete within the single European market by improved training, investment, and technology policies. However, given that the EC is founded on principles of free trade and the private ownership of capital, the consequence is that the Labour Party must either give up any remaining pretensions to be a socialist party or re-articulate socialist principles in such a way that they are compatible with private ownership and market forces.

Is it the case, then, that the UK economy has become 'globalized'? According to Auerbach (1989):

> Britain has the distinction, dubious or not, of having become a world class multinational power — as the home of multinationals which invest abroad it is second only to the US, and as a host nation it falls only behind the US and Canada in terms of the stock of foreign investments. In 1988, Britain was the world leader in foreign acquisitions, with an absolute level (£26 billion) four times as high as that of its nearest rivals. It also possessed the highest ratio in the world (34%) of foreign acquisitions to gross domestic fixed capital formation, other large countries having ratios such as 6% (France), 1.3% (the US and Japan) and 1.1% (West Germany) (*Financial Times* 13.3.89). The impact of inward investment in the UK may be seen in the fact that one in seven workers in manufacturing is employed by a foreign-owned firm (p. 263).

To this comment on manufacturing we should add the observation that the financial services sector in the UK is more highly globalized than any of its major competitors. Banking, finance business services and insurance accounted for 14 per cent of Britain's total output in 1989 and 4.1 per cent of its employment (HMSO, 1991, p. 409). Through the foreign exchange market, the International Stock Exchange, the options and financial futures market, the eurobond and eurocurrency markets, the Lloyds insurance market, and the bullion and commodity markets the City is locked into the global financial system. In 1989 it accounted for 10 per cent of worldwide equity trading and the turnover of London's foreign exchange market made it the largest such market in the world (HMSO, 1991, pp. 420–1). We return to the consequences of such an internationalized financial system below.

The UK economy has always been shaped by the world economy but the form which this now takes certainly has changed. We have the institutional presence of foreign-owned firms such as Nissan and Toyota bringing with them new approaches to employment, new production techniques, new approaches to purchasing, and new sales strategies (in this sense some observers argue that we are witnessing a process of 'Japanization'). At the same time we see British-based companies increasingly involved overseas. Meanwhile new financial markets and the free movement of capital in and out of the country have led to the creation of new organizations and new interests. In the second place, as a consequence of EC membership constraints are imposed upon economic management. It is intended by the EC that many forms of subsidy, regional aid and protection will be determined increasingly through EC institutions and with the move towards fixed exchange rates another policy instrument would be removed. Whilst recognizing that governments have never been 'free' to ignore the realities of the international economy, the institutional form through which these 'realities' are mediated is both new and significant.

These changes in the UK economy prompt questions about the extent to which British society might also be becoming 'globalized'. In the first place, the impact of world economic trends directly influence British society through changed working conditions, the changed location of industry, the shift from manufacturing to services, and through the promotion and advertising of products. This latter point may be especially important when the product being promoted is primarily a cultural artefact itself. Thus many would claim that the sale of Coca-Cola or hamburgers across the world tells us more about shared cultural values than about food. In relation to Europe, the EC Commission has argued consistently that since one consequence of economic integration is localized dislocations the EC should evolve a social policy capable of responding to this (see Commission of the European Communities, 1988, 1989a and 1989b). It has also expressed the concern that a Single Market may worsen poverty across Europe and this gave rise to the EC Programme to Combat Poverty (see Room, 1991). Through the European Social Fund and other Structural Funds, as well as through public health initiatives, the Commission's intention has been to enhance EC influence over social change.

However, as with economic change, it makes more sense to consider the changed modalities of global and European influence over British society rather than to project such influences as a novelty. Clearly, the global marketing of a fizzy drink and the slow emergence of a European social policy are both examples of quantitatively new developments but there is an important context to this. First, global factors have always shaped British society through such things as the location of industry in the workshop of the world, mass mobilization for war, international cultural movements. Second, whilst global and European factors are important these are heavily mediated by institutions and cultural practices which are obviously 'British'.

The fact that Britain was the first country to industrialize, and that since then neither revolution nor military occupation has shaken up its institutions and values, has created a peculiarly British 'prism' through which global and European processes make themselves felt. In addition, there is more to the political economy of the UK than simply its capacity to shape, and be shaped by, global processes. The institutions and processes of the UK form a distinctive analytical terrain. Without entirely abandoning our concern with international determinations, now might be the time to focus more directly upon these domestic institutions and processes. The first set of institutions considered is the state which, with its domestic constituencies and tax base, is perhaps the most firmly located in its own nation.

3 The state

'The state' includes the whole of the public sector such as parliament and the Cabinet, the civil service, public bodies, nationalized industries, the police and local government. Its peculiarly national claims to sovereignty and legitimacy give it an institutional separation from global processes which is in marked contrast to, say, multinationals. However, the maintenance of its tax base depends upon the capacity of domestic capital to compete in international markets and the maintenance of its institutional integrity depends upon (amongst other things) its capacity to resist military threats. State managers are therefore forced to place global factors high up on their strategic agenda. In this sense, the modern state is institutionally separate from, but strategically locked into, global processes.

For many neo-liberals in the 1980s there was a sense that the British state was in dire need of modernization. In pursuit of this, they drew upon what had become standard arguments and claims made by the new right in a number of countries (and not least in the USA). Here we will focus on three of these; the 'new public management', the centralization of the state, and the 'rolling back of the state'.

The so-called 'new public management' has been identified by Hood (1991) as comprising:

1   a focus on management, not policy, and on performance appraisal and efficiency;

2   the disaggregation of public bureaucracies into agencies which deal with each other on a user-pay basis;

3   the use of quasi-markets and contracting out to foster competition;

4   cost-cutting;

5   a style of management which emphasizes *inter alia* output targets, limited term contracts, monetary incentives and freedom to manage.

(Summarized in Rhodes, 1991, p.548)

Examples of this 'new public management' can be found across the state system. A couple of examples might help us to assess it.

In the health service, as we saw in Chapter 9, there is a clear expression of the 'new public management'. There has been created an internal market in which Health Authorities 'buy in' services in order to meet perceived medical needs. Hospitals can apply for trust status, through which they become self-governing organizations. Competition between hospitals plus 'private sector' management techniques is hoped to secure economies of scale and improvements in efficiency. Finally, in pursuit of these objectives, the medical profession's power over policy implementation and policy formulation has been circumscribed.

Critics of the reforms claim that in the place of medical values, new contractual relationships emphasize financial values and undermine the quality of care. This debate concerns the extent to which quality and standards can be written into contracts and absorbed into 'private sector management techniques'. Even where it is possible to write quality into contracts the cost of monitoring these standards and penalizing shortcomings may still be more expensive than the former more hierarchical system. It may also be the case that the political will to maintain standards conflicts with the political will to contain costs and that, in practice, financial disciplines place a more immediate constraint on health managers.

In the light of this debate, the White Paper which proposed these reforms (*Working for Patients*) was viewed as a radical departure in the history of the National Health Service. In terms of challenging the power of the medical profession, introducing new values to the implementation process and creating a new administrative structure this is certainly the case (although these may have unintended consequences). However, at another level the reforms have been highly conservative. A radical approach to health policy might have ensured that the deployment of health resources more closely matched the incidence of morbidity and causes of premature death. This might have two implications. First, preventative health care would be given priority. Secondly, health policy would be linked to the reduction of inequality in health standards. The general healthiness of the nation can most easily be improved by raising the health standards of the least healthy. In addition to these changes, a pro-active health policy would be planning for changes in provision to meet such predictable trends as the growing proportion of elderly people within the population. The health strategies pursued since 1979 should be assessed not only in terms of the administrative improvements hoped from them but also in terms of their wider adequacy in the face of a changing world.

Chapter 11 on the civil service provides a second example of the 'new public management'. During the 1970s, new right thinking in the US and in Britain had been shaped by works such as Niskanen (1973) which argued that a public bureaucracy tended to be inefficient and self-serving, and Bacon and Eltis (1977) which claimed that the expansion of public services was a major cause of Britain's relative economic decline because it involved an expansion of unproductive economic activity. In line with these, Conservative governments in the 1980s pursued three important areas of reform which are considered in detail in Chapter 11; the Rayner reviews, the Financial Management Initiative, and *The Next Steps*. Each of these involved 'a focus on management, not policy, and on performance appraisal and efficiency'. The third also involved a dramatic 'disaggregation of public bureaucracies into agencies which deal with each other on a user pay basis'.

As with the Health Service reforms, the view has been rightly taken that these constitute a significant break with the past. However, as one analysis comments on *The Next Steps* reforms:

> Conspicuous by its absence is any sustained attempt to change the way that core departments do their own work. The challenge to their traditions is at least the equivalent of the challenge facing operational managers. Preparing the strategic specification of policy, and then negotiating its implementation calls for skills of a new order. No department seems to be taking a strong line on this, and the project manager's attention seems to be directed almost solely at the task of getting agencies into shape, and ticking them off on a list.

> *(Metcalfe and Richards, 1990, p. 235)*

Furthermore, the doctrine of ministerial responsibility, by which a minister is held responsible for everything in his or her department, has been left untouched. Yet this is a myth which conceals civil service secrecy, inhibits parliamentary scrutiny, and deprives entrepreneurial civil servants of a sense of property over their own ideas. Furthermore, it does nothing to clarify the confusion over civil servants' duty to the government as an expression of the Queen in parliament and duty to the government as the expression of a political party intent on winning the next election.

Once again, one could conclude that the radicalism of the 'new public management' may be less deep than was at first believed. If this is the case, what might it imply for the management of the state in the 1990s? In the first place, it has been noted, more political energy was put into management, performance appraisal and efficiency than was put into policy. This was encouraged by the neo-liberal belief that if only the state can be contained and managed efficiently, the spontaneous order of the market and of family life will meet economic and social needs. Thus, for example, enhancing parental power and encouraging schools to opt out of local education authorities is seen as a solution to educational problems in itself. Similarly, privatizing previously public utilities was expected to remove them as political problems.

In the second place, the new public management depends upon the success of disaggregated public bureaucracies and agencies and this in turn depends *inter alia* upon the formulation of policies capable of being encapsulated in the framework agreements. In the case of the Benefits

Agency, for example, it is much easier to establish quantitative performance indicators rather than more qualitative criteria such as having a 'user-friendly' service (see Adler, 1992 and Adler and Sainsbury, 1990). Even where qualitative criteria are politically desired the cost of producing incontestable data may prohibit its use. A separate problem associated with a disaggregated civil service is that it also creates the potential for costly inter-agency conflicts.

In terms of the models deployed in this volume, we can readily understand that disaggregating the state involves a move from hierarchy to quasi-market relationships. However, it is never possible to produce an exhaustive marketized contract; there will always remain gaps between performance indicators. However, the successful completion of many tasks depends upon characteristics addressed in Chapter 3 and more typically associated with networks; trust, altruism, loyalty and solidarity. This is true for both inter- and intra-organizational relationships. We may find, as we monitor the outcomes of a 'contract culture' that the contracts themselves erode these characteristics without removing the need for them. In this interpretation, the new public management undermines the effective coordination of public organizations.

These problems also apply when disaggregation involves contracting out. Contracting out may encourage the organization which wins the contract to comb through it for technicalities which allow it to meet the contract at lower costs. Similar incentives are created by internal markets (despite the absence of profit as the key measure of success). Thus, to take a well-known example, where the number of patients treated is a key criterion it may create a perverse incentive to have patients leave hospital as soon as possible even if this is likely to lead to a re-admission. Re-admissions may cost more but would count as two patients and thus show up as a positive performance indicator.

On the other hand, disaggregation and contracting out can produce benefits and savings. This is especially true where policy objectives are clear, quantifiable and de-politicized. It will also help if there exists only a limited need for inter-agency cooperation. These 'benefits' to the state might take the form of lower salaries and/or poorer working conditions and a more flexible workforce, providing that poor morale and loss of good will do not swamp such savings. But they may also take the form of genuine improvements in efficiency and effectiveness through more effective deployment of resources and better-informed managerial choices. It is also likely that the most successful public and private examples of hived-off agencies and winners of public contracts will succeed in part by constructing networks within their own organization and with other external organizations. Various outcomes are possible.

If the 'new public management' has provided one area of debate on the British state, a second debate concerns its alleged centralization.

This includes part of the debate about the new public management (in as much as it is intended to enhance the strategic capacity of the centre) but it also goes beyond that debate to consider the way the local state has been more tightly controlled by the centre. The term 'local state' is intended to convey a sense of not only elected local authorities but also the institutions of urban intervention, the police, local aspects of the health system and the education system, the organization of the personal social services at the local level and so forth. However, much of the literature on the local state has focused on elected local government and this is discussed in Chapter 10. The centralizing tendencies in housing, education and health are also discussed in this volume.

Probably the dominant interpretation of the changed position of local government has been that successive governments since 1979 have been highly centralizing. Bogdanor (1988, p.7; quoted in Stoker 1990, p. 141) captured this flavour when he wrote:

> The Conservative Government elected in 1979 has been the most centralist since the Stuart monarchs of the seventeenth century. The government appears to have taken the view that other centres of power in society, such as local authorities, are somehow illegitimate, and must be curbed. For the Conservatives, there seems to be only one power centre which is truly legitimate, and that is central government.

Undoubtedly, financial controls, statute, government circulars and central party discipline have altered the nature of local government. However, another account has emerged which stresses that local government was always strongly shaped by non-local factors (Dunleavy, 1980; Rhodes, 1988). These accounts stress the continuing importance of policy communities and issue networks in which groups of professionals, bureaucrats and politicians combine to form power bases beyond the boundaries of Westminster and Whitehall. These demonstrate that whatever has been transformed it was not an undiluted expression of local democracy.

If we look at the local state more widely, we can see that there have been important developments. First, there has been the creation of new institutions such as the Training and Enterprise Councils, Trust Hospitals, Urban Development Corporations and so forth. These have statutory obligations, performance indicators, a cultural make-up, and key personnel which have led it to be market-led, non-democratic, and exclusive towards the organized interests of trades unions and the local community. Secondly, institutions which were previously more corporatist or more locally based such as the Manpower Services Commission, Local Authorities and Local Education Authorities have either been abolished or recomposed. This marks the transformation of a more social democratic, participatory and consensual local state even if it does not mark the end of a utopian local democracy.

The 'centralization thesis' is also used when discussing changes in central government and it is particularly linked to the claim that Prime Ministerial power has grown. It is alleged that a network of equals in and around the Cabinet has been replaced with a hierarchical power structure with the Prime Minister at the centre. The evidence used in support of this argument includes:

1 *Important issues are not collectively discussed.* Issues such as the abolition of metropolitan authorities, the introduction of the community charge (poll tax), the handling of the Westland Affair, and the pit closure programme announced in the autumn of 1992 all appear to have been determined outside the Cabinet structure.

2 *More matters are dealt with through the Cabinet committee structure.* Routine matters have always been dealt with in Cabinet committees. The major committees include Overseas and Defence, Economic Affairs, Home Affairs, two committees to consider current and future legislation, and about fourteen standing committees. In addition, there are a large number of *ad hoc* committees (called GEN, for 'general' or MISC for 'miscellaneous'). Some 200 of these were created in the 1980s and the Prime Minister can dictate their membership and chairing. Through this method, and through promoting 'a network of trustees strategically placed in the departments' (Jenkins, 1987), the Prime Minister has a power base outside the formal Cabinet structure.

3 *The increased use of personal advisors.* Economists such as Alan Walters and Patrick Minford, other experts such as Sir Anthony Parsons at the Foreign Office, and outside think-tanks such as the Adam Smith Institute have all been used to provide Prime Ministers with a non-civil service source of advice.

4 *Tighter management of Cabinet business.* Through a subtle use of lunch-time chats, announcing policy elsewhere and in advance, controlling the agenda, and the promotion of known supporters, the Prime Minister is able to exert considerable control over the Cabinet. Despite this (or because of it) the Cabinet met only half as frequently in the 1980s as during the 1945–1975 period.

However, the batteries of Prime Ministerial power are constrained. Items cannot be permanently excluded from the Cabinet agenda and loyalty cannot be guaranteed. Losing one or two Cabinet ministers might be seen as an acceptable accident but many more may undermine the whole government. Ultimately, as the forced resignation of Mrs. Thatcher demonstrates, if the view grips on the backbenches that a Prime Minister cannot deliver the next election then departure may be abrupt.

If the centralization thesis needs to be examined with close attention to the details, the debate over the rolling back of the state needs to be handled with equal care. In expenditure terms, whilst downward pressure has been applied, the overall result has not been dramatic. Public expenditure in the UK as a percentage of GDP remained at around 47 per cent by the end of the 1980s comparing with 37 per cent in the USA, 47 per cent in West Germany and 51 per cent in Austria. Total social spending showed the UK to be at 19 per cent compared with 17 per cent in the USA, 25 per cent in West Germany and 25 per cent in Austria (all data from OECD, 1988, quoted in SPCR, 1989, p. 42).

The downward pressure did yield tax cuts, however. Between 1979 and 1986, Byrne (1987, p. 30) has calculated that tax cuts added up to some £8.1 billion of which

- one-fifth went to the richest 1 per cent
- one-third went to the richest 5 per cent
- nearly half went to the richest 10 per cent
- almost two-thirds went to the richest 20 per cent.

At the same time as the restructuring of tax policy made the rich richer, downward pressure was applied to the low wage sector by limiting and eventually abolishing Wages Councils (responsible for maintaining minimum wages in certain sectors) and through the consequences of schemes such as the Youth Training Scheme. In its own operations, the state abolished its Fair Wages Resolution, whereby private contractors working on public contracts were obliged to meet certain standards of pay and conditions. In addition, top civil servants' pay, which had been six times higher than the civil service minimum, was sixteen times higher by 1987 (Peters, 1989). All of this suggests that it is not so much a simple case of 'rolling back' as one of restructuring the state. Across the state system we find that agencies and institutions hostile to central government have indeed been rolled back (or wound up) but that other agencies with more supportive memberships and values have been created or expanded.

However, we should not confuse the centralization of decision taking with a real increase in the capacity of the central state to secure its objectives (see Jessop et al., 1988, p. 121). Controlling the state system will not deliver enhanced capacities if the state system itself is incapable of securing the objectives set. Thus, in the case of the reconstruction of urban intervention, we find that at the local level, state agencies became heavily dependent upon the choices taken by property developers. In the parallel case of training policy, we find that similar dependencies are created in relation to private sector employers through the mechanism of Training and Enterprise Councils. When businesses calculate that even substantial public financial support is insufficient to justify further private investment then government strategies grind to a halt.

What conclusions might we draw for the British state from the arguments so far in this chapter? We might conclude:

1 Despite the fact that the nation state still remains the basic unit of political organization, it is faced with a growing number of strategic

problems which are global or European in origin, and over which it has limited control.

2   Through the new public management and wider restructurings of central-local relations, the centre has secured an enhanced strategic capacity over the state system. However, the instruments thus created (market-led, contractual, disaggregated, and driven by performance indicators) may yet prove to be rigid and damaging to the overall institutional flexibility and coherence of the state.

3   This enhanced central control has been used to benefit the more privileged sections of society and create new dependencies upon key players in the private sector. These dependencies may prove to be destabilizing as economic success cannot be guaranteed and the loyalty of private capital (especially multinational capital) is limited.

If we aggregate the potential difficulties associated with each of these, the view emerges that growing political and academic attention is likely to be given to the question of the coordination of the state during the coming years.

4   The Economy

If there has been a neo-liberal underpinning to recent governmental attitudes to the public sector, attitudes to the economy have been shaped by neo-classical and Austrian economics. This led to the view that if the market relationship became more prevalent then both productive and allocative efficiency would be enhanced and the sum of social welfare maximized. To this end, a number of objectives emerged. Jackson (1992, p. 12) lists these as:

1   A rejection of Keynesian short-run demand management; a rejection of the idea of being able to fine tune the economy by manipulating policy instruments that affect demand.

2   Emphasis upon providing medium term stability in the private sector's (especially the company's) planning environment.

3   Emphasis upon promoting economic growth by introducing supply-side policies that would free up markets, expand choice and increase productivity, by reducing the distorting effects of unnecessary regulations.

4   Emphasis upon financial management and control of the money supply (i.e., sound monetary policies) to create a zero rate of inflation and the incentives for investment and growth.

5   A reduction in public expenditure and thus a rolling back of the frontiers of the State, thereby giving individuals greater freedom over their private spending plans through tax reductions; tax reductions were also to contribute to supply-side management by creating incentives that would increase work effort,

job search, savings, and risk taking (i.e., promoting entrepreneurship and the enterprise culture) and therefore generally contributing to productivity improvements.

6   Abandonment of price controls and incomes policies.

Let us consider the extent to which these policies have been pursued,
their consequences, and the implications this has for our understanding
of the British economy in the 1990s.

In the autumn of 1992 the British government under John Major was
forced to withdraw from the Exchange Rate Mechanism (ERM) when it
became clear that the British economy was unable to sustain sterling at
its existing value. Behind this decision lay a chronic balance of payments deficit. It would be wrong to imagine that a balance of payments
crisis was a unique experience for a British government, however. Examples of economic growth being choked off by such a crisis occur
throughout the post-war era. The causes of this long-term weakness are
disputed and explanations are legion. Coates (1991) is fairly typical in
suggesting that a constellation of factors after the Second World War
seriously inhibited the UK's economic performance. He emphasizes
four factors:

1   high military expenditure;
2   the overseas orientation of UK financial institutions;
3   the anti-modernization bias resulting from key social forces and
     institutions (especially government, education, banking and the
     organized working class); and
4   the lack of urgency amongst politicians and their advisors.

Other possible 'culprits' are more or less widely canvassed elsewhere. Martin Wiener (1981) argued that it was primarily the anti-
industrial culture of the British elite which led to low growth rates.
The observations that the British elite was peculiarly pre-modern in
many of its attitudes had already been made in the work of Anderson
and Nairn (for a revised outline of this see Anderson, 1987). A variation on this theme (see Ingham, 1984) was to identify the external orientation of the City–Bank of England–Treasury institutional nexus as
the cause of weak domestic growth.

What puts Nairn, Anderson, Ingham and Coates on one side of the argument and neo-classicists, Austrians and Wiener on the other is that
the latter claim that markets will produce growth and efficiency unless
social and political institutions prevent them from doing so whilst the
former insist that the institutions necessary to make capitalism work
will always be problematic and thus lurch from boom to slump. They
emphasize that a capitalist economy requires entrepreneurs, workers, a
state, financial institutions and institutions in which to buy and sell
raw materials and products. However, market mechanisms alone are
incapable of providing these. Furthermore, they argue, left to their
own devices capitalist markets may reduce the availability of all of

these.

This leads some writers such as Coates (1991) to a regulationist approach which emphasizes that periods of economic expansion are associated with historically specific institutional configurations which create 'virtuous circles' in which increasing economic output is linked to increasing consumption in a mutually reinforcing manner. Thus, at least for a period, there can be stable expansion. In contrast to the neo-classical view that growth is created by the spontaneous calculations of individual actors in the market, this approach emphasizes that leadership and active management is required if the institutional ensemble associated with growth is to be created. Typically, such analyses would stress the temporary nature of any such institutional ensembles.

In recent years, the most common term used in relation to such an institutional ensemble in the twentieth century is 'Fordism' and the claim is widely made that in Britain, as elsewhere, there is a fundamental restructuring of the economy associated with the end of Fordism (for a review of this see Smith, 1990). One immediate difficulty is that the term is used differently to describe variously the production process (mass, assembly line production), the wider changes in forms of class composition which this causes (large urbanized groups of male workers), the associated changes in consumption (mass markets met by mass-produced, very similar products), and the enhanced role of the state in guaranteeing minimum incomes, underpinning trades union rights, providing a welfare state, and manipulating aggregate levels of demand (see Jessop, 1988, pp. 4–5). Yet others emphasize that these domestic arrangements are only possible within a particular global context. Thus Overbeek (1990) emphasizes the importance of Pax Americana in providing the preconditions for the 'long boom' of the post-war era. These circumstances might be described as 'global Fordism'.

The strength of this literature is that it compels us to consider the circumstances in which a virtuous circle of growing productivity, increasing output and rising consumption held together for so long. It also compels us to ask if these circumstances have now disappeared and whether a new set of arrangements which might be called *post-Fordist* is emerging. Or, alternatively, are we seeing the break-up of the Fordist paradigm with no alternative institutional core arising?

There are two significant weaknesses which would need to be overcome if 'Fordism' was to provide a coherent conceptual alternative to neo-liberal and Austrian interpretations of the market, however. In the first instance, the precise meaning is so vague that it can apparently be used to describe a wide range of very different circumstances. What is to be included in the concept? Assembly line production? The welfare state? Collective bargaining? The global settlement? When efforts are made to specify it more precisely, one finds that few countries (the USA being one) could reasonably be described as 'Fordist' and that there are many examples of non-Fordist growth. More substantively, the causal centrality of 'Fordist' production to the long boom can be exaggerated (see Clarke 1988).

For these reasons the term 'Fordism' should be used with extreme caution, if at all, but the underlying claim that successful economies appear to be managed by a distinctive logic of virtuous circles is useful. Chapters 5 and 6, for example, suggest that the success of Japanese industry is associated with a certain institutional concertation involving financial institutions, governmental bodies, core manufacturers and their suppliers, workers, and sales outlets. The failure of such virtuous circles in the UK economy can be gauged by considering some of its major features.

One of the most striking of these is that in 1982, for the first time since the industrial revolution, the UK imported more manufactured goods than it exported and the non-oil deficit continued to worsen. The government response was outlined above. By 1992 a consumption-led boom had led to balance of payments problems and inflationary pressure culminating in a deep recession. This failure of domestic production to meet a rise in domestic demand and to compete effectively against foreign produced goods has followed every up-turn in the UK economy since the Second World War. Furthermore, it has failed at even higher levels of unemployment and wider degrees of inequality. But is the economy in a position to benefit from any global up-turn?

One crucial indicator which would help to answer this is labour productivity which has improved since the 1970s. However, it seems that this had more to do with laying off workers in the least productive sectors, employing more capital per worker, and enhanced managerial prerogatives, than with technological innovation which is the foundation of long-term growth (see Jackson, 1992; Muellbauer, 1986; and Bean and Symons, 1989). The sector which has shown a willingness to invest in new technologies has been the service sector and in particular financial services, distribution and new technologies. However, the capacity of these to erode the balance of payments deficit is strictly limited and in any case, productivity improvements in this sector have been limited (despite their substantial liberalization). In the end, the negative balance of payments can only be substantially improved by long-term improvements in the efficiency of British manufacturing. As Rowthorn and Wells (1987, p.1) state '(T)here is not the slightest doubt that the cause of Britain's relatively poor economic record is the thoroughly unsatisfactory performance of her manufacturing industry'.

Another important indicator of economic health would be labour market flexibility. This is far from easy to measure and it is further confused by the fact that success is associated with very different circumstances such as a 'hire and fire' approach from management (as in the USA) or with the promise of life-long security for core workers (as in Japan). Jill Rubery (1989, p. 173) emphasizes there are different routes but her study of the UK labour market concludes that:

...the emerging rigidities in the labour market, the scarcities of skills, the widening dispersion of earnings all suggest ... that these policies have diminished the potential contribution from the labour market to economic growth as well as adding signifi- cantly to the extent of economic misery experienced by labour market participants.

In terms of training systems, too, the record is poor. Ashton et al. (1989, p. 137) describe the British system as 'just about the worst of our international competitors' and even the Director General of the CBI was forced to conclude '(B)y international standards our work-force is under-educated, under-trained and under-qualified...The worrying thing is that the gap may be widening' (*The Guardian*, 1989). (See, also, the critical report of the Audit Commission, 1989.)

A third factor in any revival would be the availability of finance. The UK invests more of its available resources overseas than does any of its competitors, British companies depend to a greater extent than their competitors upon short-term credit in the form of overdraft facili- ties at high rates of interest, the fear of hostile take-overs lead the largest UK companies to pay 'at least twice and sometimes three times as much out of their profits in dividends compared with their counter- parts in West Germany' (Hutton, 1991), and manufacturers have a gen- erally more distant (even hostile) relationship with their bankers. As noted above, investments have been made in the service sector often where these are protected from foreign competition, but in the less se- cure markets of manufacturing industry where success depends upon long-term investments in research and development, British industrial- ists continue to face foreign firms whose financial support give them a persistent competitive advantage.

This brief survey of some of the key debates about the economy cannot hope to come to any firm conclusions. However, the evidence supports a couple of broad claims. In the first place, there is a strong body of opin- ion which claims economic success will depend upon the capacity of manufacturing, financial, labour market and public institutions to form concerted networks outside of market relationships. For example, the need for financial and manufacturing bodies to build a relationship of trust and solidarity capable of matching the mutually supportive rela- tionships found in the UK's main competitors, or the need for a national training system which is responsive to the future needs of the economy and not simply to the current demands of today's employers. The need, in sum, for what David Marquand (1988) calls a 'developmental state' capable of playing the modernizing role which markets have failed to provide.

If this is true, then the calculations and actions of players in the economy are not fully amenable to the rationalistic calculations of Aus- trian and neo-classical economics. It is a world in which being en- trepreneurial includes not always maximizing profit when this will create a loss of solidarity, but includes also the careful construction of networks out of which real mutual interests may grow as a result of the success of others, and includes the state in playing a leading role as an agent of economic change and not simply as a guarantor of the market place. It is not a world in which the state can pursue disengagement and deregulation safe in the expectation that what will emerge is a stable and vibrant economic environment.

Clearly, the type of society in the UK will be shaped by the global context, the British state and its economy. However, an important dimension of 'managing the UK' would be left out if we failed to examine British society as a separate topic and it is to this which we now turn.

5 Society

The vision embodied in the liberal beliefs of Beveridge and Keynes was that post-war Britain should be a fairer society in which everyone should have an equal opportunity to participate and succeed and where even the poorest would be cared for. Within this vision there were significant differences about the extent of equality which was desirable, the role of means testing and so forth (see Titmus, 1963, pp. 34-37 for an interesting contemporary outline of these differences). However, despite such differing emphases, there was a shared commitment to change a society which had been characterized by elitism and class.

By the 1970s there had been limited progress towards this goal. The share of total personal wealth owned by the top 1 per cent of the population had indeed been significantly reduced (from 60.9 per cent to 31.7 per cent between 1923 and 1972) but only in order to distribute it to wives, husbands, children and siblings (the share owned by the top 5 per cent grew from 5.2 per cent to 14.4 per cent at the same time) (see Urry, 1985, p. 60). By 1970, three-quarters of the clearing bank directors were from public schools and over half of them had been to Cambridge or Oxford Universities (Scott, 1982, p. 160). Over two-thirds of senior civil servants in the post-war period also went to Cambridge or Oxford and in 1970, 62 per cent had been to one of the major public schools (Scott, 1985, p. 48; see also Coates, 1991, pp. 98-9). The incoming Conservative Cabinet in 1970 comprised eighteen people of whom four were aristocrats, fourteen were middle class and none was working class. Of these, fifteen had been to public school and fifteen were Oxbridge education (Butler and Sloman, 1980, p. 79). It contained just one woman and no-one from the ethnic minority groups. Even the following Labour Cabinet included only four working-class people and eleven were Oxbridge educated. In consequence, the UK remained a deeply class-divided society in which the networks between 'the great and good' in the civil service, the City and in Parliament constituted a peculiarly British Establishment.

If by the 1970s the management of the UK was still in the hands of a propertied male Establishment the country over which it presided was changing. Scott (1979) noted how economic power was shifting from individuals and families towards impersonal organizations. Trades unions had achieved a level of participation in the affairs of the nation (although their real power appears to have been limited to the ability to disrupt). However, the community life and work-place conditions which supported a distinctive working-class culture were disappearing and this posed deepening problems for those seeking to institutionally direct working-class interests. Furthermore, the welfare state had created new opportunities for education and health care which had raised general standards (even if the ability of the middle classes to exploit free services ensured that inequalities were not reduced) and created a vast new army of professionals, semi-professionals and white collar workers. Real disposable income increased and for the first time many enjoyed a wide degree of choice over how to spend their money. For young people, this provided the economic basis for a distinctive youth culture. Women also experienced important changes during this time, most obviously in increasing participation in the labour market, but also as a result of the changing cultural context associated with feminism. By the 1970s, also, the UK was a multi-ethnic nation with something under 5 per cent of the population designated as 'non-white' and significant groups of Irish, Australians and Canadians within the population. The non-white population, in particular, experienced both intentional racism and structural inequalities and were concentrated in the inner-urban areas.

To what extent has British society changed since the 1970s? In the first place it has become more unequal. The bottom fifth of income earners secured 0.5 per cent of original income in 1979 and 0.3 per cent in 1987. For the next fifth the figures are 9 per cent and 6 per cent. The final income of the bottom fifth (after allowing for tax and benefits) fell from 7.1 per cent to 6.2 per cent whilst for the next fifth the figures are 12 per cent and 11 per cent (Bradshaw, 1992, p. 91). From this we can see that the impact of 'flexibilizing' the bottom end of the labour market and applying downward pressure on welfare expenditure has been to depress their share of original income. The tax and benefit system mitigates inequalities in original income but post-tax and benefit inequalities have also increased.

These inequalities are felt most acutely in certain sections of society. In part it has produced a spatial concentration of poverty in inner urban areas, in part it has consequences for ethnic minorities (West Indians are seven times as likely to live in inner London, Birmingham or Manchester as white, and Asians four times as likely) (Brown, 1985, p. 62), and in part it has implications for women who are disproportionately employed in low-paid and part-time work.

According to the Church of England's *Faith in the City* report:

...rich and poor, suburban and inner city, privileged and deprived, have been becoming more sharply separated from each other for many years and ... the impoverished minority has become increasingly cut off from the mainstream of our national life ... These trends add up to a pattern warranting the label of polarization in a new comprehensive and intractable form.

(Quoted in Winyard, 1987, p. 39)

For the rest of society, the 1980s saw a period of rising incomes and even more rapidly rising consumption. The gap between income and consumption was paid for in part through a large increase in personal debt which more than doubled between 1981 and 1989. Much of this was financed through credit cards. Another form of indebtedness to rise was mortgage loans in arrears. Loans in arrears by 6–12 months grew from 12,800 to 76,300 in the years 1982–90 whilst loans in arrears by over 12 months grew from 4,800 to 18,800 (HMSO, 1991, p. 145). Personal savings during the 1980s fell from 13.1 per cent of personal disposable income in 1980 to 6.7 per cent in 1989. Cuts in savings and increased use of credit fuelled the consumer boom of the late 1980s and early 1990s.

Those in work have also seen changes in the work place. The number of large work places (with over 999 employees) decreased, employment in manufacturing (and especially extractive and heavy engineering industries) declined, a 'peripheral' labour market increased as 'core' companies contract out parts of their production, and service sector jobs increased. Associated with these changes are the decline in trades union membership with the loss of jobs in the traditional heartlands of trades union support, the increased participation of women in the labour market (especially part-time), and an employers' offensive in which existing working-practices and conditions have been undermined (often linked to the need to respond to the more competitive environment of a 'contract culture'). (Increased participation of women in the labour market has not been equally matched by increasing participation in domestic work by men.) Largely as a consequence of these changes, large, urban working-class communities have given way to a suburbanized working class whose recreation, entertainment and supports are no longer community- or class-based.

The working class has also been substantially rehoused. During the 1980s the 'right to buy' (in particular) has led to a decrease in council housing as a percentage of total housing stock from 31 per cent to 23 per cent and an increase in owner occupation from 55 per cent to 67 per cent; the result being that for the first time the majority of council house tenants came from the poorest 30 per cent of household (see Kemp, 1992, pp. 71–6). Key sections of the better-off working class are now, in a sense, part of the 'property owning democracy' above a 'second nation' of council tenants which is itself (arguably) above a third nation of the homeless.

Middle-class professionals have also faced considerable changes especially (but not exclusively) in the public sector. This is partly a con-

sequence of the 'new public management' discussed above and a generally more aggressively marketed working environment. Culturally,
they have also seen the great symbols of middle-class values undergo
major changes — the BBC in particular and the mass media in general,
the Church of England, and even the Royal family no longer appear to
project the values of middle-class family life. Perhaps this accounts
for the growth in the heritage industry where a mythical reconstruction of the past can provide a safe haven from the vagaries of a changing world.

Middle-class women have fared better in the labour market than in
the past (although they are far from a position of equality with middle-class men) and continue to fare substantially better than working-
class women. By the end of the 1980s, 10 per cent of Assistant Secre-
taries and Principal posts (in the civil service) were filled by women as
were 12 per cent of both barristers and solicitors (Cashmore, 1989, p.
182). There was also an increase in the number of women elected to Parliament but even so Westminster remains one of the most male-domi-
nated assemblies in the Western world.

At the top of society things have also changed. In the 1950s, the jour-
nalist Henry Fairlie wrote:

> ...what I call the 'Establishment' in this country is more power-
> ful than ever before. By the 'Establishment' I do not mean only
> the centres of official power though they are certainly part of
> it — but rather the whole matrix of official and social rela-
> tions within which power is exercised.

> *(Quoted in Hennessy, 1989, p. 453)*

Assessing the validity of this claim in the 1990s is made more diffi-
cult by both the vagueness with which the term is conceptualized and
the secrecy which surrounds the evidence. Peter Hennessy likened the
British Establishment under Thatcher to the Russian Army conducting
a rear-guard operation against the invaders knowing that soon the long
Russian winter would set in and the enemy fall apart (Hennessy, 1989).
Karl Marx, of a very different bourgeois revolution in *The Eighteenth
Brumaire of Louis Bonaparte* wrote:

> (B)ourgeois revolutions storm quickly from success to success.
> They outdo each other in dramatic effects, men and things seem
> set in sparkling diamonds and each day's spirit is ecstatic. But
> they are short-lived; they soon reach their apogee, and society
> has to undergo a long period of regret until it has learned to as-
> similate soberly the achievements of its period of storm and
> stress.

At one level it is possible to argue that after the onslaught of
Thatcherism the country is back to being run by 'good chaps'. The more
ecstatic 'sparkling diamonds' of the 1980s such a Norman Tebbit and
Cecil Parkinson were moved to the wings and less anti-Establishment

figures have taken their place centre-stage. Even the Labour Party appears determined to outbid the Conservative Party in the stakes for probity and respectability. However, this would be to ignore deeper changes which have taken place. First, the continuing movement of economic power away from individuals and families towards corporations (and increasingly transnational corporations). Second, the City is now far more open as a result of the liberalization of financial institutions and new domestic and global players are involved in almost every market. Consequently, the cosy relationships between the City and the Treasury, consolidated in the London clubs, are no longer easy to maintain. Third, the claims made on behalf of *The Next Steps* reforms in the civil service may sometimes be exaggerated, but it is at least arguable that a cultural change is continuing to unfold within the senior civil service which is hostile to the ways of the 'Great and the Good'. Even the Church of England, through either evangelicalism or political hostility to neo-liberalism, cannot now be regarded as the 'Tory Party at prayer'. If we add to this the fact that the *English* Establishment has lost credibility in Scotland, Wales and Ireland, then the image of an unchanged 'olde England' needs to be radically qualified. Never homogeneous nor closed, the 'Establishment', for better or for worse, is but a shadow of its former self.

So what should we conclude on the nature of British society in the 1990s? We have noted changes in the workplace and community life, the changing position of women, an unresolved race question, regional differences and nationalist sentiment in Ireland, Scotland and Wales, and a loss of social and cultural leadership. At the same time, British society is being shaped by its location in a global system in which the dismal certainties of the cold war have dissolved. However, the state may be marginally shrinking but its strategic power is not; power may be shifting to corporations but we have also seen an employers' offensive consolidate power in management at the workplace; the cultural elite may have lost their privileged position but it is not clear that the repertoire of available popular culture has thereby been widened; and if there is no longer a powerful Establishment, there is certainly a disempowered poor.

6 Continuities, changes and possible futures

The chapters of this book portray a rapidly changing world. Whatever else can be said, the management of public and private organizations has been profoundly altered during the past two decades and the force of change looks set to continue unabated. In this concluding section we consider whether these changes mark simply the normal changes in a capitalist society or whether there is a deeper, more systematic shift taking place.

Earlier in this chapter it was argued that the internal management of nation-states has always been shaped by its location in an international system of nation-states. However, the extent to which non-national organizations have a direct institutional and financial presence is new. Flows of money and direct investment are now beyond the control of national governments. This establishes qualitatively new constraints and undermines attempts to manipulate a national economy primarily through domestic demand management. At the same time, it makes attempts to operate 'monetarism in one country' equally implausible. It therefore encourages the view that effective national government policies will be pursued with a combination of international cooperation and domestic strategies to secure a competitive advantage.

There are three models which help to identify such strategies. First, in the market model, the state intends to promote the power of management to innovate, to flexibilitize the labour market through enhancing managerial powers to 'hire and fire', and to attract inward investment through offering attractive tax regimes and labour-market conditions. Second, in the hierarchy model, the government uses its resources to organize research and new technologies, coordinate export drives, close down 'sunset industries' and invest in 'sunrise industries'. Third, in the network model, central governments work with strong regional governments to catalyse a concertation of technologists, trades unions, manufacturers and investors to stimulate innovation and entrepreneurship. These might be called neo-liberal, neo-statist and neo-corporatist (see Jessop, 1992).

In practice, governments are likely to partially pursue all three and none is without its problems. The market model will generally only enhance national competitiveness when there exists either one enterprise large enough to orchestrate the work of other organizations or a well-organized network. The former is unlikely at the cutting edge of technological innovation where the research and development requirements exceed the resources available to any one company. In the latter case, it is hard to sustain the sorts of loyalty and solidarity required when the benefits of participation are so long-term and uncertain. The hierarchy model has the advantage of deploying the full resources of the state in pursuit of certain strategic objectives. The problem with it (and this also applies for hierarchical private sector organizations) is that the response time required to succeed in any one industry is so short that the bureaucratic and legal requirements facing a liberal democratic state are ill-suited to provide the motor of change. With the network model, many of these problems are overcome but in their place are the problems associated with networks becoming inward-looking, defensive and hostile to change.

Although the world is changing, and the UK needs to change to succeed, change cannot be said to characterize many of its 'core' institutions. Continuities are perhaps less remarked upon because they appear to be a part of the 'natural order' of the UK. Whilst we have seen substantial changes in the civil service, education, health and indeed in almost all public sectors, pressures for reform have been displaced to the periphery in the form of new agencies, developed management and a more widespread contract culture with the intended result that more strategic power has been shifted to the central departmental/cabinet system. Rather than construct an effective system of local and regional government which could shoulder some of the workload of the central institutions we have seen the centre extend the range of its financial, legal and managerial controls over the rest of the state system. Meanwhile, a secretive political centre stunts debate and weakens effective policy making; the constitutional fictions of collective responsibility of Cabinet and ministers' individual responsibility for their departments inhibits political accountability; Parliamentary sovereignty is used as an argument for limiting the democratic process to just one conduit; and popular involvement with the judicial and police systems is tightly managed.

However, it would be naive to imagine that if only the archaism of the UK's central political institutions could be overcome then the UK as a whole would automatically be better suited to meet the challenge of the future. On the one hand, change will occur whatever the nature of the political institutions. The impact of Japanese management practices are already being felt in industry whilst in the City new players are bringing with them different financial practices and new markets are creating new opportunities for the more long-standing organizations. On the other hand, the attachment in English culture to continuity and a sense of tradition (or a hostility to change and all things 'foreign') suggests that institutional change alone may not be a sufficient stimulus to modernization.

How these developments will come together to shape the future of the UK is, as always, uncertain and social scientists would be well advised to avoid firm predictions. However, the analyses put forward in this book suggest to me that whilst the future may not be certain neither is it random. A market-led neo-liberal, a networked based neo-corporatism, and a hierarchical statist strategy provide the parameters within which public and private choices will be made in the UK. We must wait to see whether it has the state, economy and society necessary to make any or all of these succeed in the international environment.

References

Adler, M. (1992) 'Realising the potential of the operational strategy', *Benefits*, April/May.

Adler, M. and Sainsbury, R. (1990) *Putting the Whole Person Concept into Practice: Final Report (Parts I and II)*, Edinburgh, Department of Social Policy and Social Work, University of Edinburgh.

Anderson, P. (1987) 'Figures of descent', *New Left Review,* no. 161, pp. 20–7.

Ashton, D., Green, F. and Hoskins, M. (1989) 'The training system of British capitalism: changes and prospects' in Green (ed.) (1989).

Audit Commission (1989) *Urban Regeneration and Economic Development. The Local Authority Dimension,* London, HMSO.

Auerbach, P. (1989) 'Multinationals and the British economy' in Green (ed.) (1989).

Bacon, R. and Eltis, W. (1977) *Britain's Economic Problems: Too Few Producers,* London, Macmillan.

Bean, C. and Symons, J. (1989) 'Ten years of Mrs. T.', *NBER Macroeconomics Annual,* Cambridge, MA, MIT Press, pp. 13–60

Bogdanor, V. (1988) *Against the Overmighty State: A future for Local Government in Britain,* London, Federal Trust for Education and Research.

Bradshaw, J. (1992) 'Social Security' in Marsh and Rhodes (eds.) (1992).

Brown, C. (1985) *Black and White in Britain: the Third PSI Survey,* Aldershot, Gower.

Bulpitt, J. (1983) *Territory and Power in the United Kingdom. An Interpretation,* Manchester, Manchester University Press.

Butler, D. and Sloman, A. (1980) *British Political Facts 1900–1979,* fifth edition, London, Macmillan.

Byrne, D. (1987) 'Rich and poor: the growing divide' in Walker and Walker (eds.) (1987).

Cashmore, E.E. (1989) *United Kingdom? Class, Race and Gender Since the War,* London, Unwin Hyman.

Clarke, S. (1988) *Keynesianism, Monetarism and the Crisis of the State,* Edward Elgar, Aldershot.

Coates, D. (1991) *Running the Country,* Sevenoaks, Hodder and Stoughton.

Dunleavy, P. (1980) *Urban Political Analysis,* London, Macmillan.

Dunleavy, P., Gamble, A. and Peele, G. (eds.) (1990) *Developments in British Politics 3,* London, Macmillan.

Green, F. (ed.) (1989) *The Restructuring of the UK Economy,* Hemel Hempstead, Harvester Wheatsheaf.

Guardian, The (1989) 21 November.

Hennessy, P. (1989) *Whitehall,* London, Secker and Warburg.

HMSO (1991) *Britain 1991 An Official Handbook,* London, HMSO.

Hood, C. (1991) *Beyond the Public Bureaucratic State,* London, London School of Economics Inaugural Lecture.

Hutton, W. (1991) 'Why Britain can't afford the City', *Management Today,* September, pp. 46–51

Ingham, G.K. (1984) *Capitalism Divided? The City and Industry in British Social Development,* London, Macmillan.

Jackson, P.M. (1992) 'Economic policy' in Marsh and Rhodes, (eds.) (1992).

Jenkins, P. (1987) *Mrs. Thatcher's 'Revolution' the Ending of the Socialist Era,* London, Jonathan Cape.

Jessop, B. (1988) 'Regulation theory, post Fordism, and the state: more than a reply to Werner Bonefeld', *Capital and Class,* no.34, pp.147–69.

Jessop, B. (1992) *Changing Forms and Functions of the State in an Era of Globalization,* paper presented at EAPE Conference, Paris, 1992.

Jessop, B., Bonnett, K., Bromley, S. and Ling, T. (1988) *Thatcherism, a Tale of Two Nations,* Cambridge, Polity Press.

Kemp, P. (1992) 'Housing' in Marsh and Rhodes (eds.) 1992.

Marquand, D. (1988) *The Unprincipled Society: New Demands and Old Politics*, London, Fontana.

Marsh, D. and R.A.W. Rhodes (eds.) (1992) *Implementing Thatcherite Policies: Audit of an Era*, Buckingham, Open University Press.

Metcalfe, L. and Richards, S. (1990) *Improving Public Management* (2nd edition) London, Sage.

Muellbauer, J. (1986) 'Productivity and competitiveness in British manufacturing', *Oxford Review of Economic Policy*, 2 (3), Autumn, 1-25.

Niskanen, W. (1973) *Bureaucracy: Servant or Master?* London, Institute of Economic Affairs.

OECD (1988) *The Future of Social Protection*, Paris, OECD.

Overbeek, H. (1990) *Global Capitalism and National Decline*, London, Unwin Hyman.

Peters. B.G. (1989) *Comparative Public Administration*, Tuscaloosa, Alabama, University of Alabama Press.

Rhodes, R.A.W. (1988) *Beyond Westminster and Whitehall*, London, Unwin Hyman.

Rhodes, R.A.W. (1991) 'Theory and methods in British public administration: the view from political science' in *Political Studies*, vol. XXXIX, no. 3.

Room, G. (1991) 'Towards a European welfare state?' in Room (ed.) (1991) *Towards a European Welfare State*, Bristol, SAUS, pp. 533–54.

Rowthorn, R.E. and Wells, J.R. (1987) *De-industrialization and Foreign Trade*, Cambridge, Cambridge University Press.

Rubery, J. (1989) 'Labour market flexibility in Britain' in Green (ed.) (1989).

Scott, J. (1979) *Corporatism, Classes and Capitalism*, London, Hutchinson.

Scott, J. (1982) *The Upper Classes: Property and Privilege in Britain*, London, Macmillan.

Scott, J. (1985) 'The British upper class' in Coates, D., Johnston, G. and Bush, R. (eds.) *A Socialist Anatomy of Britain*, Cambridge, Polity Press, pp. 29–54.

Smith, C. (1990) 'Flexible specialisation, automation and mass production', *Work Employment and Society*, vol.3, no.2, pp. 203–20.

SPCR (1989) *British Social Attitudes: Special International Report: the Sixth Report*, Jowell, R., Witherspoon, S., and Brook, L.(eds.), Aldershott, Gower.

Stoker, G. (1990) 'Government beyond Whitehall' in Dunleavy et al. (eds.) (1990).

Titmuss, R.M. (1963) *Essays on 'the Welfare State'*, London, George Allen and Unwin.

Urry, J. (1985) 'The class structure' in Coates, D., Johnston, G., and Bush R., (eds.) *A Socialist Anatomy of Britain*, Cambridge, Polity Press, pp. 55–75.

Walker, A. and Walker, C. (eds.) (1987) *The Growing Divide*, London, CPAG.

Wiener, M. (1981) *English Culture and the Decline of the Industrial Spirit 1850–1880*, Cambridge, Cambridge University Press.

Winyard, S. (1987) 'Divided Britain' in Walker and Walker (eds.) (1987).

Notes on the authors

Alan Cawson	Professor of Politics, University of Sussex
Alan Cochrane	Senior Lecturer in Applied Social Sciences, The Open University
Keith Dowding	Senior Tutor in Government, Brunel University
Peter Hamilton	Lecturer in Sociology, The Open University
Chris Hamnett	Senior Lecturer in Geography, The Open University
Rosalind Levačić	Senior Lecturer in Education, The Open University
Tom Ling	Senior Lecturer in European Social Policy, Anglia Polytechnic University
Richard Maidment	Senior Lecturer in Politics, The Open University
Jeremy Mitchell	Lecturer in Politics, The Open University
Christopher Pollitt	Professor and Head of Government, Brunel University
Grahame Thompson	Senior Lecturer in Economics, The Open University

INDEX